Essential Dispute Resolution for SQE1

Ben Waters

Routledge
Taylor & Francis Group
LONDON AND NEW YORK

Designed cover image: amtitus / Getty Images

First published 2023
by Routledge
4 Park Square, Milton Park, Abingdon, Oxon OX14 4RN

and by Routledge
605 Third Avenue, New York, NY 10158

Routledge is an imprint of the Taylor & Francis Group, an informa business

British Library Cataloguing-in-Publication Data
A catalogue record for this book is available from the British Library

ISBN: 978-1-032-11122-3 (hbk)
ISBN: 978-1-032-11117-9 (pbk)
ISBN: 978-1-003-21850-0 (ebk)

DOI: 10.4324/9781003218500

Typeset in The Sans
by Deanta Global Publishing Services, Chennai, India

Essential Dispute Resolution for SQE1

Essential Dispute Resolution for SQE1 explains the key principles of dispute resolution in a clear, easy-to-follow style. Principles are introduced and illustrated with reference to realistic examples, commonly used court forms, and tables. The book provides an overview of three processes for resolving civil disputes, forming part of the dispute resolution continuum, followed by a fluent narrative account of key principles of civil procedure. The guide also includes a range of supporting features:

- Chapter overviews
- Revision points: each chapter concludes with a concise list of key revision points
- Multiple-choice questions: each section of the book provides multiple-choice questions following the SQE1 question format (with answers to enable you to test your knowledge)

In a series of books aimed at those preparing for SQE1, this concise and accessible text provides a clear understanding of the dispute resolution element of SQE1 in relation to contract and tort. An invaluable resource for any SQE candidate wishing to develop the assessment skills needed to pass the exam.

Ben Waters is a Principal Lecturer at Canterbury Christ Church University; he is also a qualified solicitor (non-practising) and an accredited mediator. Ben has a particular interest in dispute resolution and specifically mediation, areas in which he has active teaching, scholarly, and research interests.

Essential Law for SQE1

Series editor: Wendy Laws

Essential Law for SQE1 is a series of concise textbooks aligned to the latest SQE1 curriculum. Providing candidates with an accessible summary of the core principles in each area of law, the style of each book is precise, with bullet-point lists summarizing key information and revision points concluding each chapter. The books also feature multiple choice questions with answers, example problem questions and a glossary of key cases.

For more information about this series, please visit: www.routledge.com/

Essential Tort Law for SQE1

Wendy Laws

Essential Dispute Resolution for SQE1

Ben Waters

Contents

Figures

Tables

Introduction

This book provides a clear, concise explanation of key principles of dispute resolution. Its focus is on those areas which fall within the assessment specification for the Solicitors Qualifying Examination Part 1 Functioning Legal Knowledge (SQE1).[1]

In so doing, the book begins with a practical introductory chapter on the characteristics of three different options available for dispute resolution, in particular arbitration, mediation, and litigation as appropriate mechanisms to resolve a civil dispute founded in either contract or tort. It then proceeds to focus on the pre-litigation phase of civil court procedure, before dealing substantively with the process and procedure involved in litigation from both the claimant's and the defendant's perspective, with reference to the Civil Procedure Rules.

The style of the book reflects the SQE1 assessment specification.

The book reflects the style of the examination by using short factual scenarios in many places throughout to illustrate principles and, in particular, those where the Civil Procedure Rules are applicable as part of the litigation process.

The SQE1 assessment requires knowledge and understanding of fundamental legal principles and the ability to apply them.

Candidates are not required to recall specific case names or statutory provisions (except where they are normally used in practice to describe a principle of civil practice).

Candidates will be tested on the current law and will not be tested on the historical development of the law.

In order to reflect these requirements, the book explains the current key principles of dispute resolution in relation to contract and tort in a clear, easy-to-follow style. Principles are introduced and illustrated by reference to realistic factual examples. Limited references

1 See: SQE1 Functioning Legal Knowledge Assessment Specification, updated 14 October 2020, published by the Solicitors Regulation Authority. Available at: www.sqe.sra.org.uk/exam-arrangements/assessment-information/sqe1-assessment-specification.

to key cases and statutes are provided because this is a guide which essentially assists candidates to gain an understanding of civil practice procedures.

This approach enables the book to provide a fluent narrative account of key principles that is clear and accessible, making it easier for the reader to understand the principles, remember them, and apply them in an assessment.

Solicitors Qualifying Examination – SQE1

This book covers the areas of dispute resolution in the SQE1 assessment specification:

- Analysis of merits of claim or defence
- Arbitration, mediation, and litigation as appropriate mechanisms to resolve a dispute
- Pre-action considerations and steps
- Commencing, responding to, or progressing a claim
- Case management and any interim applications relevant to a claim
- The evidence needed and disclosure steps required in commencing, responding to, progressing, or defending a claim
- Preparation of a case for a trial, the trial, and any post-trial steps
- Procedures and processes relevant to costs involved in dispute resolution

Key features to assist learning

Revision points: each chapter concludes with a concise list of key revision points.

Multiple-choice questions: the SQE1 assessment uses multiple-choice questions to test understanding of key principles. Multiple-choice questions, following the SQE format, are provided at the end of each section of the book (with answers at the end of the book).

Case conduct skills: this book provides a useful guide for any law student, trainee, or qualified solicitor who has conduct of cases with causes of action founded in either contract or tort. This spans from early case conduct and the consideration of the requirements to provide clear advice about dispute resolution process choices to an awareness of the pre-action protocols and, if court proceedings are commenced, the overriding objective of the procedural rules of civil procedure for all cases conducted in the courts of England and Wales. The book also provides substantive guidance on the conduct of a case once proceedings are commenced to trial and beyond, from both the perspective of the claimant and the defendant.

All references to the Civil Procedure Rules and civil procedure are as stated as of 1 March 2022 and the Civil Procedure Rules and their related practice directions can be accessed at www.justice.gov.uk/courts/procedure-rules/civil/rules.

PART 1

Different options for dispute resolution

1 Introduction

Arbitration, mediation, and litigation as appropriate mechanisms to resolve a civil dispute

1.1 Chapter overview

This introductory chapter provides an overview of three approaches to dispute resolution: arbitration, mediation, and litigation, the first two being described as processes of alternative dispute resolution (ADR). Arbitration is addressed first, starting with its origin and history, followed by a consideration of its advantages and disadvantages, before going on to look at the process in both the domestic and international arenas. Mediation and its process principles are considered next, and this increasingly popular process of ADR is evaluated in terms of its usefulness for resolving a range of civil disputes.

Finally, the chapter introduces litigation, which will be the main focus of the guide in relation to civil claims founded in contract and tort. By appreciating that the rule of law is foundational to any system of civil justice, the objectives and reasons for litigating are identified before we briefly evaluate the civil justice reforms which have taken place since the mid-to-late 1990s. The recommendations made by Lord Woolf in his Access to Justice Report of 1996, which led to the introduction of the Civil Procedure Rules, are addressed and an overview of a civil claim is provided. The chapter concludes with a brief consideration of the effect of the 'Woolf Reforms' and the associated civil procedure changes.

1.2 Introduction: the dispute resolution continuum

Solicitors practising in the area of dispute resolution should be aware that when representing a client in a matter relating to a dispute between their client and a third party, they have a professional duty to consider the dispute resolution options available to their client. In so doing, they should discuss whether mediation, or some other alternative dispute resolution (ADR) procedure, may be more appropriate than litigation, arbitration, or other formal processes (since updated, but this requirement was originally included in the new Solicitors Regulation Authority's (SRA) Code of Conduct 2011).

When contemplating litigation, parties and their lawyers should be aware that the Practice Direction on pre-action conduct promotes pre-issue settlement and requires parties to consider ADR. It is a reminder that litigation as a dispute resolution process should be chosen as a last resort. As part of a relevant pre-action protocol or this

DOI: 10.4324/9781003218500-2

Practice Direction, the parties should consider whether negotiation or some other form of ADR might enable them to settle their dispute without commencing proceedings. There can be costs sanctions imposed at the conclusion of litigation if a party has failed to consider using ADR. Even if litigation is eventually chosen as the dispute resolution forum, the Civil Procedure Rules and associated Practice Directions remind the parties that judicial case management extends to encouraging the use of ADR; Rule 1.4(2)(e), for instance, requires the court to encourage parties seeking litigation to use ADR if it considers that appropriate. Rule 26.4 enables the court to stay cases for ADR to take place, and the Practice Direction to Part 29 enables the court to give directions regarding ADR on their own initiative without a hearing.

1.3 Arbitration

1.3.1 Origin and history

Arbitration is a private dispute resolution process which operates outside the structure of the civil justice system. It is a less formal and more flexible process than litigation, which involves the parties choosing a neutral third party (the arbitrator) to consider the evidence and the arguments in the case and then make a decision (the arbitral award).

The process of arbitration developed differently around the world, but its historical evolution can be traced back to Ancient Indian, Egyptian, Greek, and Roman times. In Anglo-Saxon times in England, it was often the village elder, or during the Middle Ages, the Lord of the Manor who was chosen to be the arbitrator for a range of disputes arising from the local community. Historically, the current domestic process of arbitration can be more easily traced to the procedures emerging from the Merchant Court, the Mayor's Court of the City of London created in 1424, the Star Chamber created in 1475, and the Merchant Guild Courts in Tudor and Stuart times. Modern-day arbitration is derived from arbitral processes operating during the reign of William III and then developed during the Victorian period with the enactment of the Common Law Procedure Act 1854.

The Arbitration Acts between 1889 and 1934, and thereafter in modern times the Arbitration Acts of 1950 and 1996, have developed the legislative framework for arbitration procedures in the UK we know today. It is also considered that modern-day arbitration is heavily influenced by developments in the USA and the process has been adopted globally as a method of dispute resolution for a range of domestic, international, cross-border commercial, and contractual disputes. As a process for resolving disputes, arbitration has proved popular and successful in the world of commerce.

Arbitration has been closely associated with, if not viewed as being part of the range of processes considered to be alternative to litigation and therefore often described as a process of alternative dispute resolution (ADR). Arbitration is essentially a process whereby most commonly a commercial dispute is referred to an independent third-party neutral for a decision. The arbitrator's award, for which reasons must generally be given unless the parties agree otherwise, is usually final and binding on the parties. In fact, in most jurisdictions around the world, there are limited opportunities to legally challenge an arbitral award in the courts. See later the procedural aspects of the UK Arbitration Act of 1996, which in certain circumstances does allow the opportunity to appeal an arbitral decision. Arbitration therefore involves the parties to a dispute agreeing to submit their disagreement to a person whose expertise they trust and whose decision they are willing to accept.

1.3.2 Advantages and disadvantages of arbitration

1.3.2.1 Advantages

Arbitration is a hybrid process of ADR, meaning that whilst it is an alternative to litigation and lacks many of the formalities of that process, it still requires adjudication in that the arbitrator makes the final decision. Arbitration is informal and far more flexible than some other adjudicative processes (notably litigation) as it gives the parties the opportunity to choose the procedure and one that suits the nature of the dispute; it can be oral or written depending on the requirements of the parties.

The arbitrator, like a judge, is a third-party neutral and the parties can even choose the arbitrator. This might be advantageous if an arbitrator is chosen for his or her technical knowledge and understanding of the area relating to the dispute in question; the arbitrator will often be an expert in the subject. The neutrality of the arbitrator is important, especially for international disputes. The process takes place in private, and the proceedings are confidential to those who are party to the arbitration.

The decision made by the arbitrator is known as an 'award' and can be enforceable by the court. In limited circumstances, an arbitration award can be appealed to the Court of Appeal. The process of arbitration is often less costly and quicker than many other adjudicative processes.

1.3.2.2 Disadvantages

Unlike a judge, the arbitrator must be paid by the parties and there may be a delay whilst the parties decide which arbitrator to use. There may also be a delay in the delivery of the award by the arbitrator as many arbitrators will want to have time to consider the evidence and the arguments put forward before making the award.

The arbitrator has limited powers; he/she cannot compel parties to attend the arbitration and there are no cost penalties imposed on the parties for failure to comply with arbitral proceedings. Arbitration awards are often criticised for being inconsistent, there is no formal reporting of arbitration proceedings and as such there can be conflicting awards.

1.3.3 International aspects of arbitration

On the international stage, arbitration has become well established. The Geneva Protocol of 1923 presented an opportunity for nation states to have cross-border commercial disputes resolved by a 'World Court', and thereafter in 1927, the Geneva Convention provided recognition for the enforcement of foreign arbitral awards. Pressure from the International Chamber of Commerce (ICC) due to disaffection with the operational structures and procedures of the Geneva Treaties led to the establishment of the New York Convention 1958 which now provides international recognition of arbitration awards in more than 150 countries.

The UNCITRAL arbitration rules 1976, the UNCITRAL model law 1985, and the Revised model law 2010 give recognition to an international system of arbitration and agreement awards, their enforcement, and also the conduct of arbitration proceedings. These rules provide a framework for procedures concerning the agreement to arbitrate, the appointment of an arbitral tribunal, arbitral decisions (awards), and the enforcement of arbitration awards. There are also rules governing arbitral proceedings provided by the International Chamber of Commerce (ICC), the London Court of International Arbitration (LCIA), the Chartered Institute of Arbitrators (CIArb), and the Construction Industry Model Arbitration Rules (CIMAR).

1.3.4 Domestic arbitration

Domestic arbitration is governed by legislation and in particular, the Arbitration Act 1996, which provides guidance and a framework for conducting arbitration proceedings, including the requirement that agreements to arbitrate disputes must be in writing (ss.6–8), the ability to stay legal proceedings for arbitration to take place (s.9), the arbitration commencement provisions (ss.12–14), the appointment procedure of an arbitral tribunal (ss.15–22), and the procedure involved in the removal of an arbitrator (ss.23–29). The Arbitration Act 1996 also deals with questions of jurisdiction (ss.30–32) and the powers and duties of the tribunal in the general conduct of arbitral proceedings (ss.33–41).

Whilst arbitration is a much more flexible process than litigation, the 1996 Act also provides helpful guidance to enable the parties to the dispute to understand what procedure is allowed by the arbitral tribunal (s.34), when and where the arbitration will take place, the language to be used, whether or not written statements of claim are required, whether or not disclosure of documents should take place, and what questions should be asked. Strict rules of evidence do not apply to arbitral proceedings and the arbitrator will often take the initiative and act inquisitorially by asking searching questions of the parties and witnesses. Fundamentally, the arbitral tribunal will decide whether the hearing will take place orally or by way of written evidence and/or submissions and the arbitrator may impose time limits on the parties to arbitration to ensure procedural compliance.

The award made by the arbitrator is dealt with under ss.46–58, and these provisions require that the award must be cogent, i.e., clear and unambiguous, complete, and deal with all matters in dispute. In any arbitral proceedings, it should be clear that the award is final and not contingent, in other words, bringing the award into effect should not depend on someone else or a future event taking place. It is possible for a party to appeal the arbitrator's decision, and ss.69(2)–(8), 70 and 71 allow this, but only on a question of law arising from the arbitral proceedings. The enforcement of arbitral awards is dealt with by s.66 and the costs provisions of the arbitration proceedings by ss.59–65.

The Arbitration Act 1996 is therefore designed to be a very comprehensive piece of legislation that deals with all matters relating to arbitral tribunal proceedings taking place in England and Wales.

1.4 Mediation

1.4.1 Mediation defined

Simply put, mediation is a voluntary, confidential, and empowering process whereby the parties to a dispute have the opportunity to resolve their differences in a structured, yet informal setting, with the guidance of an impartial mediator who does not take sides. Mediation is essentially a facilitated or assisted process of negotiation, with all elements of negotiation being present. In addition, a neutral, impartial, non-aligned third party is present to help the parties attempt to negotiate and achieve a resolution to the dispute; the person assisting the parties is often described as a 'third-party neutral'.

Key elements of mediation include the potential for avoiding the expense, delay, and risk of adjudication. Full participation and control over the process allow the parties participating in mediation to experience another key element: self-determination, which gives the parties invested in the process a voice and often choice in terms of settlement outcomes. It is arguable that better outcomes can be achieved through mediation than some other dispute resolution processes, due to the parties being able to generate creative problem-solving opportunities.

In the context of civil and commercial-type disputes arising from contractual disputes, for instance, continued and sometimes better business relationships can be achieved. Each of the foundational principles of mediation will be considered.

1.4.1.1 Voluntary (nature of the process)

There is no compulsion to attend mediation in the UK and the parties to a dispute are not forced to engage in it as a means of resolving their dispute. In some other common-law jurisdictions, notably the USA and Canada, mediation is to varying degrees mandatory for certain civil and private family law disputes.

If the parties want to avoid the dispute escalating and wish to explore resolution options, by choosing mediation the parties must understand that they are required to share a mutual desire to reach an agreement. Being a voluntary process there is no requirement for the parties to remain at the 'mediation table' and they may withdraw from the process at any time.

The parties have to want to engage in the process of mediation for it to have any chance of success. Research suggests that compelling parties to participate in mediation does not always provide the best conditions for achieving settlement of a civil dispute.

1.4.1.2 Confidentiality (of the process)

Mediation is a confidential process which takes place in private. Parties bringing their civil dispute to mediation will generally sign an agreement at the commencement of the mediation which requires them to be bound by confidentiality. Essentially this means that the parties agree not to repeat anything discussed during the course of the mediation once the mediation is over.

Similarly, the process is accepted by the parties as being without prejudice, implying that if the dispute does not settle following the mediation and litigation commences or resumes, neither party can use any information (orally or in writing) disclosed or used during the course of the mediation in a genuine attempt to settle the dispute, as evidence of admissions against the interest of the party which made them, in subsequent court proceedings.

An extra layer of confidentiality exists during the course of the mediation process and applies to the private meetings that the mediator has with individual parties. The mediator is responsible for protecting confidentiality during the process at all times. The 'without prejudice' rule also applies to mediation.

1.4.1.3 Empowerment (of the parties)

The parties to mediation will have full control over the process and its outcome, which means that they can bring the mediation to a close at any time. Depending on the nature of the dispute, the parties may with the assistance of the mediator explore a whole range of settlement options.

Many of the settlement options that are potentially available to the parties at mediation, will be unavailable to a judge. All decision-making during mediation rests with the parties and in this way, the process is both flexible and empowering, as mediation enables the parties to find their own solutions and ones which, whilst not necessarily optimal for them, will enable the parties to reach an amicable solution that they can both live with.

The process of mediation is sometimes described as being future-focused; this is because above all, the process looks to the future and does not dwell on past events associated with the dispute.

1.4.1.4 Neutral facilitation (by the mediator)

The mediator is often chosen by the parties; if a mediation service is used and it has a panel of mediators, then they may recommend a certain mediator whom they consider might be best suited to the nature of the dispute. Whichever mediator is chosen, the mediator will have no stake in the dispute or its outcome, although they might be an expert in the area of the dispute or perhaps from a legal background.

The mediator is essentially an impartial and neutral facilitator and as such he or she must be free of prejudice, preconceptions, and assumptions. It is the responsibility of the mediator to create a suitable environment for mediation to take place. The mediator will encourage communication and information exchange between the parties and will assist with discovering the parties' interests, help the parties search for options, and assess the possibilities for a settlement agreement. The mediator will help the parties negotiate more effectively towards a self-determined outcome.

1.4.2 Why mediate?

Following are some of the reasons why parties to a civil dispute may wish to pursue mediation as an option for resolving the dispute. The parties may want to:

- Avoid the expense, delay, and risk of adjudication. Predicting the outcome of adjudicative processes like litigation and arbitration is risky. Mediation offers the possibility of an acceptable conclusion or at least one that the parties to the dispute can live with. Litigation can be slow and expensive and arbitration, whilst a hybrid ADR process, is still adjudicative despite being more informal
- Add structure to the existing or ongoing negotiation process
- Help establish more effective communication and information exchange
- Enable the parties to explore the opportunity for settlement in a conducive environment
- Help to remove barriers to resolution
- Enable the mediator to work with the parties to uncover interests, develop, and assess options
- Enable the mediator to test the respective parties' positions, and uncover their interests (in confidence)
- Empower the parties; self-determination enables the parties to have time and place to tell their stories and be heard. Options for settlement can be developed which are responsive to parties' needs and the process permits creative solutions. So the parties retain control over the process and outcome
- Enhance or maintain relationships
- Ensure privacy, as the process is private and the outcome is confidential to the parties.

There is international recognition of cross-border dispute settlement via mediation, for instance, the United Nations supports the online resolution of cross-border electronic commerce transactions disputes. The United Nations Commission on International Trade Law (UNCITRAL) has supported the Singapore Convention on the Enforcement of Mediated Settlement Agreements, which opened for signature in August 2019, and which seeks to provide a harmonised legal framework for the right to invoke and enforce settlement agreements achieved at mediation, including the promotion of mediation clauses in contracts, the use of mediation before arbitration or litigation, and the encouragement of increased certainty on the enforceability of mediated settlement agreements.

1.5 Litigation

1.5.1 The rule of law

The object of rule of law in any rules-based society is to substitute violence for peaceful ways of resolving disputes. Peace cannot be guaranteed by legislation, treaties, or agreements alone and the courts are essential to the rule of law; they are the agencies of rights enforcement. The rule of law, through the operation of the civil justice system, ensures democratic judgment, protection against abuse of power, and the principle of regularity, i.e., similar cases are treated similarly.

The court system allows for reasoned disposition of controversies by the application of the law, i.e., statutes/treaties or in their absence, precedent, and is based on fairness and equity. The rule of law therefore should assure a litigant's 'day in court', which is the right of every citizen as recognised by article 6 ECHR, which states that 'in the determination of [a citizen's] civil rights and obligations ... everyone is entitled to a fair and public hearing within a reasonable time by an independent and impartial tribunal established by law'. Lord Neuberger has claimed that access to the courts is the bedrock of the rule of law:

> Rights are valueless if they cannot be realised ... and it is therefore essential that all ... citizens have fair and equal access to justice.[1]

Enforcement of rights therefore depends on an accessible and effective litigation system that provides adequate remedies.

Case example

Bremner v South India Shipping Corporation [1981] AC 909

> Every civilised system of government requires that the state should make available to all its citizens a means to a just and peaceful settlement means of disputes between them as to their respective legal rights. The means provided are the courts of justice to which every citizen has a constitutional right of access in the role of [claimant] to obtain the remedy to which he claims to be entitled in consequence of an alleged breach of his legal or equitable rights by some other citizen, the defendant.
>
> (Lord Diplock)

1 Lord Neuberger, *Justice in an Age of Austerity*, Tom Sargant Memorial Lecture 2013. Available at: www.supremecourt.uk/docs/speech-131015.pdf.

1.5.2 The object of litigation

Litigation is the process of taking a case through the civil justice court system to enforce a civil right. 'Litigants' is the term used for those parties who are involved in court proceedings. The process of litigation is initiated not by the state (as with criminal proceedings), but by an individual or a collection of individuals (a company for example). The claimant is the person or organisation bringing the claim, and the defendant is the party defending the claim. The civil justice system provides established court procedures which include guiding procedural rules, strict rules of evidence, the application of substantive law (case law and statute), and the application of the system of precedent (stare decisis). It is an adjudicative process with the decision maker being a judge who is an impartial third party. In other words, litigation is a process of dispute resolution involving a judicial approach to problem-solving.

The civil justice system is institutionalised, state-sponsored, and a socially recognised authority involving an adversarial approach to finding the truth. It is, however, arguably more about which party has the best argument and whose evidence is favoured. The outcome is binary in that there is always a winner and a loser (one party is considered to be right and the other wrong). At the conclusion of the case at trial, the judge delivers a judgment which is binding on the parties and enforceable. Judicial decisions reflect society's views based on decided case law and statute.

1.5.3 Why litigate?

Where one party cannot gain the cooperation of another party in a civil dispute, litigation is one way of ensuring that the other party takes notice of the claim being made. The process of commencement of civil court proceedings, or in other words 'issuing a claim', places the parties on a formal footing. Upon payment of a fee to the court, the party bringing the claim (the claimant) will arrange for the claim form to be served on the defendant, and the defendant will then be required to respond. If the defendant takes no action and ignores the claim, the case will reach an early conclusion with judgment being entered in favour of the claimant.

The parties may have attempted negotiation; however, if those negotiations have proven fruitless, then litigation may be an alternative to negotiation. It may be that the party bringing the claim requires vindication and/or reputational affirmation. This can be provided through litigation if the case proceeds to trial and the claimant is successful, as openness and publicity are assured. This can work both ways of course, and the consequences will be very different if the claimant loses at trial.

A party bringing a case may want to set a precedent for future cases based on or associated with the same area of law. Bringing a successful case through the civil courts and being awarded judgment may therefore help to develop and shape the law; decisions in the higher courts, particularly the Court of Appeal and above, can achieve this.

1.5.3.1 The importance of precedent

Civil litigation outcomes, known as judgments, provided by the more superior or higher courts (High Court, Court of Appeal Civil Division, and the Supreme Court [formerly the House of Lords]) are reported. The current system of published law reporting dates back to 1865 with the introduction of the Modern Law Reports; these include, by way of example, judgments from cases heard in the higher courts: the Appeal Cases (AC), the Chancery Division of the High Court (Ch), the Family Division of the High Court (Fam), and the King's (or Queen's) Bench Division of the High Court (KB/QB). Other law reports providing the judgments from the higher courts include the Weekly Law Reports (WLR) and the All England Law Reports (All ER).

The law reports are therefore where 'case law' is found. They document the development of our common law and provide guidance for subsequent disputes, arguably clarifying the law and producing 'legal normalcy'. Precedents create 'civil' rights and affect society's behaviour; civil litigation is therefore the process by which civil rights or entitlements are enforced.

1.5.3.2 Formality

Litigation is a structured and formalised process governed by rules (the Civil Procedure Rules or CPR) and, being state-sanctioned, is rule-bound. Clarity of procedure should be provided for the parties involved in litigation, and the parties will be aware of the procedural stages and steps associated with the process through application of the CPR. These include timetables, deadlines, and procedural requirements. Strict rules of evidence apply to civil proceedings through application of the Civil Evidence Acts, and witnesses can be required to appear before the civil court to give evidence at trial through the subpoena procedure.

1.5.3.3 Decision-making

Litigation is an adjudicative process and, in most cases brought before the civil courts, the adjudicator at trial is a judge sitting alone in the County Court and High Court, with three judges considering an appeal from the High Court and at least five judges considering a civil appeal from the Court of Appeal sitting in the Supreme Court. The civil court judge is effectively a referee who has no prior judicial consideration of the evidence and has no investigative duties (unlike his/her continental counterpart). The function of the civil judge is to regulate the admissibility of evidence and determine the facts of the case and issues of law associated with it, following which the judge is required to give a considered and reasoned judgment. The importance of evidence in the judicial decision-making process is therefore paramount.

Litigation is often favoured by parties to a civil dispute who want to have a decision made by a third party, with the assistance of a process that ensures disclosure of evidence and the compliance of their opponent. Judicial decisions or judgments are binding and enforceable, although judicial decisions can be appealed.

Parliament has the primary law-making role; however, the judiciary also plays a major role in the creation of new law. Much of the law of England and Wales is case law made by judges, and some examples of judicial activism through 'judge-made' law can be found in the substantive law areas of contract and tort. Parliament has often created statute by consolidating the common law, and examples found in these areas of law include the Consumer Rights Act 2015, the Occupiers Liability Acts of 1957 and 1984, and the Animals Act 1971.

Judges are often required to interpret and apply the law with regard to a number of factors; e.g., where there is no clear precedent, judges have to make a decision and can create new law in this way. Judges have been left to define their own role and although they have traditionally assumed the role of declaring what the law is, parliament has retained the overall right to make new law through the creation of legislation, statutes, or Acts of Parliament.

1.5.4 Reform of the civil justice system

During the early 1990s, the government became increasingly concerned with the state of the civil justice system, mainly due to the cost involved in bringing litigation. Often the simplest of cases incurred the highest costs in proportion to the value of the claim. The government was also concerned about the slowness of the system in bringing cases to trial; the average waiting time for a county court case was 79 weeks. The complex nature of court rules and associated procedures often meant that lawyers were always needed to assist parties to bring their civil disputes before the courts and even when the party bringing the claim (then called the plaintiff) was successful, enforcing a judgment which the defendant refused to comply with was not straightforward and claimants were often left to chase the judgment debtor themselves.

In 1994 the Master of the Rolls (the head of the civil justice system), Lord Woolf, was invited to undertake a review of the civil justice system in England and Wales, and after two years he produced his report entitled 'Access to Justice' or commonly called the Woolf Report, in 1996.

The Woolf Report revealed a lack of equality between the powerful, wealthy litigant and the under-resourced litigant. Woolf considered the system too uncertain in terms of forecasting the cost of litigation and its duration, believing it also to be incomprehensible to many litigants. Above all, Woolf viewed the system as too organisationally fragmented. There was no clear overall responsibility for the administration of civil justice; it was far too adversarial with cases being party-led, and the rules of court, all too often, were being ignored by the parties and not enforced by the court.

The government took note of Woolf's findings and the Woolf Report led to wholesale reform. The Woolf Reforms, as they are to be commonly referred to, included the introduction by Parliament of the Civil Procedure Act 1997 and a new civil procedural code in the form of the Civil Procedure Rules. Two years later the Access to Justice Act 1999 was passed which placed an emphasis on avoiding litigation.

1.5.5 Civil Procedure Rules

The Civil Procedure Rules (CPR) came into force on 26 April 1999 and their overall goal was to fundamentally change the prevailing litigation culture. This guide will be predominantly concerned with the CPR and their application to the litigation process.

1.5.5.1 The overriding objective

As articulated in his report of 1996, Lord Woolf's vision of a civil justice system was one which should be just in the results it delivers, fair in its treatment of litigants, easily understood, and user-friendly. Woolf also hoped that the new system of civil justice would provide appropriate procedures at a reasonable cost, deal with cases with reasonable speed, and be responsive to the needs of those who use it. Woolf also strongly recommended that government ensure that the civil justice system should be effective, adequately resourced, and organised.

Overall, the administration of civil justice should be controlled by the judiciary and court officers rather than being party-led. Case management would therefore be introduced enabling the judiciary to determine how a case should progress through the system with a strict timetable being imposed on the parties, including directions for certain steps to be taken. A system of sanctions would be introduced to ensure that parties comply with the rules.

The overriding objective of the reform process is set out in rule 1.1 of the CPR 1998 as follows:

(1) These Rules are a new procedural code with the overriding objective of enabling the court to deal with cases justly.
(2) Dealing with a case justly includes, so far as is practicable:
   (a) ensuring that the parties are on an equal footing;
   (b) saving expense;
   (c) dealing with the case in ways which are proportionate –
      (i) to the amount of money involved;
      (ii) to the importance of the case;
      (iii) to the complexity of the issues; and
      (iv) to the financial position of each party;
   (d) ensuring that it is dealt with expeditiously and fairly; and,
   (e) allotting to it an appropriate share of the court's resources, while taking into account the need to allot resources to other cases; and,
   (f) enforcing compliance with rules, practice directions and orders.

Table 1.1 Advantages and disadvantages of litigation

Advantages and disadvantages of litigation	
Advantages	Disadvantages
• Compels participation	• Lack of control, process, outcome
• A clear formalised process	• Outcome uncertain
• Binding decision guaranteed	• Binary – win/lose
• Precedents can be set	• Remedies limited
• Law can be clarified	• Expense/time
• Costs recoverable	• Impersonal, acrimonious, stressful
• Decisions can be appealed	• The best argument wins
• Skilled advocates used	

1.5.6 An overview of a civil claim

1.5.6.1 Preliminary matters – dispute resolution process choice

It is incumbent on lawyers practising in the area of civil justice dispute resolution to provide legal advice about the choice of dispute-resolution process. The new Solicitors Regulation Authority's (SRA) Code of Conduct 2011 stated:

> When considering the options available to the client if the matter relates to a dispute between your client and a third party, you should discuss whether mediation or some other alternative dispute resolution (ADR) procedure may be more appropriate than litigation, arbitration, or other formal processes.[2]

A solicitor should therefore not advise a client to issue court proceedings without having regard to his or her professional obligations and litigation should be treated as the process choice of last resort; this follows the spirit of the Access to Justice Act 1999. The court can punish a client in costs sanctions if litigation is launched with disregard for legal advice given in this regard. A solicitor advising a client about process choice should also take into consideration the client's means, their ability to fund litigation, the legal issues involved in the case, and the likely prospects of success.

The pre-action protocols introduced as part of the Woolf Reforms and endorsed by the Ministry of Justice (see Chapter 2) provide guidance for parties in dispute on pre-action conduct for specific disputes such as personal injury, clinical negligence, and professional negligence. Where there is no approved pre-action protocol for the parties' dispute, the Practice Direction on Pre-action Conduct and Protocols applies.

2 See the SRA Code of Conduct 2011. Available at: www.sra.org.uk/solicitors/handbook/code/history/.

1.5.6.2 Using alternative dispute resolution

It should be noted that the CPR provide various opportunities for ADR to be used even once court proceedings have been commenced. Consider the following rules and associated Practice Directions: the Practice Direction (Pre-action Conduct) promotes pre-issue settlement and requires parties to consider ADR. The pre-action protocols require disputing parties to consider whether some form of ADR is appropriate (there can be later costs sanctions); CPR 1.4 dealing with judicial case management extends to encouraging the use of ADR; CPR 26.4 gives the court power to stay cases to enable ADR to take place; the Practice Direction to CPR 29 provides that the court can give directions regarding ADR on its own initiative without a case management conference (see Chapter 6 on case management); CPR 44.3 provides that the court can consider parties conduct on issues of costs (relating to the pre-action protocol period); and CPR 44.5 provides that the court can consider parties' conduct on issues of costs during the proceedings (see Chapter 13).

1.5.6.3 Letter of claim

The party bringing the claim will be known as the proposed claimant. The proposed claimant will be required to send a letter of claim (letter before action) to the proposed defendant setting out the nature and details of the claim. The approved protocols for particular types of civil action or in the absence of one for the nature of the claim, the Practice Direction on Pre-action Conduct should be followed. Clarity is crucial as the proposed claimant must set out full details of the claim including what is required at this stage by way of information including any documents relevant to the claim being made. Sufficient information is required to enable the proposed defendant to make the necessary investigations. It is at this stage that the proposed claimant should set out any proposals for ADR with a view to bringing the dispute to an early settlement.

1.5.6.4 Letter in response

The Practice Direction on Pre-action Conduct and Protocols and the approved protocols for particular types of civil action provide guidance on the matters to be dealt with in the letter of response by the party required to respond to the claim (the proposed defendant). The proposed defendant should acknowledge the letter of claim and make any admissions at this stage. If the claim is founded in tort, then this should include any admissions of liability and any allegations of contributory negligence. If liability is not admitted, then the proposed defendant should provide brief details of, and reasons for, the denial.

1.5.6.5 Commencing proceedings

If after three months of receiving the letter of claim the claim has not been settled, then court proceedings can be commenced by the proposed claimant. This is done by the proposed claimant issuing a claim form either by post or online (see Chapter 4). The claim form should set out brief details of the claim, the likely value, and particulars of the claim, either endorsed on the claim form or served as a separate document. Once the claim form is issued upon payment of a required court fee, the proposed claimant will be known as the claimant and the proposed defendant known as the defendant.

The court will serve the defendant with the claim form (and particulars of the claim if endorsed) and if the defendant proposes to defend the claim, then a defence should be filed with the court, a copy of which will be sent to the claimant. If the claim is to be defended, the court will send each party an allocation questionnaire, which once completed should be returned to the court.

The court will then exercise its case management powers and allocate the case to a particular track. For claims not exceeding £10,000, the case will be allocated to the small claims track; for cases exceeding £10,000 and not exceeding £25,000, the case will usually be allocated to the fast track; and for cases exceeding a value of £25,000, the case will be allocated to the multi-track. Claims in excess of £100,000 (£50,000 for personal injury claims) can be issued on the High Court; otherwise, the County Court will be the venue where most cases are commenced.

1.5.6.6 Case management

Once the case has been allocated to a track, the court will manage the case. A timetable will be agreed upon and approved by the court, and the parties (now formally known as litigants) will be required to comply with directions to assist the case proceeding towards trial. For cases allocated to the small claims and fast claims track, it is usual for such directions to be given without a court hearing. For those cases of greater value and complexity, a case management conference is usually required. The parties or their legal representatives will attend this, at which the district judge will consider the matters in dispute and determine what steps are required to progress the case to trial. During this interim period of a case any applications can be issued by the parties (see Chapter 6 generally).

1.5.6.7 The civil trial

A small-claims-track trial is usually conducted informally at the discretion of the judge. A fast-track trial will usually be heard in a day, whereas multi-track trials can last for many days depending on complexity and the number of witnesses involved. At the conclusion of the trial, the judge will make a decision and deliver a judgment. The issue of costs will be dealt with at this stage; in other words, the judge will decide who should pay the costs of the case and the amount of those costs; in a fast-track trial, this is known as summary assessment. The costs of a multi-track case may have to be decided at a later date before another judge by way of detailed assessment.

1.5.6.8 Post-trial

Unless the judge's decision is appealed, if the successful party at trial is awarded damages, then the judgment delivered by the trial judge will include details of the damages and costs to be paid to the winning party (the judgment creditor) by the losing party (the judgment debtor) by a certain date. Should the judgment debtor fail to honour the judgment debt, then enforcement proceedings can be commenced by the judgment creditor (see Chapter 12 for methods of enforcement).

1.5.7 Have the reforms met any of Woolf's objectives?

Since the introduction of the CPR in 1999, the pre-action protocols have produced much more settlement activity; on average less than 4 per cent of cases commenced in either the County Court or High Court come to trial. The number of 'out of court' settlements has increased. There has been a significant drop in the number of litigated cases; using the County Court as an example of litigation activity, in the year 2000 the total number of cases issued in the County Court was 1,943,513; of those, 71,233 or 3.66 per cent went to trial. In 2019, whilst there was a slight increase in the number of cases issued at 2,029,248, fewer cases, 54,747 or 3.19 per cent, went to trial.[3] This is broadly reflective of similar activity in the higher courts over the same period.

Case management has assisted with the administration of justice and cases are now disposed of more quickly. It is, however, arguable that the system of civil justice still costs too much and is unaffordable for many. There has been an exponential rise in court fees, partly driven by the need to fund the civil justice system, but arguably also to discourage parties from using litigation. HMCTS is now undoubtedly better resourced than its equivalent agency was 25 years ago and the simplified and standardised procedure for both the County Court and the High Court has generally improved access to justice.

Chapter 1 revision points

Arbitration, mediation, and litigation as dispute resolution processes

- Arbitration – a private dispute resolution process which operates outside the structure of the civil justice system. The decision (the award) is made by the arbitrator:
  - The international and domestic aspects of arbitration
  - The Arbitration Act 1996
  - Advantages and disadvantages of arbitration
- Mediation – a voluntary, confidential, and empowering process whereby the parties to a dispute have the opportunity to resolve their differences in a structured, yet informal setting, with the guidance of an impartial mediator who does not take sides:
  - Voluntary, confidential, empowering, and neutrally facilitated
  - The reasons to mediate
  - Advantages and disadvantages of mediation
- Litigation is the process of taking a case through the civil justice court system to enforce a civil right through judicial decision-making, litigators being those parties involved in court proceedings:

3 Civil Justice Statistics. Available at: www.gov.uk/government/collections/civil-justice-statistics.

- The rule of law
- The object of litigation and the reasons to litigate
- Civil justice reform – Woolf Reforms and Access to Justice
- Litigation procedure – an overview of a civil claim
- The object of litigation and the reasons to litigate
- Advantages and disadvantages of litigation

Multiple-choice question for Part 1

1. A residential property owner seeks legal advice from his solicitor about what he should do to prevent his neighbour from building a summer house on his property which he says will be an 'eyesore' and obstruct the light to his property. The building work is due to take place imminently.

*Which one of the following situations **best** explains what advice the solicitor should provide the client?*

A. Without recourse to advice about any other possible dispute resolution process, the solicitor should advise his client to apply for an injunction, allow him to draft an N1 claim form, and arrange for it to be issued and served on his client's neighbour without delay.

B. Despite the perceived urgency of the matter, and recognising his professional obligation, the solicitor must, before taking any action on his client's behalf, discuss with his client whether mediation or some other alternative dispute resolution procedure may be more appropriate than litigation.

C. Whilst the solicitor considers the matter to be urgent, he should advise his client that the best course of action would be to wait until the building work starts and then apply for an injunction preventing any further work to take place.

D. The solicitor should advise his client that as negotiation, mediation, or any other alternative dispute resolution procedure may prove fruitless, taking immediate action and reporting the matter to the police, asking that they take immediate action to stop the neighbour from commencing the building work, would be the desired advice.

E. The matter is urgent, and a civil wrong is about to take place. As such, the solicitor should immediately ask for his client's instructions to write a letter of claim to his client's neighbour without delay, threatening court proceedings (an application for an injunction) and giving a deadline of 24 hours for the neighbour to respond confirming that all building work will not take place.

PART 2

Pre-action considerations and steps

2 Resolving a dispute through a civil claim

Preliminary considerations: limitation, pre-action protocols

2.1 Chapter overview

This chapter will help understand the importance of the pre-action period for enabling parties to a civil dispute to take the opportunity to try to resolve it without the need for court proceedings. Encouraging the parties to be more open in relation to their differences so that they might enter into negotiations was one of the aims of the Woolf Reforms, and this approach will be underlined in this chapter.

Parties and causes of action will be defined, and the importance of observing limitation periods for claims in contract and tort will be emphasised before the pre-action protocols, their purpose, and consequences for failure to follow their terms and requirements are outlined.

2.2 Introduction: pre-action considerations

Before a claim can be commenced there are various preliminary considerations which must be taken into account. These include establishing whether the claim is 'within time' for the purposes of limitation. Statutory limitation periods will apply to all potential civil claims, and the legal adviser will need to be aware of the important provisions of the Limitation Act 1980 (LA Act 1980) (as amended). The LA 1980 prescribes time periods for certain claims to be brought, and failure to issue proceedings within the prescribed time limits will cause the action to be 'statute barred' for limitation purposes. This may have disastrous consequences for the claimant's ability to pursue the action, as the defendant will be able to plead limitation as a legitimate ground for defence, which if upheld will cause the action to be struck out and the claim will fail. Beware the solicitor that misses the limitation date; their firm could be sued by their client for professional negligence! Limitation will be considered further in the following.

2.2.1 The Woolf Reforms

Should the claim be within the limitation period, the potential claimant must follow the relevant pre-action protocol period as prescribed by the Civil Procedure Rules (CPR) and associated Practice Directions, which provide clear guidance on pre-action

DOI: 10.4324/9781003218500-4

conduct. This is a requirement following the Woolf Reforms of the mid-1990s, which were introduced due to prevailing concerns about the state of the civil justice system in England and Wales, and broadly identified by Lord Woolf in his Access to Justice Report 1996, as being too costly, too slow in its delivery of justice, and procedurally too complex. This then culminated in the introduction of the Civil Procedure Rules by way of the Civil Procedure Act 1997.

The CPR came into force on 26 April 1999 and introduced a standardised set of the rules of civil procedure for the County Court and High Court in England and Wales, the main features of which concerned the introduction of pre-action protocols (to encourage early dispute resolution), the allocation of cases to tracks (based on value/complexity), and case management (including tough sanctions for procedural breaches).

2.2.2 The overriding objective

Remember Part 1 of the CPR articulates the overriding objective of the new procedural rules of civil procedure for all cases conducted in the courts of England and Wales, namely that:

(1) These Rules are a new procedural code with the overriding objective of enabling the court to deal with cases justly and at proportionate cost.
(2) Dealing with a case justly includes, so far as is practicable –
  (a) ensuring that the parties are on an equal footing;
  (b) saving expense;
  (c) dealing with the case in ways which are proportionate –
    (i) to the amount of money involved;
    (ii) to the importance of the case;
    (iii) to the complexity of the issues; and
    (iv) to the financial position of each party;
  (d) ensuring that it is dealt with expeditiously and fairly; and,
  (e) allotting to it an appropriate share of the court's resources, while taking into account the need to allot resources to other cases;
  (f) enforcing compliance with rules, practice directions and orders.

The Woolf Reforms brought about by far the most comprehensive developments in civil justice in England and Wales over the last 30 years. The civil justice reform process is ongoing, however, and there have been subsequent civil justice developments brought about following the reviews of Lords Justice Jackson in 2010 and Briggs in 2016.

In this part, we will also consider the principles and purpose of pre-action protocols governing particular claims and consequences for failure to follow their terms, and the applicable law. We will also consider the mechanisms to determine which country's laws apply to a contractual or tortious claim issued in the courts of England and Wales.

2.3 Parties and causes of action

2.3.1 Parties to an action

The parties to an action are those who are in dispute and if proceedings are commenced, they become legal entities. It is important for the potential claimant to identify the correct legal entity or defendant to sue. For instance, if a potential claimant has a dispute with a company, it is pointless to proceed against a representative of the company with whom the potential claimant may have had all personal dealings. In those circumstances the claim, once issued, would likely be struck out for having sued the wrong legal entity and the claimant would have to commence proceedings all over again, ensuring that any further attempt to issue and serve proceedings is effected against the correct defendant, i.e., the company.

In the example used in Figure 2.1, which summarises details of a potential claim against the owners of a farm shop, the correct defendant needs to be identified. It would be dangerous to assume that the defendant is simply 'Dotheboys Farm'. Enquiries of its insurers will confirm the correct legal entity and therefore defendant, for example, Dotheboys Farm Ltd (if an incorporated company), or Arthur Squeers trading as Dotheboys Farm (if not incorporated and acting on his own account).

In summary, the correct parties to a civil action are defined in terms of their legal entities as:

- Individuals – sue and are sued using their full names
- Limited companies – sue and are sued in the company/corporate name (a company search can check the correct title to use for the defendant)
- Partnerships – normally sue and are sued in the name of the firm (not necessary to use individual partners' names)
- Sole traders – usually sue in their own name and are sued under the trade name of the defendant, e.g., Arthur Squeers T/A Dotheboys Farm.

2.3.2 Causes of action

The cause of action is quite simply the basis upon which a person, company, partnership, or sole trader (the potential claimant) believes they have a right to a remedy from the legal entity (the potential defendant) allegedly causing the civil wrong. Such causes of action may exist in common law in tort or in contract, as well as in statute. Causes of action can be drafted to include multiple claims for breach of common law and/or statute. For tortious causes of action, some examples might commonly include breach of negligence, trespass, and copyright infringement and any applicable statutory provisions, e.g., the Occupiers Liability Act 1957. For contractual causes of action, some examples might include fundamental breach of contract, misrepresentation and frustration, and any applicable statutory provisions, e.g., the Unfair Contract Terms Act 1977.

Client	Madeline Bray		
Opponent	Dotheboys Farm		
Cause of Action	Negligence and Breach of statutory duty (OLA 1957)		
Elements to Establish	**Facts**	**Evidence Obtained**	**Evidence Required**
Duty of Care	At approx. 3.45pm on Monday 13th December 2021 Madeline Bray visited Dotheboys Farm Shop. It was raining and as MB went to enter the farm shop she tripped/slipped on a very uneven, broken concrete step outside the entrance to the shop. Part of the step which caused MB's accident had a very obscure curve on the front of it, and in front of that, was a puddle which gave a false impression that the ground was all one level.	Photos of the entrance to the farm shop.	Site inspection (if negligence denied)
Breach of Duty	The owner(s) of Dotheboys Farm Shop (thought to be Arthur Squeers) failed to ensure that their premises were safe to all visitors, in particular in failing to warn of a potential hazard, presented by the uneven and obscurely curved step at the entrance to the Farm Shop. Common law breach of duty. The provisions of the *Occupiers Liability Act* 1957, *s.2.2* of which imposes and obligation on the occupier of the premises to ensure the safety of all lawful visitors to their premises.	Photos of the entrance to the farm shop.	Site inspection (if negligence denied)
Damage	Injury: As a result of her accident, MB sustained a broken right wrist (Colles' fracture) and cuts/bruising to her face, together with consequential headaches and dizziness for several weeks after the accident. Financial Losses: MB was required to take several weeks off work as a secretary (she was unable to type or lift), and she has other consequential losses.	Photos of injuries	Medical evidence Payslips Receipts for medication and any other losses

Figure 2.1 Instructions received from a client having suffered personal injury and loss.

2.3.3 An example: breach of negligence (tort)

The example in Figure 2.1 comprises notes of instructions received from a client having suffered personal injury and loss. These record details of a cause of action for a public (occupiers) liability claim (a tortious cause of action) for a lady who suffered a fall on farm shop premises.

2.4 Calculating limitation periods for claims in contract and tort

2.4.1 The general rule

The Limitation Act 1980 prescribes the periods within which claims founded in both contract and tort must be brought, otherwise, they will be 'statute barred' for the purposes of litigation. This places a burden on the legal advisor instructed to ensure that the limitation period is determined upon receipt of instructions to act. It is possible to issue a claim form without serving it with the particulars of the claim for four months, to ensure that the claim is brought 'within time' and protected for the purposes of limitation. The procedure governing the commencement of proceedings is dealt with under CPR Part 7.

The general rule is that claims founded in contract and tort must be brought within six years of the date of the contract or the event giving rise to a cause of action in tort. There are, however, some notable exceptions to this rule:

- Damages for personal injury and death – three years from the date of the accident or date of knowledge of injured party (s.11 LA 1980)
- Trespass to the person – six years (s.2 LA 1980)
- Defective premises and latent damage – six years or three years from the date of knowledge (s.14 LA 1980)
- Fraud or concealment – six years from the date of knowledge of the fraud, concealment, or mistake (s.32 LA 1980).

2.4.2 Extending time for service of the claim form

Parties to a claim can agree to extend the period of time for service of proceedings beyond the four-month period following the issue of the claim form under CPR Part 7(6). This may be required if the legal adviser received instructions from the claimant at the eleventh hour before the limitation expired. For instance, in the aforementioned case, if Mrs Bray did not provide instructions to her legal advisor to act until 30 November 2024, only 14 days before the expiry of the limitation period for personal injury claims, then her legal adviser would be well advised to issue (but not serve) proceedings and then obtain the required evidence to support the cause of action, e.g., obtaining a medical report to establish the nature and extent of the injury, before then serving the claim form with full particulars of claim and supportive medical evidence, within four months of the date when the claim form was issued.

2.5 Practice Direction – pre-action conduct

The pre-action protocols were introduced as part of the Woolf Reforms and implemented through the Civil Procedure Rules 1998. The protocols are designed to enable parties to a particular type of civil dispute to consider the possibility of settlement without the need to commence formal court proceedings (litigation). There are several specific protocols, namely for debt, personal injury, clinical negligence, construction and engineering, defamation, family law, judicial review, media and communications, disease and illness, package travel claims, possession claims, housing disrepair, low-value personal injury claims in road traffic accidents, dilapidations (commercial property), and low-value employers' and public liability.

Even where there is no 'tailor-made' pre-action protocol, the claimant must still write to the potential defendant informing him/her of the claim. A claim should not be commenced until three months have elapsed following the issue of this letter or protocol. The aim is to achieve a settlement without the need for litigation through the courts. Provided in Figure 2.2 is an example of a letter of claim to an employer of a client concerning a tripping/slipping public liability accident. It provides confirmation of its intention and then goes on to summarise the facts and consider the relevant law.

The general purpose of the letter of claim is to confirm that the legal representative of the potential claimant has received instructions to act for their client in a civil claim for damages against the person or organisation they are writing to. It provides an outline of the issues concerning the matter, including the circumstances of the accident, the reason fault is alleged (including details of both common law and statutory breach), brief details of the injury and loss sustained by the potential claimant, and concludes with the required action which should be taken. Note that it includes a request for disclosure of documents and other information which may be relevant as well as a request that the organisation's insurers be informed of the claim.

2.6 Principles and purpose of pre-action protocols governing particular claims and consequences for failure to follow terms

The Practice Direction for those disputes not covered by a protocol and those approved pre-action protocols are designed to:

(a) Enable parties to settle the issue between them without the need to start court proceedings
(b) Encourage the parties to exchange sufficient information about the matter to allow them to understand each other's position
(c) Enable the parties to make informed decisions about settlement and how to proceed
(d) Encourage the parties to consider using a form of alternative dispute resolution (ADR)

The Manager
Dotheboys Farm Shop
Hollies Road
Staffordshire
ST23 4PU

Our Ref: 040898/RD/Y/402
3rd March 2022

Dear Sir,

Re: Client: Madeline Bray

We are instructed by the above named born on **2nd May 1963** of **25 Mulberry Terrace, Melbourne, Staffs.** in connection with a claim for damages for personal injury and loss arising out of an accident which occurred on **13th December 2021** at Dotheboys Farm Shop in Melbourne.

Please confirm the identity of your insurers. Pease note that your insurers will need to see this letter as soon as possible as it may affect your insurance cover and/or the conduct of any subsequent legal proceedings if you do not send this letter to them. A further copy of this letter is enclosed for your use.

The Circumstances of the Accident are:

At approximately 3.45pm on Monday 13th December 2021 our client visited Dotheboys Farm Shop. It was raining and upon entering the farm shop she tripped/slipped on a very uneven, broken concrete step outside the entrance to the shop. Part of the step which caused our client's accident had a very obscure curve on the front of it, and in front of that, was a puddle which gave a false impression that the ground was all one level.

The Reason for Alleging Fault is:

In our opinion the owners of Dotheboys Farm Shop failed to ensure that their premises were safe to all visitors, in particular in failing to warn of a potential hazard, presented by the uneven and obscurely curved step at the entrance to the Farm Shop.

Together with a common law breach of duty to our client, we believe that you are also in breach of the provisions of the Occupiers Liability Act 1957, s.2.2 of which imposes and obligation on the occupier of the premises to ensure the safety of all lawful visitors to their premises.

A Description of our Client's Injuries is as Follows:

As a result of her accident, our client sustained a broken right wrist and cuts/bruising to her face, together with consequential headaches and dizziness for several weeks after the accident. She was required to take several weeks off work following her accident, and she has suffered loss of earnings as a result together with other consequential losses.

At this stage of our enquires we would expect disclosure of copies of any documents which may be relevant to this action, including those in the attached schedule pursuant to the Pre-Action Personal Injury Protocol standard disclosure list for public liability claims.

A copy of this letter is enclosed for your insurers. Finally, we expect an acknowledgment of this letter within 21 days.

Yours faithfully,

Figure 2.2 Letter of claim (public liability – tripping accident).

(e) Support the efficient management by the court and the parties of proceedings that cannot be avoided.

2.6.1 Failure to follow the required pre-action protocol procedure

If court proceedings are commenced following the pre-action protocol period, the court may be alerted to a party's conduct which may amount to a failure to comply with the Practice Direction and/or follow the pre-action conduct applicable to the nature of the dispute. If, as a consequence of court proceedings having been commenced, it is considered that a party has been put to unnecessary expense due to the failure to follow the required pre-action protocol procedure, the matter is dealt with under the pre-action conduct Practice Direction and may give rise to sanctions. The court will look at the overall effect of non-compliance on the other party when deciding whether to impose sanctions. If, in the opinion of the court, there has been non-compliance, the sanctions that the court may impose include:

(a) Staying (suspending) proceedings until steps which ought to have been taken have been taken
(b) Ordering that the party at fault pays the costs, or part of the costs, of the other party or parties (this may include an order under Rule 27.14(2)(g) in cases allocated to the small claims track)
(c) An order that the party at fault pays those costs on an indemnity basis (Rule 44.4(3) sets out the definition of the assessment of costs on an indemnity basis)
(d) If the party at fault is the claimant in whose favour an order for the payment of a sum of money is subsequently made, an order that the claimant is deprived of interest on all or part of that sum, and/or that interest is awarded at a lower rate than would otherwise have been awarded
(e) If the party at fault is a defendant, and an order for the payment of a sum of money is subsequently made in favour of the claimant, an order awarding interest on that sum for a specified period at a higher rate (not exceeding 10 per cent above base rate) than the rate which would otherwise have been awarded.

2.7 Applicable law: mechanisms to determine which country's laws apply to a contractual or tortious claim issued in the courts of England and Wales

In cases where litigation is contemplated concerning a case with a foreign element, it is important for the legal adviser to ensure that the claim is issued in the correct jurisdiction. Jurisdiction means the court system where the dispute will be dealt with or in other words the forum. Jurisdiction is distinct from the 'governing law' of a country, as the governing law is the law which will often be chosen to be used (sometimes agreed in a contract) within the jurisdiction hearing the case. If instructions are received from a client abroad, or a client wishes to pursue a claim against another party based outside the UK, then the question of which country's laws should apply also arises and needs to be considered. In such circumstances, the legal adviser must decide in which country the case should be best brought and proceedings commenced. There are rules that govern this.

2.7.1 EU countries

It should be noted that despite the UK's formal departure from the EU on 31 December 2020, the European (Withdrawal Agreement) Act 2020, preserves and incorporates most EU legislation within the domestic law of the UK. However, there is currently no current post-Brexit agreement about issues of jurisdiction, which the UK originally had agreed under the terms of Lugano Convention 2007 which is equivalent to the Recast Brussels Regulation, the regulation of the European Parliament and of the Council on jurisdiction and the recognition and enforcement of judgments in civil and commercial matters between EU member states.

Under the Lugano Convention 2007, if a defendant is based in the EU or the parties have agreed to litigate the dispute within an EU Member State, Council Regulation 1215/2012 (of the Recast Brussels Regulation) provides guidance on which jurisdiction should provide the forum for determination of the dispute. Whilst the Civil Jurisdiction and Judgments Act 1982 incorporates these provisions into English law, it is important to note the situation is unclear post-Brexit.

The general rule, as provided by Article 4 of Council Regulation 1215/2012, is that the jurisdiction governing the defendant's place of domicile or where a company's registered office is located is where the defendant should be sued. If, for example, the dispute concerns a company registered in Germany, the German company should be sued in the German courts. There are, however, specific rules applying to cases concerning contract and tort.

2.7.1.1 Contract cases

Article 7(1) provides that the state where the contract was performed will determine jurisdiction. For example, where the dispute involves the sale of goods, the forum will be the jurisdiction where the goods were delivered. In a dispute concerning the provision of services, the forum will be the jurisdiction where the services were to be provided.

It is usual for commercial contracts to incorporate governing law clauses to ensure clarity about which laws should prevail in the event of a dispute. Article 3(1) provides that a contract will be governed by the law chosen by the parties. However, if there is no governing law clause, this will present potential problems for the disputing parties, as the rules associated with determining the governing law are complex. In such circumstances, the parties will undoubtedly be required to have the issue concerning the appropriate governing law dealt with as a preliminary issue, and this will add to the litigation costs.

As a starting point, however, Article 4(1) provides guidance in particular instances. For example, for disputes concerning the sale of goods, the applicable law will be the law of the country where the seller has habitual residence, and with disputes concerning the supply of services, the applicable law will be that of the country where the supplier has habitual residence.

2.7.1.2 Tort cases

Cases concerning a cause of action arising in tort are dealt with under Article 7(2). This provides that the state where the tort was committed or where the harm/damage caused by the tortious action occurred will be the best forum for the case to be heard.

2.7.2 Outside the EU

2.7.2.1 Contract and tort cases

Where there is no governing law clause, the general rule is that the defendant should be sued in the courts of the member state where it is domiciled. If, therefore, the claimant is domiciled in England, but the defendant is domiciled in the USA, the presumption is that the defendant should be sued in its home state, the USA.

Regardless of where the cause of action arose, if a foreign defendant was served with proceedings when in England, it can be sued in the courts of England and Wales. A defendant from another member state may however object to being sued in the courts of England and Wales if the cause of action arose in their home state. For example, a US citizen alleged to have caused injury to an English person whilst on holiday in Florida will probably succeed in insisting that the claimant commence proceedings in the US courts.

The parties are, however, free to agree that the courts of a particular country are to have jurisdiction.

If the proposed defendant is based outside the jurisdiction, then the claimant must apply to the court for permission to serve proceedings.

The Hague Convention on Choice of Court Agreements provides a voluntary worldwide framework of rules on jurisdiction and the recognition and enforcement of judgments in civil and commercial matters. The provisions are incorporated into domestic law under the Private International Law (Implementation of Agreements) Act 2020.

2.8 Funding litigation

Whilst there is an increasing number of litigants who are self-representing, mainly as a consequence of legal aid being unavailable for most types of litigation concerning claims founded in contract and tort, the majority of parties involved in litigation will retain the services of a solicitor. Solicitors are under a professional duty to provide their clients with clear information about the different kinds of litigation funding available (legal aid, legal expenses insurance, or union funding for instance), and keep them regularly informed about continuing costs. In some cases, solicitors will undertake work on a fixed-fee basis (perhaps to simply draft documents or to attend a hearing within the litigation process). Where a client is paying 'privately', which is more common, the solicitor should explain the steps to be taken and the likely costs involved. For instance, hourly charging rates must be disclosed and the level of 'fee earner' within the firm who will be undertaking the work should be confirmed. It is not unusual for the client to make a payment 'on account' to his/her solicitor and then for regular interim bills for work undertaken to be rendered to the client.

2.9 Basic charging agreements

Basic charging agreements are probably the most commonplace. With such funding agreements, the solicitor should advise the client about the difference between solicitor and own-client costs (the amount the client should pay his/her solicitor) and those costs incurred between parties.

It is usual for the unsuccessful party in litigation to pay his own solicitor's costs. In addition, Rule 44.2(2)(a) of the CPR 1998 provides that the unsuccessful party will also be ordered to pay the costs of the successful party. Unless the parties can reach an agreement on the costs payable, the court will usually be required to assess the amount considered to be reasonable that the unsuccessful party must pay the successful party in costs and make the appropriate order for costs.

At the outset of the case, the client should always be informed by his/her solicitor that even if he/she wins the case, not all costs may be recovered. This is because even if the client wins the case, he/she will be required to pay his/her solicitor's costs, and the amount recovered from the opponent may not always cover these. Remember the successful party will only be awarded costs that the court considers reasonable.

2.10 Conditional fee agreements (CFAs)

A conditional fee arrangement or agreement is defined by s.58(2)(a) of the Courts and Legal Services Act (1990) as an agreement with a person providing advocacy or litigation services which provide for his/her fees and expenses, or any part of them, to be payable only in specified circumstances. The specified circumstances are where he/she succeeds in winning or successfully defending the claim. CFAs are not available for criminal cases, family cases, or those cases involving children.

CFAs are sometimes called 'no win no fee' agreements because the solicitor entering into such an agreement with a client will not receive any payment in legal fees if the client loses the case. If the client wins the case, then the solicitor may under s.58(2)(b) of the Courts and Legal Services Act (1990) receive in addition to the usual costs payable a success fee which can be up to 100 per cent of the solicitor's usual hourly charging rate.

CFAs must comply with s.58(3) and (4) Legal Services Act (1990), and:

- Be in writing
- Not relate to proceedings which cannot be the subject of an enforceable CFA

- State the percentage uplift payable if successful (and must not exceed the percentage specified in relation to the description of proceedings to which the agreement relates).

2.10.1 The success fee

Because there is considered to be a risk to the solicitor in taking on the case (if the client loses the solicitor will not receive any fees), a success fee can be charged in the event that the client wins his/her case. The solicitor should carry out a risk assessment and the level of risk is reflected in the success fee which is a percentage increase on basic costs (the solicitor's hourly charging rate).

Due to the application of the indemnity principle (see Chapter 13 on costs), whilst the winning party's solicitor is entitled to claim recovery of their reasonable costs (this will usually be ordered by the court) from the losing party, this does not include the success fee. That will be payable by the client.

2.10.2 After-the-event insurance

It has been commonplace for a client who has entered into a CFA with his/her solicitor to take out after-the-event (ATE) insurance. This will normally cover (usually the claimant in proceedings) the legal costs which a claimant must pay to a defendant if the claim is unsuccessful. It can also cover the disbursements (litigation expenses) incurred by the claimant's own solicitor.

2.11 Legal expenses insurance

When taking instructions from a new client, the solicitor should always check to see if the client has an insurance policy that covers him/her for the legal expenses of the case. This type of legal expenses insurance policy is called before-the-event (BTE) insurance. It is common for this kind of insurance to be purchased with a policy of household or motor insurance.

2.12 Contingency fees or damages-based agreement

These agreements allow a solicitor to recover a share of the client's damages in costs if the claim is successful. Contingency fees or damages-based agreements (DBAs) have been only available in England and Wales since 1 April 2013 pursuant to s.45 Legal Aid, Sentencing and Punishment of Offenders Act 2012 (LASPO), which amended s.58AA of the Courts and Legal Services Act 1990 to permit DBAs.

Through the application of the indemnity principle which also applies to DBAs, if successful in his/her claim, the claimant can recover costs from the defendant but cannot recover more in costs than is required to pay to his/her own solicitor. Therefore, if the agreed contingency fee is lower than the figure decided through the assessment of costs by the court, the defendant will only have to pay the lower amount in costs.

2.13 Third-party funding

Traditionally third-party funding of litigation or 'champerty' was not lawful in England and Wales. However, the rules have been relaxed now and it is possible for a third party unconnected with the litigation to assist with funding a client's case in return for a fee.

If the client is a member of a trade union or other professional organisation, it may be possible for the client's costs to be paid by the union or organisation. It is not usual with these kinds of agreements for the funder to receive a separate fee, however.

2.14 Public funding

Following successive civil justice reviews of the public funding system or legal aid in England and Wales, the most recent culminating in the enactment of the LASPO, very few areas of law now remain 'within scope' of legal aid funding administered by the Legal Aid Agency. For instance, personal injury claims, a significant area of tort law where legal aid was available for those eligible, were removed from scope following the enactment of the Access to Justice Act 1999. There may, however, be very limited situations where clients are eligible to receive legal aid funding for civil litigation.

Chapter 2 revision points

Resolving a dispute through a civil claim

- Pre-action considerations:
  - Statutory limitation periods apply to all potential civil claims
  - The overriding objective – CPR Part 1.1
  - Parties – legal entities
  - Causes of action – the basis upon which the potential claimant believes they have a right to a remedy from the legal entity, the potential defendant
- Pre-action conduct:
  - Pre-action protocol rationale
  - Sanctions for failure to comply
- Applicable law:
  - Pre-action protocol rationale Jurisdiction – where the dispute (case) will be heard (the court system)
  - Governing law – applies to rules and laws that will govern the dispute

  - The distinction between EU and non-EU countries and approaches to dispute resolution
- Litigation funding:
  - Basic charging agreements
  - Conditional fee agreements
  - The success fee
  - After-the-event insurance
  - Legal expenses insurance (before-the-event insurance)
  - Contingency fee agreements
  - Third-party funding
  - Public funding

Multiple-choice questions for Part 2

1. Shortly before limitation expires on 30 November, a claimant pursuing a claim for damages for personal injury and loss failed to attend a pre-arranged appointment with a medical expert. No medical report is available, which is a requirement to accompany the service of court proceedings. The next medical appointment cannot be made until 10 April next year. The claimant issues proceedings but does not serve the claim form.

*Which one of the following **best** explains what advice should be provided to the claimant?*

A. An application should be made to extend the time to serve the claim form with the particulars of the claim with supportive medical evidence under CPR Rule 8.6.
B. An application should be made to dispense with service of the claim form with the particulars of the claim and medical evidence under CPR 6.16.
C. An application should be made to extend the time to serve the claim form with the particulars of the claim with supportive medical evidence under CPR Rule 7.6.
D. No application is needed, it is sufficient for the claimant to write to the court explaining the situation and that the claim form will be served late.
E. An application should be made to extend the time to serve the claim form with the particulars of the claim with supportive medical evidence under the provisions of the Administration of Justice Act 1920.

2. Nearly three years ago, whilst on holiday in California, A, a UK citizen, was involved in a car accident on the Pacific Highway in which he suffered a broken arm and other soft tissue injuries. A alleges that B, a US citizen, was responsible for the accident. Limitation expires in a month and A must serve proceedings if the claim is to be pursued. An enquiry agent employed by A has established that B has business interests in the UK and will be in the UK on business next week. Hurriedly, A's legal adviser arranges for proceedings to be commenced in the jurisdiction of England and Wales and will be served on B when in England.

*Which one of the following situations **best** explains in which jurisdiction the claim will proceed once proceedings are issued by A and served on the defendant B?*

A. Under the terms of the Lugano Convention 2007, the case must proceed in England and Wales because that is where the defendant B's company is based.
B. Under the Hague Convention, B can object to the claim proceeding in the courts of England and Wales by arguing that the best forum would be where he is domiciled, i.e., the USA.
C. There is no provision that insists that the case must proceed under the jurisdiction of England and Wales because the parties to the action do not have a governing law or jurisdiction agreement.
D. As he has been served in England, B has no grounds to object to the case proceeding in England and, due to place of service, must accept that the correct jurisdiction will be that of England and Wales.
E. The claimant can object to the case proceeding in England under Article 7(2) and insist that the state where the alleged tort was committed will be the best forum for the case to be heard.

PART

3

Commencing, responding to, or progressing a claim

3 Where to start proceedings

3.1 Chapter overview

The situation in which parties are unable to resolve their dispute during the pre-action protocol period and court proceedings are to be contemplated will give rise to the consideration of preliminary issues such as choice of court and the allocation of business between the High Court and the County Court. These matters will be dealt with in this chapter as well as an overview of the court structure in England and Wales.

The work of the main courts and the jurisdiction of the specialist courts will be explained, so as to determine which court forum should be chosen once the decision to commence court proceedings has been taken by the proposed claimant.

3.2 Introduction: choice of court

Once the pre-action protocol period has passed and the parties to a civil dispute have not reached a settlement, the potential claimant may then have no other option but to resort to litigation. Once the decision has been taken to pursue litigation and commence court proceedings, the claimant must then decide where proceedings will be started, or to use the technical term, 'issued'. Part 7 CPR 1998 (Part 7) provides the guidance for this, and for claims founded in contract and tort it is based on the value of the claim. Practice Direction (PD) 7A, para 2.1 states that if the claim does not exceed £100,000, then the case must be issued in the County Court. If the claim exceeds £100,000, then it can be issued in the High Court. Although, PD 7A, para 2.2 provides that claims for damages for personal injuries can be started in the High Court if the value of the claim is £50,000 or more.

3.3 Allocation of business between the High Court and the County Court

Where the claimant has a choice of where to start proceedings (either the High Court or the County Court), under PD 7A 2.4, the claimant should start the claim in the High Court if by reason of:

(1) the financial value of the claim and the amount in dispute, and/or
(2) the complexity of the facts, legal issues, remedies, or procedures involved, and/or

DOI: 10.4324/9781003218500-6

(3) the importance of the outcome of the claim to the public in general, the claimant believes that the claim ought to be dealt with by a High Court judge.

3.3.1 The County Court

The County Court was founded in 1846 and as of 2021, there are 170 County Courts in England and Wales. All civil claims can be started here and, other than claims founded in contract and tort, the court's jurisdiction includes recovery of land, divorce and family matters, and the small claims procedure. The County Courts are served by circuit judges, district judges, and deputy district judges.

The Part 7 procedure applies only to claims for money and therefore is generally the correct procedure to use for claims founded in contract and tort. Claims for either a specified or non-specified amount of money should be sent by post, using the appropriate form (N1 Claim Form) with the issue fee, to the County Court Money Claims Centre, at:

County Court Money Claims Centre
PO Box 527
Salford
M5 0BY

Money claims for a fixed amount of a value less than £100,000, can alternatively be issued online by visiting the Money Claims Online Court (MCOL) website.[1] The claim must be against no more than two people or organisations and the service can be used from anywhere in the UK, but only against someone with an address in England or Wales.[2]

3.3.2 The High Court

The High Court was established by the Judicature Act 1873, which created what is technically (and perhaps confusingly) called the Supreme Court comprising three Administrative Divisions, namely: the King's Bench Division (KBD), the Chancery Division, and the Family Division. There are also Divisional Courts that deal with appeals from the inferior (lower) courts. The High Court is served by High Court judges and masters. For the purposes of this book, we are mainly concerned with the operation of the King's Bench Division of the High Court, although the specialist civil courts and their association with both the King's Bench Division and the Chancery Division are considered in the following.

1 See www.moneyclaim.gov.uk/web/mcol/welcome.
2 Ibid.

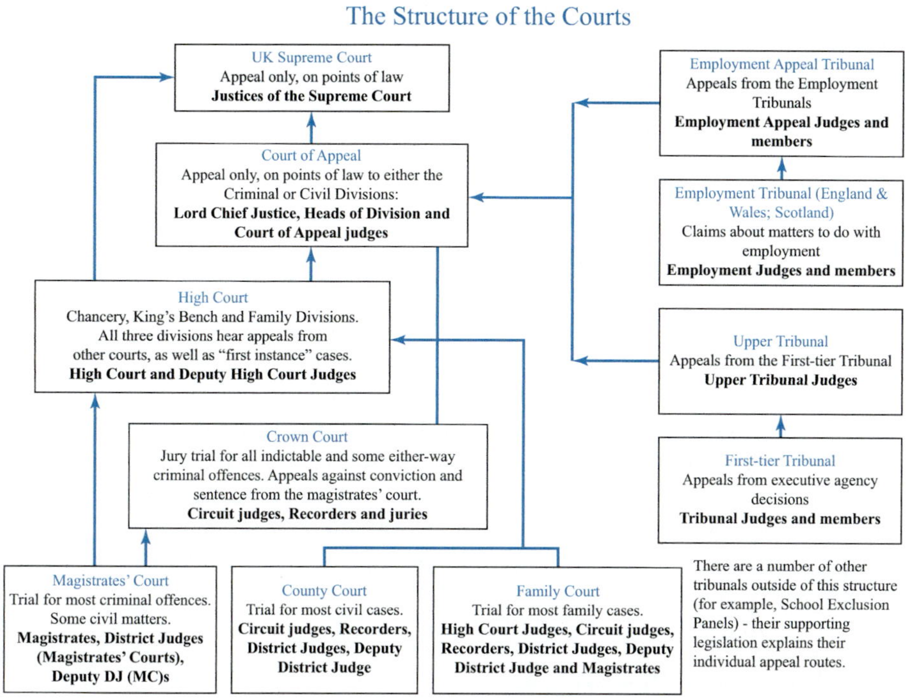

Figure 3.1 Structure of the courts in England and Wales (including tribunals). Source: Courts Tribunals and Judiciary website. Available at: www.judiciary.uk/about-the-judiciary/the-justice-system/court-structure/courts-structure-0715-2/.

The King's Bench Division is where all claims for contract and tort will be dealt with. The court has a designated website[3] which states that the cases most commonly dealt with are personal injury, negligence, breach of contract, breach of statutory duty, breach of the Human Rights Act 1998, libel, slander and other torts, non-payment of a debt, and 'enforcement orders' which allow the court to ensure that a party complies with a judgment against them.

The King's Bench Division of the High Court is based at the Royal Courts of Justice in London and at district registries across England and Wales. Hearings at the Royal Courts of Justice are heard by a High Court judge (or sometimes a deputy High Court judge or circuit judge) while other issues (e.g., case management, listing, and most applications) are handled by a 'master'. Outside London, hearings are heard by circuit judges while the work of masters is handled by district judges.[4]

3 www.gov.uk/courts-tribunals/queens-bench-division-of-the-high-court.
4 Ibid.

The Chancery Division of the High Court is based at the Rolls Building in London and at district registries across England and Wales. The nature of the work commonly dealt with in the Chancery Division includes disputes relating to business, property or land, disputes over trusts, competition claims under either European or UK competition law, commercial disputes (domestic and international), intellectual property issues, and disputes over the validity of a will ('probate disputes').[5]

3.4 Jurisdiction of the specialist courts

There are some specialist courts, such as the Administrative Court, the Admiralty Court, the Commercial Court (formerly the Mercantile Court), the Technology and Construction Court, and the Intellectual Property Enterprise Court (IPEC) (formerly the Patents Court) that deal with particular types of subject matter in cases which do not necessarily need to be heard in the High Court. Whilst these specialist courts are associated with either the King's Bench Division or the Chancery Division of the High Court, since 2017 some of them have been brought under the auspices of the Business and Property Courts for specialist civil jurisdiction within England and Wales.

3.5 The specialist courts

3.5.1 Administrative Court

The Administrative Court is a specialist court within the King's Bench Division based at the Royal Courts of Justice, London, and at centres in Birmingham, Cardiff, Leeds, and Manchester. The court reviews decisions made by people or bodies with a public law function, e.g., local authorities and regulatory bodies. The court can carry out a judicial review of decisions made by other courts, tribunals, and public bodies and can hear challenges to decisions made by certain people or bodies (e.g., ministers or local government) where legislation has given the right to challenge.[6]

3.5.2 Admiralty Court

The Admiralty Court is part of the recently created Business and Property Court within the King's Bench Division based in the Rolls Building, London. The Admiralty Court deals with shipping and maritime disputes which include collisions between ships, disputes over the transport of cargo, salvage of a ship, cargo, or crew, disputes over goods supplied to a ship, disputes over mortgages and other security over ships, claims by passengers for injuries suffered, claims by ship crew for unpaid wages, and claims by shipowners to limit liability for loss or damage.[7]

5 www.gov.uk/courts-tribunals/chancery-division-of-the-high-court.
6 www.gov.uk/courts-tribunals/administrative-court.
7 www.gov.uk/courts-tribunals/admiralty-court.

3.5.3 Commercial Court

The Commercial Court is also part of the Business and Property Court within the King's Bench Division based in the Rolls Building, London, and deals with complex national and international business disputes. Cases that we hear include disputes over contracts and business documents, insurance and reinsurance, sale of commodities, import, export, and transport ('carriage') of goods, issues relating to arbitration awards, banking and financial services, agency and management agreements, and construction of ships.[8]

3.5.4 Technology and Construction Court

The Technology and Construction Court is also part of the Business and Property Court within the King's Bench Division. The court covers both High Court and County Court claims. The High Court work is handled at the Rolls Building, London, and at district registries across England and Wales. The County Court work is handled at court centres across England and Wales. The court deals with disputes about buildings, engineering, and surveying, including claims about services provided by engineers, architects, surveyors, and other professionals in this sector, claims about local authority duties relating to land and buildings, environmental claims (e.g. pollution), claims resulting from fires, and challenges to decisions of arbitrators in construction and engineering disputes.

The court generally does not handle cases with a value of less than £250,000 unless there is a good reason, e.g., the case involves a new or difficult point of law or the case is of an international nature.[9]

3.5.5 Intellectual Property Enterprise

The Intellectual Property Enterprise Court is also part of the Business and Property Courts within the Chancery Division of the High Court, based at the Rolls Building in London. The court deals with cases relating to intellectual property disputes, including registered designs, patents, registered trademarks, copyrights, and other intellectual property rights. If the amount sought (damages) is under £500,000 then the case can also be heard by the Patents Court or the Chancery Division. These two courts will hear cases where the amount sought is over £500,000 unless all parties agree that we may hear it.

Certain intellectual property disputes where the amount sought is £10,000 or less will be handled by the court's 'small claims track'.[10]

8 www.gov.uk/courts-tribunals/commercial-court.
9 www.gov.uk/courts-tribunals/technology-and-construction-court.
10 www.gov.uk/courts-tribunals/intellectual-property-enterprise-court.

3.5.6 Patents Court

The Patents Court, whilst under the specialist auspices of the Business and Property Court, sits within the Chancery Division of the High Court based at the Rolls Building in London. The Patents Court deals with cases relating to intellectual property, and particularly disputes about patents, registered designs, and plant varieties.

If the value of the claim exceeds £500,000, then the Patents Court will normally handle the case unless all the parties to the case have agreed that the Intellectual Property Enterprise Court may hear it.[11]

Chapter 3 revision points

Where to start proceedings

- Choice of court
- Allocation of business – value, complexity, public importance (of outcome):
    - County Court
    - High Court
- Specialist courts:
    - Administrative Court
    - Admiralty Court
    - Technology and Construction Court
    - Intellectual Property Enterprise Court (IPEC) (formerly the Patents Court)

11 www.gov.uk/courts-tribunals/patents-court.

4 Issuing and serving proceedings

4.1 Chapter overview

Once the decision has been taken to commence court proceedings, the procedure for issuing and serving proceedings will be explained in this chapter. The importance of completing the claim form accurately will be stressed before other matters such as adding or substituting parties once court proceedings have been commenced and serving the particulars of claim separately are addressed.

The chapter will also consider methods, place, and deemed dates of service (with time limits) and the procedure for service of a claim form outside the jurisdiction (with or without the court's permission), as well as the mechanisms for effecting valid service in another jurisdiction.

4.2 Introduction: issuing and serving proceedings

Once the choice of court has been established, the claimant must now issue and serve proceedings on the defendant. This is a crucially important stage, and it is vital that the claim form is drafted accurately, and the correct court fee is paid. Otherwise, the court issue desk may refuse to issue the claim form and will return it unserved to the claimant, or their legal representative. The importance of 'getting it right' the first time, not least to save time and money, may also be an issue if the limitation date (discussed in Chapter 2) is looming. If for instance limitation for the purposes of court proceedings expires on 1 May, the claimant or its legal representative would be well advised to ensure that all attempts to issue proceedings are made well before this date, in early April ideally. For the purposes of limitation, the date when the court receives the claim form is the date when proceedings are considered to have started. Failure to issue proceedings within the limitation period may cause the claim to be 'statute barred' for limitation purposes and the claim will likely be struck out. In those circumstances, the claimant will have lost the opportunity to use litigation to resolve the dispute.

4.3 Issuing a claim form

Part 7 CPR 1998 (Part 7) and the Practice Directions for this part provide guidance on how to start proceedings using a claim form. CPR 7.2 states that proceedings

DOI: 10.4324/9781003218500-7

are started when the court issues a claim form at the request of the claimant and a claim form is issued on the date entered on the form by the court (although see the point made above regarding limitation). Part 16 and its Practice Directions should also be referred to as these provide guidance on Statements of Case, contents of the claim form, statements of value, and particulars of claim. A copy of the N1 claim form used in the case of *Madeline Bray v Arthur Squeers trading as Dotheboys Farm* appears in Figure 4.1.

To assist in completing the claim form, the Court Service provides a very helpful guidance document. See Figure 4.2 for the N1a Notes for Claimant on Completing a Claim form. As well as the CPR and Practice Directions, these guidance notes should be referred to when considering the following information which will need to be included in the claim form.

4.3.1 Claimant's and defendant's details

In order to complete the claim form with accurate details of the parties to litigation, the Practice Direction to Rule 16 provides helpful guidance and should be referred to. Practice Direction 16.2 specifies the following matters which the claim form must contain:

(1) An address at which the claimant resides or carries on business. This paragraph applies even though the claimant's address for service is the business address of his solicitor.

(2) Where the defendant is an individual, the claimant should (if he/she is able to do so) include in the claim form an address at which the defendant resides or carries on business. This paragraph applies even though the defendant's solicitors have agreed to accept service on the defendant's behalf.

(3) Any address which is provided for the purpose of these provisions must include a postcode or its equivalent in any European Economic Area (EEA) state (if applicable), unless the court orders otherwise. Postcode information for the United Kingdom may be obtained from www.royalmail.com or the Royal Mail Address Management Guide.

(4) If the claim form does not show a full address, including postcode, at which the claimant(s) and defendant(s) reside or carry on business, the claim form will be issued but will be retained by the court and will not be served until the claimant has supplied a full address, including postcode, or the court has dispensed with the requirement to do so. The court will notify the claimant.

(5) The claim form must be headed with the title of the proceedings, including the full name of each party. The full name means, in each case where it is known:

    (a) in the case of an individual, his full unabbreviated name and title by which he is known;

In the	County Court Money Claims Centre
Fee Account no.	
Help with Fees - Ref no. (if applicable)	H W F - -

Claim Form

You may be able to issue your claim online which may save time and money. Go to www.moneyclaim.gov.uk to find out more.

	For court use only
Claim no.	
Issue date	

Claimant(s) name(s) and address(es) including postcode

Madeline Bray
75 Spring Lane
Calmforth
Yorks HD9 1DT

SEAL

Defendant(s) name and address(es) including postcode
Arthur Squeers T/A Dotheboys Farm
Nettleton Road
Calmforth
Yorks HD9 7BR

Brief details of claim

The Claimant claims damages for personal injury and loss arising out of an accident on 13th December 2021 at Dotheboys Farm.

Value

The Claimant's cliam includes a claim for personal injuries and the amount she expects to recover in damages for pain, suffering, and loss of amenity is greater than £1,000 but not more than £10,000

You must indicate your preferred County Court Hearing Centre for hearings here *(see notes for guidance)*

Huddersfield

Defendant's name and address for service including postcode

Arthur Squeers T/A Dotheboys Farm
Nettleton Road
Calmforth
Yorks HD9 7BR

	£
Amount claimed	
Court fee	410.00
Legal representative's costs	
Total amount	

For further details of the courts www.gov.uk/find-court-tribunal.
When corresponding with the Court, please address forms or letters to the Manager and always quote the claim number.

N1 Claim form (CPR Part 7) (10.20)

Figure 4.1 N1 claim form (page 1).

Notes for claimant on completing a claim form

Before you begin completing the claim form

- You must think about whether alternative dispute resolution (ADR) is a better way to reach an agreement before going to court. The leaflet 'I'm in a dispute - What can I do?' explains more about ADR and how you can attempt to settle your claim.
- Please read all the notes which follow the order in which information is required on the form.
- Before completing this form, consider whether you might prefer to issue online www.moneyclaim.gov.uk
- If you are filling in the claim form by hand, please use black ink and write in block capitals.
- Copy the completed claim form and the defendant's notes for guidance so that you have one copy for yourself, one copy for the court and one copy for each defendant.
- If the claim is for a sum of money then you must send it to the County Court Money Claims Centre, PO Box 527, Salford, M5 0BY.
- If it is a High Court claim or is a claim for anything other than money you should send the form and the fee to a court office.
- You can get additional help in completing this form from the Money Claim helpdesk - phone 0300 1231372. If you need legal advice you should contact a solicitor or a Citizens Advice Bureau.

Further information may be obtained from Direct.gov.uk or from the court in a series of free leaflets.

Notes on completing the claim form

Heading

You must fill in the heading of the form to indicate the name of the court where you want the claim to be issued. If you want the claim to proceed in the County Court and it is for money only, you must enter 'County Court Money Claims Centre'.

The claimant and defendant

As the person issuing the claim, you are called the 'claimant'. Please enter your name and address. The person you are suing is called the 'defendant'. Please enter their name.

You must provide the following information about yourself and the defendant according to the capacity in which you are suing and in which the defendant is being sued.

Providing information about yourself and the defendant

full address including postcode

You should provide the address including postcode for yourself and the defendant or its equivalent in any European Economic Area (EEA) state (if applicable).

If an address does not have a postcode you will need to ask the judge for permission to serve the claim with this information missing. There is no additional fee for this, but the court will not allow your claim to be served without the postcode, unless you have permission from the judge.

When suing or being sued as:-

an individual:

You must enter his or her full name where known, including the title (for example, Mr., Mrs., Ms., Dr.) and residential address postcode and telephone number. Where the defendant is a proprietor of a business, a partner in a firm or an individual sued in the name of a club or other unincorporated association, the address for service should be the usual or last known place of residence or principal place of business.

Where the individual is:

trading under another name

you must enter his or her full unabbreviated name where known, and the title by which he or she is known and the full name under which he or she is trading, for example, 'Mr. John Smith trading as Smith's Groceries'.

suing or being sued in a representative capacity you must say what that capacity is for example, 'Mr Joe Bloggs as the representative of Mrs Sharon Bloggs (deceased)'.

suing or being sued in the name of a club or other unincorporated association add the words 'suing/sued on behalf of' followed by the name of the club or other unincorporated association.

an unincorporated business - a firm

In the case of a partnership (other than a limited liability partnership) you must enter the full name of the business followed by the suffix 'a firm' for example, 'Bandbox - a firm' and an address including postcode for service. This may either be one of the partners residential addresses or the principal or last known place of business of the firm.

a company registered in England and Wales or a Limited Liability Partnership

In the case of a registered company or limited liability partnership, enter the full name followed by the appropriate suffix (for example, 'Ltd'.) and an address including postcode which is either the company's registered office or any place of business in the UK that has a connection with the claim e.g. where goods were bought.

N1A Notes for claimant (07.14)

Figure 4.2 Form N1a Notes for claimant on completing a claim form.

a corporation (other than a company)
enter the full name of the corporation and any suffix and the address including postcode in the UK which is either its principal office or any other place where the corporation carries on activities and which has a connection with the claim.

an overseas company (defined by s744 of the Companies Act 1985)
enter the company's full name and any suffix if appropriate and address including postcode. The address must either be the registered address under s691 of the Act or the address of the place of business having a connection with the claim

under 18 write '(a child by Mr Joe Bloggs his litigation friend)' after the name. If the child is conducting proceedings on their own behalf write '(a child)' after the child's name.

a patient within the meaning of the Mental Health Act 1983 write '(by Mr Joe Bloggs his litigation friend)' after the patient's name.

Brief details of claim

You must set out under **this** heading:

- a concise statement of the nature of your claim
- the remedy you are seeking e.g. payment of money

Value

If you are claiming a **fixed amount of money** (a 'specified amount') write the amount in the box at the bottom right-hand corner of the claim form against 'amount claimed'.

If you are not claiming a fixed amount of money (an 'unspecified amount') under 'Value' write "I expect to recover" followed by whichever of the following applies to your claim:

- 'not more than £10,000' **or**
- 'more than £10,000 but not more than £25,000' **or**
- 'more than £25,000'

If you are **not able** to put a value on your claim, write 'I cannot say how much I expect to recover'.

Personal injuries
If your claim is for 'not more than £5,000' and includes a claim for personal injuries, you must also write 'My claim includes a claim for personal injuries and the amount I expect to recover as damages for pain, suffering and loss of amenity is' followed by either:

- 'not more than £1,000' **or**
- 'more than £1,000'

Housing disrepair
If your claim is for 'not more than £5,000' and includes a claim for housing disrepair relating to residential premises, you must also write 'My claim includes a claim against my landlord for housing disrepair relating to residential premises. The cost of the repairs or other work is estimated to be' followed by either:

- 'not more than £1,000' **or**
- 'more than £1,000'

If within this claim, you are making a claim for other damages, you must also write:

'I expect to recover as damages' followed by either:

- 'not more than £1,000' **or**
- 'more than £1,000'

Preferred Court

You may be asked to send this claim to a court centre that is not convenient for you to attend. If attendance is required the court will transfer the case to make it easier for one or all of the parties to attend. A list of County Courts hearing centre can be found at: hmctscourtfinder.justice.gov.uk State your preferred court where indicated. The court will take it into account if transfer is required.

Defendant's name and address

Enter in this box the title, full names, address and postcode of the defendant receiving the claim form (one claim form for each defendant). If the defendant is to be served outside the UK or any other state of the EEA, you may need to obtain the court's permission.

Legal representative's costs

These fixed sums may only be claimed where a legal representative has been instructed to make the claim on your behalf.

Particulars of claim

You must set out under this heading:

- a concise statement of the facts on which you rely
- a statement (if applicable) that you are seeking aggravated damages or exemplary damages
- details of any interest which you are claiming
- any other matters required for your type of claim as set out in the relevant practice direction

Statement of truth

This must be signed by you, your solicitor or your litigation friend.

Where the claimant is a registered company or a corporation the claim must be signed by either the director or other officer of the company or (in the case of a corporation) the mayor, chairman, president or town clerk.

Address for documents

Please note that the service regulation provides that cross-border service by any direct means including fax or email is not permitted within the EEA.

Figure 4.2 Continued.

(b) in the case of an individual carrying on business in a name other than his own name, the full unabbreviated name of the individual, together with the title by which he is known, and the full trading name (for example, John Smith 'trading as' or 'T/A' 'JS Autos');
(c) in the case of a partnership (other than a limited liability partnership (LLP))
  (i) where partners are being sued in the name of the partnership, the full name by which the partnership is known, together with the words '(A Firm)'; or
  (ii) where partners are being sued as individuals, the full unabbreviated name of each partner and the title by which he is known;
(d) in the case of a company or limited liability partnership registered in England and Wales, the full registered name, including suffix (plc, limited, LLP, etc), if any;
(e) in the case of any other company or corporation, the full name by which it is known, including suffix where appropriate.

As mentioned earlier, it is vitally important that the correct address for service is provided on the claim form, otherwise, the court will be unable to effect proper service of the court documents. If the claimant does not have an address for the defendant, then an application to dispense with service of the claim form can be made, the procedure for which is dealt with under CPR Part 6 and its associated Practice Directions.

4.3.2 Brief details of claim

The full particulars of the claim should not be placed here. As the heading suggests and notes on completing the claim form state, only brief details are required, and Rule 16 2(1) provides that the claim must:

(a) contain a concise statement of the nature of the claim;
(b) specify the remedy which the claimant seeks.

4.3.3 Value/amount claimed

The wording to be used for the value or the amount claimed will depend on the nature of the claim and whether it is a claim for a fixed amount or for a claim for an unspecified amount such as for personal injuries. Rule 16 2(1) provides that the claim must:

(a) where the claimant is making a claim for money, contain a statement of value in accordance with rule 16.3;
(b) where the claimant's only claim is for a specified sum, contain a statement of the interest accrued on that sum.

Rule 16.3(2) requires that the claimant must indicate the amount claimed, or if for an unspecified amount of money, whether or not the claimant expects to recover:

(a) not more than £10,000;
(b) more than £10,000 but not more than £25,000; or

(c) more than £25,000; or
(d) that the claimant cannot say how much is likely to be recovered.

Providing details of value/amount will indicate the amount of the court issue fee payable (see the following). It will also assist the county court in allocating the claim to the appropriate track: either the small claims track (claims of less than £10,000), the fast track (claims of between £10,000 and £25,000), or the multi-track (claims of greater than £25,000). Note that personal injury claims of less than £1,000 will be allocated to the small claims track and clear guidance for the wording to be included in the value section for such claims is provided in the Notes for Claimant in Completing a Claim form.

If the claim is to be commenced in the High Court due to the fact that the claim involves an unspecified sum of money, under Practice Direction 7A, para 3.6, the claimant should state that the amount expected to be recovered is greater than £100,000.

4.3.4 The court fee

The claimant must pay the correct court fee when asking the court to issue proceedings. This will be based on the value of the claim and the claimant should refer to the current Civil and Family Court Fees guidance document (EX50), available from the UK Government website.[1]

4.3.5 Legal representative's costs

If the claim is issued by the claimant's legal representative and the amount claimed is for a specified amount of money, then the amount of 'fixed costs', then the claimant will be entitled to claim fixed costs in the event that the defendant admits the claim. The amount of fixed costs will vary depending on the nature of the claim. Guidance on the amount to include for fixed costs is provided in CPR Part 45. It is acceptable for a claim for an unspecified amount of money for the claim form to be completed with the words 'to be assessed', and the court will then determine the amount payable by the defendant should the claimant be successful.

4.3.6 Particulars of claim

The claimant must either complete (endorse) the particulars of claim on page two of the claim form or serve separate particulars of claim within 14 days of service of the claim form. The words 'attached' or 'to follow' should therefore be struck out depending on which applies.

4.3.7 Contents of the particulars of claim

Rule 16.4 provides that the particulars of claim must include:

(a) a concise statement of the facts on which the claimant relies;
(b) if the claimant is seeking interest, a statement to that effect;

1 www.gov.uk/government/publications/fees-in-the-civil-and-family-courts-main-fees-ex50.

(c) if the claimant is seeking aggravated damages or exemplary damages, a statement to that effect and his grounds for claiming them;
(d) if the claimant is seeking provisional damages, a statement to that effect and his grounds for claiming them.

It is usual for the claimant to seek interest and in which case he/she must:

(a) state whether he/she is doing so –
    (i) under the terms of a contract;
    (ii) under an enactment and if so which; or
    (iii) on some other basis and if so, what that basis is; and
(b) if the claim is for a specified amount of money, state –
    (i) the percentage rate at which interest is claimed;
    (ii) the date from which it is claimed;
    (iii) the date to which it is calculated, which must not be later than the date on which the claim form is issued;
    (iv) the total amount of interest claimed to the date of calculation; and
    (v) the daily rate at which interest accrues after that date.

4.3.8 Statement of truth

CPR Part 22 provides that various documents used in the course of litigation need to be verified by a statement of truth. The claim form is one such document. The form of the statement of truth verifying a statement of the case, a response, an application notice, a certificate of reasons, or a notice of objections should, in accordance with PD 22 para 2.1, be as follows:

> [I believe] [the (claimant or as may be) believes] that the facts stated in this [name document being verified] are true. I understand] [The (claimant or as may be) understands that proceedings for contempt of court may be brought against anyone who makes, or causes to be made, a false statement in a document verified by a statement of truth without an honest belief in its truth.

Practice Direction 22, para 3.1 provides guidance on who may sign the statement of truth. Essentially, in a statement of case, a response, or an application notice, the statement of truth must be signed by:

(1) the party or his litigation friend, or
(2) the legal representative of the party or litigation friend.

4.3.9 Signing the claim form

The claim form should be signed by the claimant or the claimant's legal representative/solicitor. The wording to be used is as follows: 'I believe that ...' or '[name of party] believes that ...'.

In the case of an organisation or company, for instance, a person authorised to sign on behalf of that organisation/company should sign. In which case the following wording should be added: 'I am duly authorised by [name of party] to sign this statement'.

Failure to sign the claim form, or otherwise verify its contents with a statement of truth, may mean that the claim will be struck out by the court on its own initiative or upon application by the defendant, according to Practice Direction 22 para 4. If the claimant knowingly verifies a statement of case containing a false statement, r 32.14 provides that proceedings for contempt of court may be brought against the person making the false statement.

4.4 Adding or substituting parties

If the parties are individuals of full age, then their full names should appear on the claim form. There may, however, be special considerations where the claimant is a partnership, limited company, sole trader, child, or other protected party.

Partnerships should sue or be sued in the name of the firm, e.g., Nickleby, Noggs, and Knag (a firm). Sole traders should sue and be sued in the name of the individual, e.g., Wackford Squeers trading as, or T/A for short. A limited company should sue or be sued in its company name, e.g., Linkinwater Mantalini Millinery Limited. It is recommended that a company search of Companies House be undertaken to determine the correct name of the company and its registered office, where the claim form should be served.

A child is deemed to be a person under the age of 18, and a protected person is considered to be a person who is incapable of managing his or her affairs by virtue of the Mental Capacity Act 2005. Guidance for these litigants is provided under CPR Part 21. In these circumstances, the claimant will require a litigation friend to conduct the litigation on their behalf.

Occasionally the claimant will find it necessary to add or substitute a defendant to the proceedings and under r 19.1, any number of defendants may be joined as parties to the claim. For instance, in a claim for damages for personal injuries, this may arise if the claimant discovers that in place of, or as well as the defendant already sued, another party may be at fault entirely or as well. The rules governing the addition of a party to proceedings are governed by r 19.2:

(2) The court may order a person to be added as a new party if –
    (a) it is desirable to add the new party so that the court can resolve all the matters in dispute in the proceedings; or
    (b) there is an issue involving the new party and an existing party which is connected to the matters in dispute in the proceedings, and it is desirable to add the new party so that the court can resolve that issue.

(3) The court may order any person to cease to be a party if it is not desirable for that person to be a party to the proceedings.

(4) The court may order a new party to be substituted for an existing one if –
  (a) the existing party's interest or liability has passed to the new party; and
  (b) it is desirable to substitute the new party so that the court can resolve the matters in dispute in the proceedings.

4.5 Service of the claim form within the jurisdiction – methods of service

Once the claim form has been issued it will need to be served on the defendant(s). Rule 7.5 and PD 6A provide the guidance for service within the jurisdiction. The permitted methods of service within the jurisdiction are as follows:

(a) personal service;
(b) first class post, Document Exchange or other service which provides for delivery on the next business day;
(c) leaving it at a place;
(d) fax or other means of electronic communication;
(e) any method authorised by the court.

It is usual for the claimant to send sufficient copies of the claim form for each defendant plus one copy for the court file. The court will then choose the appropriate method of service; usually, this will be by first-class post.

Rule 7.5(1) provides that where the claim form is served within the jurisdiction, the claimant must complete the step required by the following table in relation to the particular method of service chosen, before 12.00 midnight on the calendar day four months after the date of issue of the claim form. Table 4.1 illustrates the various methods of service and the required steps that should be taken.

Table 4.1 Steps required depending on the method of service used

Method of service	Step required
First-class post, Document Exchange, or other service which provides for delivery on the next business day	Posting, leaving with, delivering to, or collection by the relevant service provider
Delivery of the document to or leaving it at the relevant place	Delivering to or leaving the document at the relevant place
Personal service under Rule 6.5	Completing the relevant step required by Rule 6.5(3)
Fax	Completing the transmission of the fax
Other electronic method	Sending the e-mail or other electronic transmission

4.5.1 First-class post or Document Exchange (DX)

Service can be made on the next working day if the claim form is sent by first-class post. If the defendant or their solicitors have agreed to accept service via a DX box, PD 6A para 2.1 allows for this, unless the defendant or their solicitor has indicated in writing that they are unwilling to accept service by DX.

4.5.2 Personal service

Rule 6.22 requires that in certain circumstances personal service of the claim form must take place. In other cases, a document may be served personally except where the party to be served has given an address for service under or in any proceedings by or against the Crown.

Rule 6.5(3) provides that the claim form should be served personally on:

(a) an individual by leaving it with that individual;
(b) a company or other corporation by leaving it with a person holding a senior position within the company or corporation; or
(c) a partnership (where partners are being sued in the name of their firm) by leaving it with
  (i) a partner; or
  (ii) a person who, at the time of service, has the control or management of the partnership business at its principal place of business.

4.5.3 Service by fax or by other means of electronic communication

Practice Direction 6A para 4.1 provides the guidance here and requires that the party must previously have indicated in writing to the party serving that the party to be served or the solicitor is willing to accept service by fax or other electronic means.

Where a party intends to serve a document by electronic means (other than by fax) that party must first ask the party who is to be served whether there are any limitations to the recipient's agreement to accept service by such means (for example, the format in which documents are to be sent and the maximum size of attachments that may be received).

4.5.4 Where to serve the claim form

The nature of the defendant will determine the place where the claim form should be served, as illustrated in Table 4.2. Rule 6.9 provides guidance where personal service, service of the claim form on the solicitor, and the defendant gives address at which the defendant may be served, apply.

4.5.5 Deemed service

Other than personal service, the claim form is deemed served on the second business day after the event listed in Table 4.3.

Table 4.2 Place of service depending on the nature of the defendant

Nature of defendant to be served	Place of service
Individual	Usual or last known residence
Individual being sued in the name of a business	Usual or last known residence of the individual or principal or last known place of business
Individual being sued in the business name of a partnership	Usual or last known residence of the individual or principal or last known place of business of the partnership
Limited liability partnership	Principal office of the partnership or any place of business of the partnership within the jurisdiction which has a real connection with the claim
Corporation (other than a company) incorporated in England and Wales	Principal office of the corporation or any place within the jurisdiction where the corporation carries on its activities, and which has a real connection with the claim
Company registered in England and Wales	Principal office of the company or any place of business of the company within the jurisdiction which has a real connection with the claim
Any other company or corporation	Any place within the jurisdiction where the corporation carries on its activities or any place of business of the company within the jurisdiction

4.5.6 Dispensing with service

The court has the power to dispense with service of the claim form under CPR Rule 6.16, but only in exceptional circumstances, and an application for an order to dispense with service may be made and must be supported by evidence, and may be made without notice.

4.6 Procedure for service of a claim form outside the jurisdiction (with or without the court's permission) and mechanisms for effecting valid service in another jurisdiction

Rule 6.32(2) allows the claimant may serve the claim form on a defendant in Scotland or Northern Ireland where each claim made against the defendant to be served and included in the claim form is a claim that the court has the power to determine.

Rule 6.33(2) allows the claimant to serve the claim form on a defendant out of the UK where each claim made against the defendant to be served and included in the claim form is a claim that the court has the power to determine.

Table 4.3 Deemed date of service depending on service method

Method of service	Deemed date of service
First-class post (or other service which provides for delivery on the next business day)	The second day after it was posted, left with, delivered to, or collected by the relevant service provider provided that day is a business day; if not, the next business day after that day
Document Exchange	The second day after it was left with, delivered to, or collected by the relevant service provider provided that day is a business day; if not, the next business day after that day
Delivering the document to or leaving it at a permitted address	If it is delivered to or left at the permitted address on a business day before 4.30 p.m. on that day; in any other case, on the next business day after that day
Fax	If the transmission of the fax is completed on a business day before 4.30 p.m. on that day; in any other case, on the next business day after the day on which it was transmitted
Other electronic method	If the e-mail or other electronic transmission is sent on a business day before 4.30 p.m. on that day; in any other case, on the next business day after the day on which it was sent
Personal service	If the document is served personally before 4.30 p.m. on a business day on that day; in any other case, on the next business day after that day

4.6.1 Permission for service

This is required where Rules 6.32 or 6.33 do not apply. The claimant in those circumstances may serve a claim form out of the jurisdiction with the permission of the court if any of the grounds set out in paragraph 3.1 of Practice Direction 6B apply. Such applicable examples include: a contractual claim where the contract was made within the jurisdiction, was made by or through an agent trading or residing within the jurisdiction, or is governed by English law; or a claim in tort where damage was sustained, or will be sustained, within the jurisdiction or where damage which has been or will be sustained results from an act committed, or likely to be committed, within the jurisdiction.

4.7 Deemed dates of service and time limits for serving proceedings

Any document, other than a claim form, served within the UK is deemed to be served on the day shown in Table 4.3.

4.8 Extending time for service of the claim form

As we have already learnt, the claim form must be served on the defendant before 12.00 midnight on the calendar day four months after the date of issue of the claim form. There are circumstances where the court may allow the claim form to be served after the expiry of the prescribed period. In those circumstances, the claimant must apply to the court for an order to extend the time for service before the expiry of the four-month period under Rule 7.6(2). It is still possible to apply for an order once the four-month period has expired, but such an order under Rule 7.6(3) will only be granted if the court has failed to serve the claim form or the claimant has taken all reasonable steps to try to serve the claim form but has been unable to do so; in either case, the claimant has acted promptly in making the application.

4.8.1 Service of the particulars of claim

Under PD 7.6, where the claimant does not include the particulars of the claim in the claim form, they may be served separately, either at the same time as the claim form or within 14 days after service of the claim form provided that the service of the particulars of the claim is within four months after the date of issue of the claim form (or six months where the claim form is to be served out of the jurisdiction). If the particulars of the claim are not included in or have not been served with the claim form, the claim form must contain a statement that the particulars of the claim will follow.

Chapter 4 revision points

Issuing and serving proceedings

- Issuing a claim form – required details:
  - Claimant's and defendant's details
  - Brief details of claim
  - Value/amount claimed
  - Court fee
  - Legal representative's costs
  - Particulars of claim
  - Statement of truth
- Adding/substituting a party
- Possible methods of service:
  - Personal service
  - First-class post, Document Exchange, or other service which provides for delivery on the next business day
  - Leaving it at a place
  - Fax or other means of electronic communication
  - Any method authorised by the court
- Procedure for service of a claim form outside the jurisdiction

5 Responding to a claim

5.1 Chapter overview

This chapter provides an overview of civil procedure once the claim form has been served on the defendant with the response pack. The requirements for acknowledging service, indicating what the defendant intends to do, will be addressed and the procedure involved in filing and serving a defence, if the case is to be defended, will be explained.

The chapter will also consider the early disposal of a case through voluntary settlement (the use of Tomlin orders will be explained), default judgment, and the Part 36 offer procedure for settlement of claims. Settlement through the recommendation of alternative dispute resolution (ADR), and the costs consequences of failing unreasonably to accept an offer to attempt ADR will also be discussed. Finally, the effect and consequences of discontinuance of a claim and the abandonment of parts of a claim will be explained.

5.2 Introduction: responding to a claim

Once served with the proceedings by the court or the claimant, it is important that the defendant does not ignore the papers that have been served. Failure to file an acknowledgement of service or defence will mean that the claimant will be able to enter judgment in default of the defendant having failed to respond to the claim. That will bring proceedings to an early conclusion and the claimant will have effectively won the case.

If the defendant is served with the claim form which indicates that the particulars of the claim are to follow (which is allowed), the defendant need not respond until the particulars of the claim have been served. This makes sense because only once the defendant sees the particulars of the claim (full information and details about the cause of action) can a decision be taken as to how to respond to the claim.

Accompanying service of the claim form will be the N1C Notes for the defendant on replying to the claim form, which provide helpful guidance for the defendant on how

DOI: 10.4324/9781003218500-8

to respond to the claim. The guidance explains that the defendant has three options on how to respond at this stage of proceedings, namely:

- Pay the total amount, i.e., the amount claimed, the court fee, and solicitor's costs (if any)
- Admit all or part of the claim and ask for time to pay, or
- Dispute the claim.

The Notes provide guidance for the defendant on what happens next depending on the defendant's proposed response. A copy of the N1C Notes appears in Figure 5.1.

5.2.1 The response pack

The defendant will have 14 days from deemed service of the claim form (including particulars of the claim), or from service of the particulars of the claim (if served separately) to file an acknowledgement of service, defence, or admission. Accompanying the claim form will be a Response Pack (Form N9). Included in this pack are:

- The Admission Form N9A (if the claim is for a specified amount)
- The Admission Form N9C (if the claim is for an unspecified amount or is not a claim for money)
- A Defence and Counterclaim Form N9B (if the claim is for a specified amount)
- A Defence and Counterclaim Form N9D (if the claim is for an unspecified amount or is not a claim for money)
- An acknowledgement of service.

The acknowledgement of service should be completed with the defendant's full name and address for service and indicate whether the claim is to be admitted in full or in part or if the claim is to be defended. It should be signed by the defendant or his/her solicitor. The completed acknowledgement of service form should then be sent to the court where the claim form was issued and once received, the court will forward a copy to the claimant. See Figure 5.2 for a sample response pack.

5.3 Time limits for responding to a claim

It is important for the defendant to be aware of the time limits imposed by the CPR once proceedings have been served. Rule 2.8 (2) provides that to calculate any period of time for doing any act, a period of time is expressed as being as 'clear days'. This does not include the day on which the period begins, and if the end of the period is defined by reference to an event, the day on which that event occurs. For instance, if the particulars of the claim must be served within 14 days of service of the claim form and the claim form is served on 2 May, the last day for service of the particulars of the claim is 16 May.

Rules 2.9 and 2.10 explain dates and the meaning of 'month' in judgments, etc. Where the court gives a judgment, order, or direction which imposes a time limit for doing any act, the last date for compliance must, wherever practicable, be expressed as a

If you admit liability for the claim and offer an amount of money to satisfy the claim, complete Form N9C and send it to the court within 14 days. The claimant will be sent a copy and asked if the offer is acceptable. The claimant must reply to the court within 14 days and send you a copy. If a reply is not received, the claim will be stayed. If the amount you have offered is **accepted** -

- the claimant may request the court to enter judgment against you for that amount.
- if you have requested time to pay which is not accepted by the claimant, the rate of payment will be decided by the court.

If your offer in satisfaction is **not accepted** -

- the claimant may request the court to enter judgment against you for an amount to be decided by the court, and costs; and
- the court will enter judgment and refer the court file to a judge for directions for management of the case. You and the claimant will be sent a copy of the court's order.

Disputing the claim

If you are being sued as an individual for a specified amount of money and you dispute the claim, the claim may be transferred to a local court i.e. the one nearest to or where you live or carry on business if different from the court where the claim was issued.

If you need longer than 14 days to prepare your defence or to contest the court's jurisdiction to try the claim, complete the Acknowledgment of Service form and send it to the court within 14 days. This will allow you 28 days from the date of service of the particulars of claim to file your defence or make an application to contest the court's jurisdiction. The court will tell the claimant that your Acknowledgment of Service has been received.

If the case proceeds as a defended claim, you and the claimant will be sent a Directions Questionnaire. You will be told the date by which it must be returned to the court. The information you give on the form will help a judge decide whether your case should be dealt with in the small claims track, fast track or multi-track. After a judge has considered the completed questionnaires, you will be sent a notice of allocation setting out the judge's decision. The notice will tell you the track to which the claim has been allocated and what you have to do to prepare for the hearing or trial. **Leaflets telling you more about the tracks are available from the court office.**

Claim for specified amount

If you wish to dispute the full amount claimed or wish to claim against the claimant (a counterclaim), complete Form N9B and send it to the court within 14 days.

If you admit part of the claim, complete the Defence Form N9B and the Admission Form N9A and send them both to the court within 14 days. The claimant will decide whether to accept your part admission in satisfaction of the claim (see under 'Admitting the Claim - specified amount'). If the claimant does not accept the amount you have admitted, the case will proceed as a defended claim.

If you dispute the claim because you have already paid it, complete Form N9B and send it to the court within 14 days. The claimant will have to decide whether to proceed with the claim or withdraw it and notify the court and you within 28 days. If the claimant wishes to proceed, the case will proceed as a defended claim.

Claim for unspecified amount/return of goods/non-money claims

If you dispute the claim or wish to claim against the claimant (counterclaim), complete Form N9D and send it to the court within 14 days.

Personal injuries claims:
If the claim is for personal injuries and the claimant has attached a medical report to the particulars of claim, in your defence you should state whether you:

- agree with the report **or**
- dispute all or part of the report **and** give your reasons for doing so **or**
- neither agree nor dispute the report **or** have no knowledge of the report

Where you have obtained your own medical report, you should attach it to your defence.

If the claim is for personal injuries and the claimant has attached a schedule of past and future expenses and losses, in your defence you must state which of the items you:

- agree **or**
- dispute **and** supply alternative figures where appropriate **or**
- neither agree nor dispute or have no knowledge of.

Address where notices can be sent

This must be either the business address of your solicitor or European Lawyer or your own residential or business address within the UK or in any other European Economic Area state.

Statement of truth

This must be signed by you, by your solicitor or your litigation friend, as appropriate.

Where the defendant **is a registered company or a corporation** the response must be signed by either the director, treasurer, secretary, chief executive, manager or other officer of the company **or** (in the case of a corporation) the mayor, chairman, president or town clerk.

Figure 5.1 N1C Notes for the defendant on replying to the claim form.

Response pack

You should read the 'notes for defendant' attached to the claim form which will tell you when and where to send the forms.

Included in this pack are:

- either **Admission Form N9A** (if the claim is for a specified amount)
  or **Admission Form N9C** (if the claim is for an unspecified amount or is not a claim for money)
- either **Defence and Counterclaim Form N9B** (if the claim is for a specified amount)
  or **Defence and Counterclaim Form N9D** (if the claim is for an unspecified amount or is not a claim for money)
- **Acknowledgment of service** (see below)

	Complete
If you admit the claim or the amount claimed and/or you want time to pay	the admission form
If you admit part of the claim	the admission form and the defence form
If you dispute the whole claim or wish to make a claim (a counterclaim) against the claimant	the defence form
If you need 28 days (rather than 14) from the date of service to prepare your defence, or wish to contest the court's jurisdiction	the acknowledgment of service
If you do nothing, judgment may be entered against you	

Acknowledgment of service

Defendant's full name if different from the name given on the claim form

In the	
Claim No.	
Claimant (including ref.)	
Defendant	

Address to which documents about this claim should be sent (including reference if appropriate)

Postcode

If applicable	
Telephone no.	
Fax no.	
DX no.	
Your ref.	

E-mail

Tick the appropriate box

1. I intend to defend all of this claim ☐
2. I intend to defend part of this claim ☐
3. I intend to contest jurisdiction ☐

(My) (Defendant's) date of birth is

  / /

If you file an acknowledgment of service but do not file a defence within 28 days of the date of service of the claim form, or particulars of claim if served separately, judgment may be entered against you.

If you do not file an application to dispute the jurisdiction of the court within 14 days of the date of filing this acknowledgment of service, it will be assumed that you accept the court's jurisdiction and judgment may be entered against you.

If served outside the jurisdiction see CPR rule 6.35 and 6.37(5).

Signed

(Defendant) (Defendant's legal representative) (Litigation friend)

Position or office held (if signing on behalf of firm or company)

Date   / /

For further details of the courts www.gov.uk/find-court-tribunal. When corresponding with the Court, please address forms or letters to the Manager and always quote the claim number.

N9 Response pack (04.14)

Figure 5.2 Response pack.

calendar date, and include the time of day by which the act must be done. Where the date by which an act must be done is inserted in any document, the date must, wherever practicable, be expressed as a calendar date. Where the word 'month' occurs in any judgment, order, direction, or other document, it means a calendar month.

5.4 Admitting the claim

If the defendant admits the claim in full or in part, the appropriate sections of the response pack should be completed. This will then have a bearing on the next steps in proceedings. Part 14 deals with admissions.

5.4.1 Admission of the whole of a claim for a specified amount

If the claim for a specified amount is admitted in full, the defendant should complete the N9A Form of admission and serve it on the claimant. The defendant must indicate how much of the claim is admitted and must also provide personal and financial details of income and expenditure. The form also provides an opportunity for the defendant to make an offer of payment.

Upon receipt of the N9A Form of admission, the claimant can either accept the offer of payment either by instalments or by a certain date, in which case a request for judgment can be filed with the court.

If the claimant rejects the amount admitted or the offer of payment and wishes the proceedings to continue the claimant must file the notice and serve a copy on the defendant within 14 days after it is served. The case will be transferred to the claimant's chosen court centre under r 14.7A.

The court will then make a decision without a hearing. If a hearing is requested, however, the parties will be given seven clear days' notice of the hearing.

5.4.2 Admission of part of a claim for a specified amount

If the defendant admits part of the claim for a specified amount, the defendant should complete the N9A Form of admission and serve it on the claimant.

On receipt of the admission, the court will serve a notice on the claimant requiring the return of the notice stating that:

(a) The claimant accepts the amount admitted in satisfaction of the claim
(b) The claimant does not accept the amount admitted by the defendant and wishes the proceedings to continue, or
(c) If the defendant has requested time to pay, the claimant accepts the amount admitted in satisfaction of the claim, but not the defendant's proposals as to payment.

The claimant must then file the notice and serve a copy on the defendant within 14 days after it is served.

5.4.3 Admission of liability to pay the whole of a claim for an unspecified amount with no offer

Where the defendant admits liability for an unspecified amount but does not offer to pay a specified amount of money in satisfaction of the claim, the defendant should complete the N9C Form of admission and serve it on the claimant.

Upon receipt of the admission, the court will then serve a copy on the claimant. The claimant may obtain judgment by filing a request. If the claimant does not file a request for judgment within 14 days after service of the admission, the claim is stayed until the request is filed. On receipt of the request for judgment, the court will enter judgment. Judgment will be for an amount to be decided by the court and costs.

5.4.4 Admission of liability to pay a claim for an unspecified amount with an offer

Where the defendant admits the claim, the defendant should complete the N9C Form of admission and serve it on the claimant.

On receipt of the admission, the court will serve a notice on the claimant requiring the return of the notice stating whether or not the claimant accepts the amount in satisfaction of the claim. If the claimant does not file a request for judgment within 14 days after service of the admission, the claim is stayed until the request is filed. If the claimant accepts the offer, they may request judgment.

If the defendant has not requested time to pay, the claimant may enter judgment and indicate by when payment should be made. If the defendant has requested time to pay, the procedure indicated earlier will apply. In which case, the claimant may specify in his request for judgment the date by which the whole of the judgment debt is to be paid; or the times and rate at which it is to be paid by instalments. On receipt of the request for judgment, the court will enter judgment for the amount offered by the defendant (less any payments made) and costs.

5.5 Acknowledging service and filing a defence and/or counterclaim

If the claim is to be defended, then the defendant should still complete the acknowledgement of service indicating an intention to defend the claim and whether there will be a counterclaim. In this case, Form N9B should be completed, and the defendant should serve it on the claimant. The usual time limit of 14 clear days applies.

5.5.1 Filing a defence

If the claim is to be defended in full or in part, then the defendant must file serve the defence and the appropriate sections of the response pack should be completed. Part 15 deals with the defence protocols, and r 15.4 provides that the defence should be filed with the court:

(a) 14 days after service of the particulars of claim, or
(b) If the defendant files an acknowledgement of service under Part 10, 28 days after service of the particulars of claim.

Where the claimant serves the particulars of the claim with the claim form, under r 10.3 the defendant has 14 days after (deemed) service of the claim form to respond.

5.5.2 Content of the defence

Under r 16.5 the defendant must state in the defence:

(a) Which of the allegations in the particulars of claim are denied
(b) Which allegations are not able to be admitted or denied, but which the claimant is required to prove, and
(c) Which allegations are admitted.

Where the defendant denies an allegation, the reasons must be stated for doing so, and if it is intended that a different version of events from that given by the claimant will be put forward, that version of events must be stated.

Where the claim includes a money claim, a defendant shall be taken to require that any allegation relating to the amount of money claimed be proved unless he expressly admits the allegation.

5.5.3 Extending time for service of the defence

Unless the parties come to an agreement about extending time for service of the defence for no more than 28 days, it is possible for the defendant to apply to the court to extend time for service. This will usually be granted if sufficient grounds exist, for instance, if the claimant has not complied with the pre-action protocols by failing to provide the defendant with sufficient time and/or evidence to properly understand the nature of the claim.

If the defendant and the claimant agree to extend the period of time for filing a defence, the defendant must notify the court in writing under r 15.5.

5.5.4 Making a counterclaim

This is covered by Part 20. A defendant may make a counterclaim against a claimant by filing particulars of the counterclaim.

Pursuant to r 20.5, a defendant who wishes to counterclaim against a person other than the claimant must apply to the court for an order that that person be added as an additional party.

5.6 Disputing the court's jurisdiction

The defendant may wish to dispute the court's jurisdiction to try the claim, or argue that the court should not exercise its jurisdiction. In this case, an application to the court can be made under Part 11, for an order declaring that it has no such jurisdiction or should not exercise any jurisdiction that it may have.

A defendant who wishes to make such an application must first file an acknowledgement of service, and then within 14 days submit an application supported by evidence for an order containing a declaration that the court has no jurisdiction or will not exercise its jurisdiction. The court may also:

(a) Set aside the claim form
(b) Set aside service of the claim form
(c) Discharge any order made before the claim was commenced or before the claim form was served, and
(d) Stay the proceedings.

If the court does not grant the defendant's application and make the order about jurisdiction, then the acknowledgement of service will have no effect. In which case the defendant may file a further acknowledgement of service within 14 days or such other period as the court may direct, and the court will give directions as to the filing and service of the defence if a further acknowledgement of service is filed.

5.7 Entering judgment in default

If once the claim form is served the defendant fails to file an acknowledgement of service or a defence, the claimant may enter judgment in default in accordance with Part 12. This means that proceedings will be brought to an early conclusion without the need for a trial. Usually, no hearing is required for this step, unless some judicial decision is required, for example, if the claimant requires an injunction, which is a discretionary remedy.

A default judgment may not be obtained in the following circumstances:

(a) A claim for delivery of goods subject to an agreement regulated by the Consumer Credit Act 1974
(b) Where he uses the procedure set out in Part 8 (alternative procedure for claims), or
(c) In any other case where a practice direction provides that the claimant may not obtain default judgment.

5.7.1 Conditions required to satisfy entering judgment in default

The claimant may obtain judgment in default of an acknowledgement of service only if at the date on which judgment is entered:

(a) The defendant has not filed an acknowledgement of service or a defence to the claim (or any part of the claim) within the prescribed time limit
(b) Judgment in default of defence may be obtained only where an acknowledgement of service has been filed but at the date on which judgment is entered, a defence has not been filed within the prescribed time limit
(c) In a counterclaim, where at the date on which judgment is entered a defence has not been filed within the prescribed time limit.

5.7.2 Procedure for obtaining default judgment

A claimant wishing to apply for default judgment must follow the procedure under r 12.4 by filing a request in the relevant practice form where the claim is for:

(a) A specified amount of money
(b) An amount of money to be decided by the court
(c) Delivery of goods where the claim form gives the defendant the alternative of paying their value, or
(d) Any combination of these remedies.

5.7.3 Claims for a specific amount

Where the claim is for a specified sum of money, the claimant may specify in a request that the defendant pays the full amount by a certain date, or if by instalments, the times and rate at which it is to be paid. In which case, judgment will be entered for the amount of the claim (less any payments made) and costs. Form N225 should be used (see Figure 5.3).

5.7.4 Claims for an unspecific amount

Where the claim is for an unspecified sum of money, the court will fix a date for a hearing before a judge at the claimant's preferred hearing centre, who will decide the amount of the claim and costs. Form N227 should be used.

Where the claim is for delivery of goods and the claim form gives the defendant the alternative of paying their value, if default judgment is obtained the defendant will be required to deliver the goods or (in the alternative) pay the value of the goods as decided by the court (less any payments made) and costs.

5.7.5 Interest

Rule 12.6 provides that default judgment for a claim for a specified amount may include interest claimed to the date of judgment if

(a) the particulars of claim include the details required by rule 16.4;
(b) where interest is claimed under section 35A of the Supreme Court Act 1981 or section 69 of the County Courts Act 19843, the rate is no higher

Request for judgment and reply to admission (specified amount)

Complete section A or B.
If you complete section A you must also confirm, where applicable, that particulars of claim have been served in accordance with the rules.

In all cases you must complete sections C and D.
If the defendant has given an address on the form of admission to which correspondence should be sent, which is different from the address shown on the claim form, you must tell the court.

Remember to sign and date the form. Your signature certifies that the information you have given is correct.

In the	
Claim No.	
Claimant (including ref)	
Defendant (including ref)	

A ☐ The defendant has not filed an admission or defence to my claim

☐ I confirm that particulars of claim have been served on the defendant in accordance with the rules.

Now complete section C and all the judgment details at section D. Decide how and when you want the defendant to pay. You can ask for the judgment to be paid by instalments or in one payment.

B ☐ The defendant admits that all the money is owed

Tick only **one** box below and complete section C and all the judgment details at section D.

☐ **I accept the defendant's proposal for payment**

Say how the defendant intends to pay. The court will send the defendant an order to pay. You will also be sent a copy.

☐ **The defendant has not made any proposal for payment**

Say how you want the defendant to pay. You can ask for the judgment to be paid by instalments or in one payment. The court will send the defendant an order to pay. You will also be sent a copy.

☐ **I do NOT accept the defendant's proposal for payment**

Say how you want the defendant to pay. Give your reasons for objecting to the defendant's offer of payment on the back of this form. Send this form to the court **with defendant's admission N9A.** The court will fix a rate of payment and send the defendant an order to pay. You will also be sent a copy.

C Defendant's date of birth

☐ Defendant's date of birth is not stated in the form of reply but is known to the claimant as: ☐☐/☐☐/☐☐☐☐

☐ Defendant's date of birth is not stated in the form of reply and is not known to the claimant.

D Judgment details

I would like the defendant to be ordered to pay:

☐ immediately

☐ by instalments of £ ______ per month

☐ in full by ☐☐/☐☐/☐☐☐☐

Amount of claim as admitted	
(including interest at date of issue) Interest since date of claim (if any) Period from ______ to ______ Rate ___ %	
Court fees shown on claim	
Legal Representative's costs (if any) on issuing claim	
Sub Total	
Legal Representative's costs (if any) on entering judgment	
Sub Total	
Deduct amount (if any) paid since issue	
Amount payable by defendant	

I certify that the information given is correct.

Signed ______________________
(Claimant) (Claimant's solicitor) (Litigation friend)

Position or office held ______________________
(if signing on behalf of firm or company)

Date ☐☐/☐☐/☐☐☐☐

Please return the completed form to the court.

Please address forms or letters to the Operational Delivery Manager and quote the claim number.

N225 Request for judgment and reply to admission (specified amount) (04.13)

Figure 5.3 Request for judgment in default (specified amount).

than the rate of interest payable on judgment debts at the date when the claim form was issued; and

(c) the claimant's request for judgment includes a calculation of the interest claimed for the period from the date up to which interest was stated to be calculated in the claim form to the date of the request for judgment.

5.8 Discontinuance and settlement

Once proceedings have commenced, other than judgment by default already dealt with, at various stages during the lifetime of a case, the court rules provide the opportunity for early disposal of proceedings in a number of different ways. These include:

- Case disposal following application (dealt with in Chapter 7)
- Striking out on the court's own motion (dealt with in Chapter 6)
- Settlement during proceedings
- Part 36 offers of settlement
- Settlement through recommendation of ADR (including through procedural stays)
- Discontinuance or abandonment.

It should be noted that even though proceedings have been commenced and litigation is ensuing, negotiation can be ongoing with a view to bringing proceedings to conclusion through a negotiated settlement. This is often described as 'bargaining in the court's shadow'.

5.8.1 Settlement during proceedings

If negotiations take place between the parties or their respective lawyers and those negotiations lead to the parties agreeing to settle the claim after proceedings have been commenced, it is advisable for a consent order to be drawn up to evidence the terms of the settlement agreement. This will enable the consent order evidencing the terms of settlement to be enforced in the event that the agreement is not honoured (see Chapter 12 for methods of enforcement).

5.8.2 Procedure

Where none of the parties to the litigation is a litigant in person and has legal representation, it will be possible to draw up a consent order setting out the terms of settlement and file it with the court without the need for an application. Rule 40 applies where all the parties agree to the terms in which a judgment should be given or an order should be made.

Rule 40.6(7) provides that:

(a) the order which is agreed by the parties must be drawn up in the terms agreed;
(b) it must be expressed as being 'By Consent';
(c) it must be signed by the legal representative acting for each of the parties to whom the order relates or, where paragraph (5) applies, by the party if he is a litigant in person.

5.8.3 Tomlin orders

It is possible for the parties to agree to settle the claim by using a Tomlin order. Named after Justice Tomlin in the case of *Dashwood v Dashwood* [1927] WN 276, 64 LJNC 431, 71 Sol Jo 911, such an order keeps the proceedings alive only to the extent necessary to enable a party to enforce the terms of the settlement.

In the case of *Dashwood*, Tomlin J held that a provision in the order which required one party to refrain from running a business in competition with the other party could not be enforced unless and until the court made an order for specific performance or for an injunction. Thus, any provisions in a Tomlin order which require action by the court, such as releasing funds held in court, or an order for costs, must be included in the body of the order, not the schedule. Until a second order has been sought, it is not possible to apply to commit the party in breach for contempt of court.

A Tomlin order can be usefully used where there are complex terms to be carried out, e.g., where the defendant agrees to undertake a schedule of work (building repairs) by a certain date. Such a compromise would be outside the power of the court (as they would have no mechanism to implement the terms) and should be set out and recorded in a schedule to the Tomlin order.

The Tomlin order should also deal with the costs of the proceedings. Where one party is to pay the other party's costs, these details should be included in the schedule of the order, including the amount to be paid by whom and by when. If costs are to be assessed by the court, then that provision must be included in the schedule.

To ensure that the terms of the agreement are observed, and the steps carried out, the Tomlin order will include the words 'liberty to apply', so that in the event that a party does not carry out one or more of the steps, the other party can apply to the court to enforce the order, in other words, to bring the order into effect and carry out its terms. An example a Tomlin order is displayed in Figure 5.4.

5.8.4 Part 36 offers of settlement

Courts are keen to promote settlement where possible and costs implications and offers to settle can encourage and promote settlement. The case of *Calderbank v Calderbank* [1976] Fam 93 introduced the concept of the Calderbank offer. Through negotiation, the parties can discuss the claim and make (without prejudice) offers to settle. The Calderbank offer is the origin of the offer procedure now incorporated into the CPR under Part 36. Historically, where claims involve money, payments into court would have to be made, where an amount of money is physically lodged with the court. Whilst this used to be a requirement, payments into court can still be made.

Under the Part 36 procedure, it is important to note that either the claimant or the defendant can make a Part 36 offer.

5.8.4.1 Part 36 procedure

An offer to settle is made by the offeror, whilst the person receiving the offer is the offeree. Rule 36.5(1) requires that a valid Part 36 offer must:

(a) be in writing;
(b) state on its face that it is made pursuant to the provisions of Part 36;

(c) specify a period of not less than 21 days within which the defendant will be liable for the claimant's costs in accordance with rule 36.10 if the offer is accepted;
(d) state whether it relates to the whole of the claim or to part of it or to an issue that arises in it and if so to which part or issue; and
(e) state whether it takes into account any counterclaim.

It is very important that the time limit as set out in (c) is observed and it is best practice to ensure that information about the time limit of 21 days for acceptance (the relevant acceptance period) is included in the offer for clarity.

IN THE HUDDERSFIELD COUNTY COURT **Claim No: HU782001**

BETWEEN:

Madeline Bray

Claimant

-and-

Arthur Squeers T/A Dotheboys Farm

Defendant

TOMLIN ORDER

The Claimant and the Defendant having agreed to the terms set out in the schedule hereto

IT IS ORDERED THAT all further proceedings in this Claim be stayed except for the purpose of carrying such terms into effect

Liberty to apply as to carrying such terms into effect

SCHEDULE

1. The Defendant will pay to the Claimant the sum of £15,842.45 ("the Settlement Sum") in full and final settlement of all of claims set out in the Particulars of Claim herein.

2. The Settlement Sum will be paid by the Defendant to the Claimant's Solicitors on or before 16th June 2023.

3. Notwithstanding any costs order to the contrary, the Defendant will pay to the Claimant the sum of £5,200 ("the Costs Settlement Sum") in full and final settlement of the Claimant's costs of the action.

4. The Costs Settlement Sum will be paid by the Defendant to the Claimant's Solicitors on or before 16th June 2023.

We hereby consent to an Order in the above terms.

Figure 5.4 Tomlin order.

Part 36 offers are very commonly used for monetary claims. However, the procedure can be used for non-monetary claims, for example, an application for an injunction, so long as the terms of the offer are clear.

Under r 36.5(4), Part 36 offers for monetary claims will include all interest until the relevant acceptance period expires.

5.8.4.2 Costs consequences

There are important costs consequences which may follow once a Part 36 offer has been made and this makes the procedure a tactical step. The rules associated with Part 36 costs are covered in r 36.17 and apply once judgment has been entered. If when judgment is given:

(a) A claimant fails to obtain a judgment more advantageous than a defendant's Part 36 offer (in money terms that means better by any amount, however small, and 'at least as advantageous') or
(b) Judgment against the defendant is at least as advantageous to the claimant as the proposals contained in a claimant's Part 36 offer

the following entitlements apply. In the case of (a) (claimant fails to beat defendant's offer) the defendant will be entitled to:

(a) Costs (including any recoverable pre-action costs) from the date on which the relevant period expired, i.e., usually 21 days after the Part 36 offer was made, and
(b) Interest on those costs.

In the case of (b) (claimant beats or equals their own offer) the claimant is entitled to:

(a) Interest on the whole or part of any sum of money (excluding interest) awarded, at a rate not exceeding 10 per cent above the base rate for some or all of the period starting with the date on which the relevant period expired
(b) Costs (including any recoverable pre-action costs) on the indemnity basis from the date on which the relevant period expired
(c) Interest on those costs at a rate not exceeding 10 per cent above the base rate, and
(d) Provided that the case has been decided and there has not been a previous order about costs, an additional amount, which shall not exceed £75,000, calculated by applying the prescribed percentage set out in Table 5.1 to an amount which is:
    (i) The sum awarded to the claimant by the court, or
    (ii) Where there is no monetary award, the sum awarded to the claimant by the court in respect of costs.

See Chapter 13 for further clarification of the Part 36 costs consequences; Chapter 13 also deals with the situation where the claimant beats his/her own Part 36 offer, and the same principles apply, i.e., the claimant will be entitled to an additional amount awarded if the claimant beats his/her Part 36 offer.

Table 5.1 Additional amount awarded to the claimant if they beat or equal their own Part 36 offer

Amount awarded by the court	Prescribed percentage
Up to £500,000	10% of the amount awarded
Above £500,000	10% of the first £500,000 and (subject to the limit of £75,000) 5% of any amount above that figure

It should be noted that r 36.17 further provides that in considering whether it would be unjust to make the financial (costs and interest) orders referred to earlier, the court must take into account all the circumstances of the case including; the terms of any Part 36 offer, the stage in the proceedings when any Part 36 offer was made, including in particular how long before the trial started the offer was made, the information available to the parties at the time when the Part 36 offer was made, the conduct of the parties with regard to the giving of or refusal to give information for the purposes of enabling the offer to be made or evaluated, and whether the offer was a genuine attempt to settle the proceedings.

So, Part 36 offers can have a significant impact on litigation costs! Where the claimant beats the Part 36 offer the defendant will have to pay the judgment amount and the claimant's costs of the whole claim, usually on a standard basis (see Chapter 13) as well. Consider, though, the following example from the case of *Bray v Squeers*, a claim for damages arising from personal injury, in other words, a monetary claim, where Bray (claimant) fails to beat the Part 36 offer made by Squeers (defendant) at trial.

Example

The claim has been progressing and was allocated to the fast track. Directions were given for trial and the case is listed for a one-day trial on 1 July.

Partial liability for the accident is admitted in March and on 1 May Squeers' (defendant) solicitors make a Part 36 Offer of £3,000 to settle the case. Upon instructions, Bray's (claimant) solicitors reject the offer as being unreasonable. The case proceeds to trial.

At trial, the judge finds Madeline Bray partially responsible for her accident (to the extent of 30 per cent) and after deduction for contributory negligence, awards £2,800 to the claimant Madeline Bray. She has failed to beat the Part 36 offer made by the defendant.

The court awards the claimant Bray her costs up to and including 21 May. The court orders that Bray is liable not only for her own costs from 22 May until the end of the trial, but also Squeers' costs for the same period. The defendant Squeers' costs from 22 May (21 days after the date when the Part 36 offer was made) are £1,000; Bray's are £800. The reasoning is that Bray has wasted time and money in litigation when she could have accepted the Part 36 offer.

5.8.4.3 Split costs order

Where the defendant beats the Part 36 offer, as mentioned earlier, Rule 36.17(3) provides that the court must, unless it considers it unjust to do so, order that the defendant is entitled to:

(a) Costs (including any recoverable pre-action costs) from the date on which the relevant period expired, and
(b) Interest on those costs.

A split costs order is illustrated in the preceding example. The usual order that the court will make is that the losing party will have to pay the costs and interest on those costs of the winning party from the date of the judgment.

Table 5.2 illustrates the three possible outcomes at trial in the case of *Bray v Squeers*, including the one illustrated in the example earlier, and the costs consequences of each outcome, where a Part 36 offer was made by the defendant.

Table 5.2 Different trial outcomes and possible costs orders that the judge can make

Trial outcome	**Possible costs orders**
Judgment awarded is more advantageous than Squeers' (defendant) offer	Bray (claimant) is awarded her costs of the whole claim on a standard basis
Judgment awarded is the same as or less advantageous than Squeers' (defendant) offer (as in the example given earlier)	The court will make a split order on costs: Squeers (defendant) will be ordered to pay Bray's (claimant) costs on a standard basis up to and including 21 May. Bray (claimant) will be ordered to pay Squeers' (defendant) costs on the standard basis from and including 22 May plus interest on costs until trial when judgment is given on 1 July
Bray (claimant) loses at trial	Bray (claimant) pays Squeers' (defendant) costs of defending the claim from when first incurred to judgment on 1 July. Bray (claimant) pays interest on Squeers' (defendant's) costs from and including 22 May until trial when judgment is given on 1 July

5.8.4.4 A tactical procedure

The Part 36 procedure is undoubtedly a tactical step in proceedings and was introduced no doubt as part of the Woolf Reform process to encourage parties to settle the dispute without the need for a trial. The process arguably favours the defendant as it can put pressure on the claimant to accept an offer which they know, if not accepted, may give rise to an adverse costs order if at trial the claimant is awarded an amount less than or equal to the offer put forward by the defendant. The clever defendant will therefore make a Part 36 offer at the right stage in proceedings (usually once all evidence has been exchanged), which, if the claim involves money, is pitched at just the right figure for the claimant to be tempted to accept it for fear of failing to beat the offer at trial.

Note that the Part 36 costs consequences are further dealt with in more detail in Chapter 13.

5.8.4.5 Making more than one offer

There is no limit on the number of Part 36 offers that either the claimant or the defendant can make. If, for instance, the claimant makes a series of offers of decreasing value, the defendant may feel pressured to accept one of those offers. The pressure is applied by the financial consequences imposed on the defendant by r 36.17 if the claimant beats or equals their own offer.

Similarly, if the defendant makes a series of increasing Part 36 offers to settle the claim, if none of the offers is accepted by the claimant, the financial consequences of r 36.17 will be imposed on the claimant, should he/she fail at trial to be awarded a judgment sum which is more advantageous than the defendant's latest most advantageous offer.

5.8.4.6 Acceptance of a Part 36 offer

A Part 36 offer can be accepted by the offeree at any time, even when the offeror has made a different offer, unless of course the offer has been withdrawn in writing. Any offer can be accepted outside the relevant period, although there may be adverse costs consequences of doing so.

A Part 36 offer must be accepted in writing; a letter will suffice, as there is no prescribed court form.

Once a notice of acceptance of the Part 36 offer has been received by the offeror, proceedings will be stayed. If accepted within the relevant period (usually 21 days, remember), the offeror will be entitled to the costs of the proceedings up to the date when the notice of service is served on the offeree. If, for example, the claimant accepts the defendant's offer late, i.e., outside the relevant period, but the parties cannot agree on the liability for costs, the court must, unless it considers it unjust to do so, order that:

(a) The claimant be awarded costs up to the date on which the relevant period expired, and

(b) The claimant pays the defendant's costs for the period from the date of expiry of the relevant period to the date of acceptance.

It follows, therefore, that where the claimant's Part 36 offer is accepted by the defendant, if the parties cannot agree on the liability for costs, the court will usually order the defendant to pay the claimant's costs of the proceedings up to the date of acceptance. Thereafter each party will be ordered to pay their own costs.

5.8.5 Settlement through recommendation of alternative dispute resolution

Remember the Practice Direction on pre-action conduct and protocols makes it clear that litigation should be engaged in as a last resort for the parties in dispute. If the case proceeds to litigation, the parties can at a later stage be penalised in adverse costs orders for failing to make genuine efforts to comply with the pre-action protocol provisions, and that includes making efforts to enter into negotiations to bring the dispute to a conclusion at an early stage. Indeed Paragraph 8 of the aforementioned Practice Direction explicitly provides that the parties should consider whether negotiation, or some other form of alternative dispute resolution (ADR), might enable them to settle their dispute without the need for the party to bring the claim to commence court proceedings.

5.9 Case management and ADR

Simply because the parties in dispute have resorted to litigation does not mean that their efforts to explore and reach a settlement should not cease. The court's case management responsibilities under Rule 1.1(4) must further the aim of the overriding objective, which includes the encouragement of settlement notwithstanding the fact that litigation has been commenced. To help with this, the CPR provide various opportunities for the parties to explore the opportunity to settle the claim without the need for a trial.

In terms of promoting settlement, judicial case management (which will be dealt with in greater detail in Chapter 6), extends to the following:

- Encouraging the parties to co-operate with each other in the conduct of the proceedings (Rule 1.4(2)(a))
- Encouraging the parties to use an alternative dispute resolution procedure if the court considers that appropriate and facilitating the use of such procedure (Rule 1.4(2)(e)), and
- Helping the parties to settle the whole or part of the case (Rule 1.4(2)(f)).

Rule 26.4 allows the judge to stay the case with the parties' agreement to enable ADR to take place. When filing the completed directions questionnaire, a party can make a written request for the proceedings to be stayed while the parties try to settle the case by ADR or other means. It is usual for the proceedings to be stayed for one month if the parties agree or perhaps for longer if the court considers it appropriate. It is even possible for the court to extend the stay beyond the period specified if the parties are making a genuine effort to try to resolve the dispute and bring the proceedings to a conclusion.

Once Allocation Questionnaires have been filed by the parties, the court can under Practice Direction 29 4.9 give directions of its own initiative without fixing a case management conference. The court may then under Practice Direction 29 4.10(9) give directions requiring the parties to consider ADR. Such directions may be, for example, in the following terms:

> The parties shall by [date] consider whether the case is capable of resolution by ADR. If any party considers that the case is unsuitable for resolution by ADR, that party shall be prepared to justify that decision at the conclusion of the trial, should the judge consider that such means of resolution were appropriate, when he is considering the appropriate costs order to make.

Whilst the parties are not therefore compelled to attempt ADR, the Practice Direction does provide that a party considering the case unsuitable for ADR shall, not less than 28 days before the commencement of the trial, file with the court a witness statement giving reasons why the case was unsuitable.

5.9.1 Small Claims Mediation Service

Rule 26.4A deals specifically with the referral of cases started in the County Court, which would normally be allocated to the small claims track, to the Small Claims Mediation Service. It does not apply to road traffic accidents, personal injury or housing disrepair claims, or any claim in which any party to the proceedings does not agree to referral to mediation.

The scheme is operated by Her Majesty's Courts and Tribunals Service and where all parties indicate on their directions questionnaire that they agree to mediation, the claim will be referred to the Mediation Service. If the referred claim then settles at mediation, the proceedings will automatically be stayed, with permission to apply for judgment for the unpaid balance of the outstanding sum of the settlement agreement, or the claim to be restored for hearing of the full amount claimed, unless the parties have agreed that the claim is to be discontinued or dismissed.

5.9.2 Costs implications (of ignoring ADR)

Under Rule 44.2(5)(a), the conduct of the parties before, as well as during, the course of proceedings and in particular the extent to which the parties followed the Practice Direction on pre-action conduct and protocols or any relevant pre-action protocol will be taken into account in considering an award of costs.

Under Rule 44.4(3)(a), in deciding the amount of costs to be awarded, the court will have regard for the conduct of all the parties, including in particular the conduct before, as well as during the proceedings and the efforts made, if any, before and during the proceedings to try to resolve the dispute. This includes consideration of ADR and an invitation made by one party to another to attempt ADR. The following case example of *Dunnett v Railtrack* illustrates the court's approach with regard to the award of costs in such circumstances.

Example

The case of *Dunnett v Railtrack* Plc [2002] EWCA Civ 302, is an important decision on the application of the court's discretion to impose costs penalties on a party unreasonably rejecting an invitation to use mediation (a form of ADR). The claimant Mrs Dunnett lost her case in the High Court but was granted leave to appeal. In granting leave, the judge suggested that the claimant attempt ADR with the defendant Railtrack, who subsequently refused the request. The claimant appellant's appeal failed, and the defendant-respondent Railtrack asked for their costs relating to the appeal. The Court of Appeal concluded that Railtrack should not be awarded their costs because they had ignored the first instance judge's suggestions to attempt ADR.

Dunnett remains an important decision as it illustrates not only the risks of unreasonably rejecting an offer of ADR when the court had specifically recommended it, but also that the court considers that mediation may be suitable at any stage of proceedings, even after a party has successfully argued their case at trial.

The judicial guidance provided by *Dunnett* should however be considered in light of the subsequent decision in *Halsey v Milton Keynes*, considered in the next case example.

Example

The case of *Halsey v Milton Keynes General NHS Trust and Steel v Joy* [2004] EWCA Civ 576), involved two appeals where the court was required to determine when it should make an adverse costs order against a successful party after they had rejected an offer to use ADR. Upon hearing the appeals, the guidelines which the court produced outlined six factors that the courts should take into account when exercising discretion to award adverse costs:

(a) The nature of the dispute
(b) The merits of the case
(c) The extent to which other settlement methods had been attempted
(d) Whether the costs of ADR would be disproportionately high

(e) Whether the delay in setting up and attending ADR would have been prejudicial, and
(f) Whether the ADR had a reasonable prospect of success.

The court was keen to emphasise that whilst these factors were important in considering the question of costs in such cases, there was no single factor that was decisive in arriving at their decision.

In the case of *Halsey*, the Court of Appeal made it clear that to compel unwilling parties to engage in ADR would be a potential breach of their right of access to court as prescribed by Article 6 of the European Convention on Human Rights. The court also took the view that compelling parties' attendance at mediation would reduce mediation's effectiveness as a voluntary process.

5.10 Discontinuance and abandonment

Two further methods by which claimant can bring the claim to a conclusion prior to trial are covered by Rule 38, which deals with the procedure for discontinuance and abandonment. The former is where the whole claim is withdrawn by the claimant and the latter is where more than one remedy is sought and some part of the claim is abandoned by the claimant.

Discontinuance or abandonment could arise where the claimant has overstated his/her case, sued the wrong defendant, cannot produce the evidence to prove his/her case, or realises that the claim is now likely to fail.

A claimant who wishes to discontinue all or part of a claim where the court has granted an interim injunction, or any party has given an undertaking to the court, must obtain the permission of the court.

A claimant who has received an interim payment in relation to a claim may discontinue that claim only if the defendant who made the interim payment consents in writing, or the court gives permission.

Where there is more than one claimant, a claimant may not discontinue unless every other claimant consents in writing or the court gives permission. Where there is more than one defendant, the claimant may discontinue all or part of a claim against all or any of the defendants.

5.10.1 Procedure

To discontinue a claim or part of a claim, a claimant must file a notice of discontinuance and serve a copy of it on every other party to the proceedings stating in the notice that it has been served on every other party to the proceedings.

Where the claimant needs the consent of some other party, a copy of the necessary consent must be attached to the notice of discontinuance. Where there is more than one defendant, the notice of discontinuance must specify against which defendants the claim is discontinued.

5.10.2 Costs implications

Where the claimant discontinues it is usual for the claimant to be required to pay the defendant's costs. Where only part of the claim is abandoned then the costs associated with that part of the claim will be the defendant's costs.

Chapter 5 revision points

Responding to a claim

- Time limits for responding to a claim
- Admitting the claim:
  - Admission of the whole of a claim for a specified amount
  - Admission of part of a claim for a specified amount
  - Admission of liability to pay claim for unspecified amount with or without an offer
- Filing a defence must include:
  - Allegations that are denied
  - Allegations that are not able to be admitted or denied, but which the claimant is required to prove
  - Allegations that are admitted
- Default judgment:
  - Failure to file an acknowledgement of service
  - Failure to file a defence
- Discontinuance and settlement
  - Discontinuance and abandonment
  - Using Tomlin orders
- Part 36 offers:
  - Procedure
  - Costs consequences (of failing to accept)
  - Split costs orders
  - Acceptance

Multiple-choice questions for Part 3

1. A has suffered catastrophic and life-changing injuries as a result of a serious road traffic accident. Up until the time of the accident she was in middle management working for a global insurance company. Her likely claim for damages will far exceed £100,000, much of which will be a claim for lost and future loss of earnings and earning capacity.

*Which one of the following is the **best** reason for choosing the court venue for issuing proceedings?*

A. The claim has a monetary value of at least £100,000 and must be issued in the High Court.
B. A monetary value does not have to be placed on a personal injury claim at the outset; such claims are difficult to value without expert evidence and because of this, court proceedings can be commenced in either the County Court or the High Court.
C. Because the claim exceeds (or is likely to exceed) £25,000, then proceedings can be issued in the High Court.
D. The claim is for damages for personal injury and loss and because the monetary value is likely to exceed £50,000, proceedings can be commenced in the High Court.
E. The claim is for damages and loss arising from personal injury and proceedings must be issued in the High Court

2. You have received instructions to act for a client in a personal injury claim. Limitation for the purposes of commencing court proceedings expires next week and you know that the claim form must be issued prior to the expiry of limitation. The problem is that your client does not know where the proposed defendant lives.

*Which one of the following **best** explains the approach to take where the claimant does not have an address for the defendant?*

A. The claim form cannot be issued until your client has found an address for the proposed defendant where valid service of the claim form can be effected by the court.
B. The claimant will be able to use CPR Part 6 to request that the court allow you to dispense with service of the claim form by posting a notice of issue of proceedings against the defendant in the *Law Society Gazette*.
C. As the legal representative for the claimant, you can ask the court to return the claim form to you once issued, so that you can then effect service on the defendant yourself.
D. The claim form cannot be issued without the defendant's address unless you notify the court of a firm of solicitors that has been nominated to accept service of proceedings.
E. The claim form can be issued without the defendant's address and the claimant can make an application to the court under CPR Part 6 to dispense with service of the claim form.

3. You issue proceedings and arrange for the claim form to be served on the defendant. Upon filing the defence, it appears that another party may be partially responsible for the claimant's accident. You have instructions from your client to pursue the other party as well.

*Which one of the following **best** explains the situation?*

A. It is now too late to include another party and it will be necessary to start the proceedings again in order to pursue the other party as well.
B. It is possible to apply to the court to add a defendant to the proceedings as the CPR provide that any number of defendants may be joined as parties to the claim.
C. Whilst it is too late to include another party, if judgment is obtained against the defendant, the defendant can then pursue the other party themselves.
D. It will be necessary to obtain an order from the court, but the CPR require that the defendant must be required to make the application.
E. It is possible to apply to the court to add the other party as a defendant, but only if the existing defendant agrees to this.

4. A intends to commence proceedings against a sole trader in a contractual dispute concerning the supply of goods and services.

Which one of these methods best describes what would ***not*** *be a valid method of service?*

A. Using personal service of the claim form on the defendant.
B. Sending the claim form first class post, by document exchange, or other service which provides for delivery on the next business day.
C. Leaving the claim form at the defendant's solicitor's office.
D. Sending the claim form via fax or other means of electronic communication.
E. Serving the claim form by using any method authorised by the court.

5. A claim form with particulars of claim was sent by the claimant's solicitor to the defendant, a limited company in a commercial contractual dispute, on 4 February by first-class post to the defendant's registered office.

Which one of the following is the ***best*** *explains the approach to take where when responding to the claim form?*

A. If the defendant company intends to defend the claim, indication of an intention to defend should be made within seven days, and the defendant company must file and serve a defence within 14 days of deemed service.
B. Deemed service will be determined by the fact that the defendant is a limited company and depending on when that is, the defendant will have 28 days in which to file and serve a defence if the claim is to be defended.
C. Service of the claim form will be deemed to have taken place on 6 February, and if the defendant acknowledges service within time indicating an intention to defend, the defendant will have until 6 March to file and serve a defence.
D. As deemed service will be considered to be the day of posting, i.e., 4 February, and the defendant acknowledges service within time indicating an intention to defend, the defendant will have until 18 February to file and serve a defence.
E. Service of the claim form will be deemed to have taken place on 5 February and if the defendant files an acknowledgement of service within time indicating an intention to defend, the defence must be served by 5 March.

PART 4

Case management and any interim applications relevant to a claim

6 Case management

6.1 Chapter overview

This chapter will provide a comprehensive overview of case management by reference to the Civil Procedure Rules and associated practice directions. It starts by revisiting the overriding objective of the CPR, before moving on to deal with aspects of case allocation and the procedural aspects associated with the directions questionnaire.

The chapter also considers the importance of case summaries in the management of cases, the procedure involved in varying directions, and the consequences of non-compliance with court directions. The role of the court in costs management will be explained, and finally the effect and consequences of non-compliance with orders, the possible sanctions that can be imposed, and consideration of the circumstances where a party can apply for relief from sanctions.

6.2 Introduction: case management

An important aim and feature of the Woolf Reform process was to give greater power to the court in the active management of cases as they progress through the civil justice system. As part of the changes, cases entering litigation were to be allocated to one of three tracks on the basis of claim value: the small claims track, with a raised upper limit of £5,000, the fast track with an upper limit of £15,000 and fixed timetables, and the multi-track for cases over £15,000 and with pro-active case management. The £15,000 limit has since been raised to £25,000.

The court's general powers of management are governed by Part 3 CPR 1998, which gives the court and judges wide-ranging case management powers. The list of powers is set out in r 3.1(2), which explains that under the cases management provisions, the court can:

(a) extend or shorten the time for compliance with any rule, practice direction or court order (even if an application for extension is made after the time for compliance has expired);
(b) adjourn or bring forward a hearing; (bb) require that any proceedings in the High Court be heard by a Divisional Court of the High Court;

DOI: 10.4324/9781003218500-10

(c) require a party or a party's legal representative to attend the court;
(d) hold a hearing and receive evidence by telephone or by using any other method of direct oral communication;
(e) direct that part of any proceedings (such as a counterclaim) be dealt with as separate proceedings;
(f) stay (suspend) the whole or part of any proceedings or judgment either generally or until a specified date or event;
(g) consolidate proceedings;
(h) try two or more claims on the same occasion;
(i) direct a separate trial of any issue;
(j) decide the order in which issues are to be tried;
(k) exclude an issue from consideration;
(l) dismiss or give judgment on a claim after a decision on a preliminary issue; (ll) order any party to file and exchange a costs budget;
(m) take any other step or make any other order for the purpose of managing the case and furthering the overriding objective, including hearing an Early Neutral Evaluation with the aim of helping the parties settle the case.

The court can use its case management powers to make orders which specify certain specific conditions. For example, the court can make an order with a condition that a party pay a sum of money into court and specify the consequence of failure to comply with the order or a condition.

Where the court gives directions, it will take into account whether or not a party has complied with the Practice Direction (Pre-Action Conduct) and any relevant pre-action protocol. The pre-action protocol and the associated procedures were dealt with in Chapter 2. So, the court may order a party to pay a sum of money into court if that party has, without good reason, failed to comply with a rule, practice direction or a relevant pre-action protocol. The court may also contact the parties from time to time in order to monitor compliance with directions. The parties must respond promptly to any such enquiries from the court.

6.3 Case management and the overriding objective

Remember CPR Rule 1.1 sets out the overriding objective of the Civil Procedure Rules, which includes case management and the overriding objective of enabling the court to deal with cases fairly, expeditiously, and at proportionate cost. See Chapter 2 for details of CPR Rule 1.1 in full.

Rule 1.4 sets out the court's duty to further the overriding objective by actively managing cases, which includes:

(a) encouraging the parties to co-operate with each other in the conduct of the proceedings;

(b) identifying the issues at an early stage;
(c) deciding promptly which issues need full investigation and trial and accordingly disposing summarily of the others;
(d) deciding the order in which issues are to be resolved;
(e) encouraging the parties to use an alternative dispute resolution procedure if the court considers that appropriate and facilitating the use of such procedure;
(f) helping the parties to settle the whole or part of the case;
(g) fixing timetables or otherwise controlling the progress of the case;
(h) considering whether the likely benefits of taking a particular step justify the cost of taking it;
(i) dealing with as many aspects of the case as it can on the same occasion;
(j) dealing with the case without the parties needing to attend at court;
(k) making use of technology; and
(l) giving directions to ensure that the trial of a case proceeds quickly and efficiently.

Since the implementation of the Woolf Reforms and the introduction of the new civil procedural code, it can be seen from the Rules that the court and judges have become much more proactively involved in the management of cases.

6.3.1 Unrepresented parties

To reflect the increasing numbers of litigants in person which has arisen as a direct result of legal aid cutbacks, the court now has case management responsibilities where unrepresented parties are concerned. Therefore, when the court is exercising any powers of case management, it must have regard for the fact that if at least one party is unrepresented the rules require that both the parties and the court must, when drafting case management directions in fast-track and multi-track cases, take as their starting point any relevant standard directions. These can be found online at www.justice.gov.uk/courts/procedure-rules/civil and adapted as appropriate to the circumstances of the case.

In these cases, the court must adopt such a procedure at any hearing as it considers appropriate to further the overriding objective. Therefore, at any hearing where the court is taking evidence, this may include ascertaining from an unrepresented party the matters about which the witness may be able to give evidence or on which the witness ought to be cross-examined and putting appropriate questions to the witness.

6.4 Track allocation

6.4.1 Allocation – general

Upon the filing and serving a defence which indicates an intention to defend at least part of the claim, the court will send out a directions/allocation questionnaire to all parties to the proceedings or, if represented, their legal representatives. At the same time, the court will provisionally indicate which track is considered appropriate for the case by serving a notice of proposed allocation. This is usually in Form N181.

Part 26 CPR deals with the preliminary stages of case management and allocation to a particular track.

The notice of proposed allocation also requires that the parties complete and file the directions questionnaire with the court by a certain date, usually 14 days. If the claim has been provisionally allocated to the multi-track the following documents must also be prepared:

- A case summary
- A disclosure report
- A costs budget and budget discussion report
- A draft order for directions.

Allocation is an important litigation staging post, as the information provided in the directions questionnaire will determine the timetable for the case as it progresses through the civil court system. The parties are expected to cooperate with each other when completing the questionnaire, which must be returned fully completed with the required information by a certain date.

6.4.2 Completion of the directions questionnaire

As can be seen from Figure 6.1, the directions questionnaire is a fairly extensive court form. It is divided into ten parts A to J and each part requires the parties to provide information which will assist the court in the management of the case.

The directions questionnaire requires the parties to provide information on the following matters.

6.4.2.1 Part A – Settlement

This part reminds parties that in accordance with the Civil Procedure Rules they should make every effort to settle their case before trial. This could be by discussion or negotiation (such as a roundtable meeting or settlement conference), or by a more formal process such as mediation. The court will want to know what steps the parties have taken to try to settle the case as settling the case at this stage of proceedings can save costs, including court hearing fees.

Parties are therefore asked to confirm in this part whether they have tried to settle their dispute and, if not, the reasons why they have not made any attempts to do so. The parties can tick the box asking for a stay (suspension) of proceedings if they wish, in which case the court can 'stay' proceedings which will then enable the parties to make efforts to resolve their dispute. This is an opportunity to use ADR, particularly mediation, and the form provides the parties with a link to the Civil Mediation Council's online Directory of CMC accredited mediation service providers.[1]

1 www.civilmediation.justice.gov.uk.

Directions questionnaire (Fast track and Multi-track)

In the	Claim No.

To be completed by, or on behalf of,

who is [1st][2nd][3rd][ ][Claimant][Defendant][Part 20 claimant] in this claim

You should note the date by which this questionnaire must be returned and the name of the court it should be returned to since this may be different from the court where the proceedings were issued.

If you have settled this claim (or if you settle it on a future date) and do not need to have it heard or tried, you must let the court know immediately.

If the claim is not settled, a judge will allocate it to an appropriate case management track. To help the judge choose the most just and cost-effective track, you must now complete the directions questionnaire.

You should write the claim number on any other documents you send with your directions questionnaire. Please ensure they are firmly attached to it.

A Settlement

Notes

Under the Civil Procedure Rules parties should make every effort to settle their case before the hearing. This could be by discussion or negotiation (such as a roundtable meeting or settlement conference) or by a more formal process such as mediation. The court will want to know what steps have been taken. Settling the case early can save costs, including court hearing fees.

For legal representatives only

I confirm that I have explained to my client the need to try to settle; the options available; and the possibility of costs sanctions if they refuse to try to settle. ☐ I confirm

For all

Your answers to these questions may be considered by the court when it deals with the questions of costs: see Civil Procedure Rules Part 44.

1. Given that the rules require you to try to settle the claim before the hearing, do you want to attempt to settle at this stage? ☐ Yes ☐ No
2. If Yes, do you want a one month stay? ☐ Yes ☐ No
3. If you answered 'No' to question 1, please state below the reasons why you consider it inappropriate to try to settle the claim at this stage.

Reasons:

The court may order a stay, whether or not all the other parties to the claim agree. Even if you are requesting a stay, you must still complete the rest of the questionnaire.

More information about mediation, the fees charged and a directory of mediation providers is available online from www.civilmediation.justice.gov.uk This service provides members of the public and businesses with contact details for national civil and commercial mediation providers, all of whom are accredited by the Civil Mediation Council.

N181 Directions questionnaire (Fast track and Multi-track) (04.14) 1

Figure 6.1 Directions questionnaire.

B Court

Notes

B1. (High Court only)
The claim has been issued in the High Court. Do you consider it should remain there? ☐ Yes ☐ No

If Yes, in which Division/List?

If No, in which County Court hearing centre would you prefer the case to be heard?

High Court cases are usually heard at the Royal Courts of Justice or certain Civil Trial Centres. Fast or multi-track trials may be dealt with at a Civil Trial Centre or at the court where the claim is proceeding.

B2. Trial (all cases)
Is there any reason why your claim needs to be heard at a court or hearing centre? ☐ Yes ☐ No

If Yes, say which court and why?

C Pre-action protocols

You are expected to comply fully with the relevant pre-action protocol.

Have you done so? ☐ Yes ☐ No

If you have not complied, or have only partially complied, please explain why.

Before any claim is started, the court expects you to have complied with the relevant pre-action protocol, and to have exchanged information and documents relevant to the claim to assist in settling it. To find out which protocol is relevant to your claim see: www.justice.gov.uk/guidance/courts-and-tribunals/courts/procedure-rules/civil/menus/protocol.htm

D Case management information

D1. Applications
Have you made any application(s) in this claim? ☐ Yes ☐ No

If Yes, what for? (e.g. summary judgment, add another party).

For hearing on ☐☐/☐☐/☐☐☐☐

D1. Applications
It is important for the court to know if you have already made any applications in the claim (or are about to issue one), what they are for and when they will be heard. The outcome of the applications may affect the case management directions the court gives.

D2. Track
If you have indicated in the proposed directions a track attached which would not be the normal track for the claim, please give brief reasons below for your choice.

D2. Track
The basic guide by which claims are normally allocated to a track is the amount in dispute, although other factors such as the complexity of the case will also be considered. Leaflet ***EX305 – The Fast Track and the Multi-track***, explains this in greater detail.

2

Figure 6.1 Continued.

6.4.2.2 Part B – Court

Here the parties should confirm if there are any reasons why the case should be heard in a particular court. If the case is of a value which suggests it should be heard in the High Court, the parties should indicate whether or not the case should remain there. If it is to remain in the High Court, then the case will usually be heard in the Royal Courts of Justice in London or in other regional trial centres.

D Case management information (continued)

Notes

D3. Disclosure of electronic documents (multi-track cases only)

If you are proposing that the claim be allocated to the multi-track:

1. Have you reached agreement, either using the Electronic Documents Questionnaire in Practice Direction 31B or otherwise, about the scope and extent of disclosure of electronic documents on each side? ☐ Yes ☐ No
2. If No, is such agreement likely? ☐ Yes ☐ No
3. If there is no agreement and no agreement is likely, what are the issues about disclosure of electronic documents which the court needs to address, and should they be dealt with at the Case Management Conference or at a separate hearing?

D4. Disclosure of non-electronic documents (all cases)

What directions are proposed for disclosure?

For all multi-track cases, except personal injury.

Have you filed and served a disclosure report (Form N263) (see Civil Procedure Rules Part 31). ☐ Yes ☐ No

Have you agreed a proposal in relation to disclosure that meets the overriding objective? ☐ Yes ☐ No

If Yes, please ensure this is contained within the proposed directions attached and specify the draft order number.

E Experts

Do you wish to use expert evidence at the trial or final hearing? ☐ Yes ☐ No

Have you already copied any experts' report(s) to the other party(ies)? ☐ None yet obtained ☐ Yes ☐ No

Do you consider the case suitable for a single joint expert in any field? ☐ Yes ☐ No

There is no presumption that expert evidence is necessary, or that each party will be entitled to their own expert(s). Therefore, the court requires a short explanation of your proposals with regard to expert evidence.

3

Figure 6.1 Continued.

Practice Direction 29 governing case management in the Royal Courts of Justice provides under para 2.6 that claims suitable for trial in the Royal Courts of Justice include:

(1) professional negligence claims,
(2) Fatal Accident Act claims,

E Experts (continued)

Notes

Please list any single joint experts you propose to use and any other experts you wish to rely on. Identify single joint experts with the initials 'SJ' after their name(s). Please provide justification of your proposal and an estimate of costs.

Expert's name	Field of expertise (e.g. orthopaedic surgeon, surveyor, engineer)	Justification for expert and estimate of costs

F Witnesses

Which witnesses of fact do you intend to call at the trial or final hearing including, if appropriate, yourself?

Witness name	Witness to which facts

G Trial or Final Hearing

How long do you estimate the trial or final hearing will take?

☐ less than one day ☐ Hrs | ☐ one day | ☐ more than one day ☐ State number of days

Give the best estimate you can of the time that the court will need to decide this case. If, later you have any reason to shorten or lengthen this estimate you should let the court know immediately.

Are there any days within the next 12 months when you, an expert or an essential witness will not be able to attend court for trial or final hearing?

You should only enter those dates when you, your expert(s) or essential witnesses will not be available to attend court because of holiday or other commitments.

If Yes, please give details

Name	Dates not available

You should notify the court immediately if any of these dates change.

4

Figure 6.1 Continued.

(3) fraud or undue influence claims,
(4) defamation claims,
(5) claims for malicious prosecution or false imprisonment,
(6) claims against the police,
(7) contentious probate claims.

H	Costs	Notes

Do not complete this section if:

1) you do not have a legal representative acting for you

2) the case is subject to fixed costs

If your claim is likely to be allocated to the Multi-Track form Precedent H must be filed at in accordance with CPR 3.13.

I confirm Precedent H is attached. ☐

I	Other information

Do you intend to make any applications in the future? ☐ Yes ☐ No

If Yes, what for?

In the space below, set out any other information you consider will help the judge to manage the claim.

5

Figure 6.1 Continued.

It should be noted that under PD 29 para 2.2, a claim with an estimated value of less than £100,000 will generally be transferred to a county court.

6.4.2.3 Part C – Pre-Action Protocols

The court will have expected the parties to have complied with the provisions of the relevant pre-action protocol for the dispute. As such, before any claim is started, the

J Directions

You must attempt to agree proposed directions with all other parties. **Whether agreed or not a draft of the order for directions which you seek must accompany this form.**

All proposed directions for multi-track cases must be based on the directions at www.justice.gov.uk/courts/procedure-rules/civil

All proposed directions for fast track cases must be based on CPR Part 28.

Signature

Date
☐☐/☐☐/☐☐☐☐

[Legal Representative for the][1st][2nd][3rd][ ]
[Claimant][Defendant][Part 20 claimant]

Please enter your name, reference number and full postal address including details of telephone, DX, fax or e-mail

	If applicable	
	Telephone no.	
	Fax no.	
	DX no.	
Postcode	Your ref.	

E-mail	

Figure 6.1 Continued.

court expects the parties to have exchanged information and documents relevant to the claim to assist in settling it. To assist the parties to determine which protocol is relevant to the claim, the parties are referred to the justice.gov.uk website.[2]

The parties should then indicate clearly if they have complied with the relevant pre-action protocol, or if they have only partially complied, they are asked to explain why.

6.4.2.4 Part D – Case Management Information

It is important for the court to know if the parties have already made any applications in the claim (or are about to issue one), what they are for and when they will be heard. The outcome of the applications may affect the case management directions the court gives.

If the parties have indicated in the proposed directions attached to the form, a track which would not be the normal track for the claim, here they are asked to give brief reasons below for their choice of track.

2 www.justice.gov.uk/guidance/courts-and-tribunals/courts/procedurerules/civil/menus/protocol.htm.

Note that claims are normally allocated to a track based on the amount in dispute, although other factors such as the complexity of the case will also be considered. The parties are referred by the court to Leaflet EX305: The Fast Track and the Multi-Track, which explains this in greater detail.

6.4.2.5 Part E – Experts

There is no presumption that expert evidence is necessary, or that each party will be entitled to their own expert(s). If the parties wish to use expert evidence at trial, in this section the court will require a short explanation of the parties' proposals with regard to expert evidence. They should also indicate whether their experts' reports have been exchanged and if the case is suitable for a single joint expert.

Any proposed single joint experts and any other experts upon which the parties wish to rely should be listed in this section of the form indicating their field of expertise (e.g., orthopaedic surgeon, surveyor, engineer) and the justification for using the expert, together with an estimate of associated costs.

6.4.2.6 Part F – Witnesses

The parties must indicate which witnesses of fact they intend to call at the trial or final hearing including, if appropriate, themselves, their names, and what facts they are attesting to.

6.4.2.7 Part G – Trial

Here the parties must provide an estimate for the length of the trial or final hearing. They should give the best estimate they can of the time that they think the court will need to decide the case. The form asks the parties that they should let the court know immediately if, at a later date and for any reason, there is a need to have a longer or shorter trial time estimate.

The parties should also indicate if there are any days within the forthcoming 12 months when they, an expert, or an essential witness will not be able to attend court for trial or final hearing. They should only enter those dates when they or their expert(s) or essential witnesses will not be available to attend court because of holidays or other commitments. This is important information for listing the case for trial.

6.4.2.8 Part H – Costs

A party need only complete this section if they have representation. In which case, where the stated value of the claim on the claim form is of a value less than £50,000, but likely to be allocated to the multi-track, the legal representative must complete a costs budget estimate on a prescribed court form, and file it with the directions questionnaire or not later than 21 days before the first case management conference.

6.4.2.9 Part I – Other Information

Here the parties should indicate if they intend to make any applications in the future and set out any other information they consider will help the judge to manage the claim.

6.4.2.10 Part J – Directions

The parties must attempt to agree on proposed directions. Whether agreed or not, a draft of the order for directions which they seek must accompany the questionnaire. All proposed directions for fast-track cases must be based on CPR Part 28, which requires the parties to deal with the following matters:

- Disclosure of documents
- Service of witness statements, and
- Expert evidence.

If the court decides not to direct standard disclosure, it may direct that no disclosure should take place or specify the documents or the classes of documents which the parties must disclose.

All proposed directions for multi-track cases must be based on the directions that the questionnaire helpfully guides the parties to at www.justice.gov.uk/courts/procedure-rules/civil. These are provided as a menu of model paragraphs as follows:

- A selection of headings
- Allocation, docketing, alternative dispute resolution
- Before case management
- Case management directions
- Documents
- Evidence of fact
- Expert evidence
- Paper Order Direction
- Pre trial
- Restriction on Extension of Timetable
- Schedules of loss
- Trial.

When all parties have filed their directions questionnaires, the court will allocate the claim to a track, unless the case has been stayed according to the proceedings under r 26.4, in which case it will allocate the claim to a track at the end of the period of the stay. If a claim is referred to a mediation service provider and the court has not been notified in writing that a settlement has been agreed, the claim will be allocated to a track in accordance with this rule no later than four weeks from the date on which the last directions questionnaire is filed.

Before deciding the track to which to allocate proceedings or deciding whether to give directions for an allocation hearing to be fixed, the court may order a party to provide further information about his case. The court may hold an allocation hearing if it thinks it is necessary. Case management directions will be given for cases proceeding on the fast or multi-tracks.

6.4.3 Failure to file directions questionnaire

If the claim is for a monetary sum, and either party does not comply with the notice of proposed allocation by the date specified then the court will serve a further notice on that party, requiring them to comply within seven days. If that party fails to comply with the notice served, then that party's statement of case (claim or defence) will be automatically struck out by the court.

If a claim is not a 'money claim' and a party does not comply with the notice of proposed allocation by the date specified, the court will make such order as it considers appropriate, including;

- An order for directions
- An order striking out the claim
- An order striking out the defence and entering judgment, or
- Listing the case for a case management conference.

It is therefore in the parties' interest to comply with the court's requirements to complete and return the completed direction questionnaire promptly.

6.5 Allocation to track and case management directions

When allocating a case to an appropriate track, the usual determining factor will be the financial value of the claim. Claims will usually be allocated as follows:

- Claims of a value not exceeding £10,000 – the small claims track
- Claims of a value between £10,000 and £25,000 – the fast claims track
- Claims of a value greater than £25,000 – the multi-claims track.

Although when deciding which track is appropriate for the case, r 26.8(1) sets out the matters to which the court shall have regard, which include:

(a) the financial value, if any, of the claim;
(b) the nature of the remedy sought;
(c) the likely complexity of the facts, law or evidence;
(d) the number of parties or likely parties;
(e) the value of any counterclaim or other Part 20 claim and the complexity of any matters relating to it;
(f) the amount of oral evidence which may be required;
(g) the importance of the claim to persons who are not parties to the proceedings;
(h) the views expressed by the parties; and
(i) the circumstances of the parties.

Where the court assesses the financial value of a claim, it will disregard:

(a) any amount not in dispute;
(b) any claim for interest;
(c) costs; and,
(d) any contributory negligence.

If the claim involves more than one claim, for instance, if the defendant has raised a counterclaim, under PD 26, para 7.7 the court will not generally aggregate the claims. Instead, for the purposes of allocation, it will generally regard the largest of them as determining the financial value of the claims.

6.5.1 Allocation to the small claims track

If the claim is of a financial value not exceeding £10,000, then it will be allocated to the small claims track. CPR Part 27 deals with small claims track allocation and cases allocated here will be dealt with by the small claims court. PD 26, para 8.1(1) provides that:

(a) The small claims track is intended to provide a proportionate procedure by which most straightforward claims with a financial value of not more than £10,000 can be decided, without the need for substantial pre-hearing preparation and the formalities of a traditional trial, and without incurring large legal costs. (Rule 26.6 provides for a lower financial value in certain types of case.)
(b) The procedure laid down in Part 27 for the preparation of the case and the conduct of the hearing are designed to make it possible for a litigant to conduct his/her own case without legal representation if he/she wishes.
(c) Cases generally suitable for the small claims track will include consumer disputes, accident claims, disputes about the ownership of goods and most disputes between a landlord and tenant other than opposed claims, disputed claims for possession and demotion claims whether in the alternative to possession claims.
(d) A case involving a disputed allegation of dishonesty will not usually be suitable for the small claims track.

The court will not normally allow more than one day for the hearing of a claim allocated to the small claims track.

6.5.2 Allocation to the fast track

If the claim is of a financial value exceeding £10,000, but not greater than £25,000, then it will be allocated to the fast track. CPR Part 28 deals with the allocation of claims to the fast track, and cases allocated here will be dealt with by reference to a typical stepped timetable for case preparation as suggested by PD 28, para 3.12 as shown in Table 6.1.

The timetable will start from the date of allocation.

Table 6.1 Typical timetable for case preparation

Typical timetable for case preparation	
Step	**Timeframe**
Disclosure of documents	4 weeks
Exchange of witness statements	10 weeks
Exchange of experts' reports	14 weeks
Court to send pre-trial checklists (listing questionnaires)	20 weeks
Parties to file completed pre-trial checklists	22 weeks
Trial	30 weeks

6.5.2.1 Varying the fast-track timetable

The court may consider under PD 28, para 3.13, that some or all of the steps are unnecessary, in which case the court may omit them and direct an earlier trial. This may happen where the court is informed that the Practice Direction dealing with pre-action conduct, or any pre-action protocol has been complied with or that steps which it would otherwise order to be taken have already occurred. It may also happen where an application (for example for summary judgment or for an injunction) has been heard before allocation and little or no further preparation is required. In such a case the court may dispense with the need for a pre-trial checklist.

Under r 28.4, a party may apply to the court to vary the date which the court has fixed for:

- The return of a pre-trial checklist
- The trial, or
- The trial period.

A party may appeal other directions or orders made by the court if dissatisfied with them or apply to the court for its decision to be reconsidered. Otherwise, the parties can agree on changes to be made to the directions given between themselves. For instance, the parties can agree to extend the time for the exchange/service of witness statements. Variation by consent in this way does not need the court's consent or a court order. It is sufficient to record any variations of the timetable in correspondence. In any other case, the parties should apply to the court for an order by consent and provide a draft consent order which the court will usually grant without a hearing.

6.5.2.2 Failure to comply with case management directions

Under PD 28, para 5.1, if a party has failed to comply with a direction given by the court any other party may apply for an order to enforce compliance or for a sanction to be imposed by the court. Making such an application must be done promptly but the other party should be warned of the proposed application. The court may take any delay into account when it decides whether to make an order imposing a sanction or whether to grant relief from a sanction imposed by the rules or any practice direction.

In the spirit of the overriding objective to deal with cases justly, PD 28 makes it clear, however, that it will not allow a failure to comply with directions to lead to the postponement of the trial unless the circumstances of the case are exceptional. If it is practicable to do so the court will exercise its powers in a manner that enables the case to come on for trial on the date or within the period previously set. In those circumstances, the court will assess what steps each party should take to prepare the case for trial, direct that those steps are taken in the shortest possible time, and impose a sanction for non-compliance. The practice direction provides that any such a sanction may, for example, deprive a party of the right to raise or contest an issue or to rely on evidence to which the direction relates.

In a situation where one or more issues are or can be made ready for trial at the time fixed while others cannot, the practice direction enables the court to direct that the trial will proceed and deal with the issues which are or will be ready, and order that no costs will be allowed for any later trial of the remaining issues or that those costs will be paid by the party in default.

In circumstances where the court has no option but to order postponement of the trial, it will do so very much as a last resort and for the shortest possible time. It will give directions for any necessary steps to be taken in the meantime and as rapidly as possible.

6.5.3 Allocation to the multi-track

If a claim is of a value greater than £25,000, it will be allocated to the multi-track where the court is required to deal with disputes of widely differing values and complexity. The court is expected to be flexible in the way it will manage a multi-track case and in a way appropriate to its particular requirements. Multi-track cases comprise a wide range of dispute types, from straightforward (higher value) money claims to more complex disputes involving millions of pounds. CPR Part 29 deals with the allocation of claims to the multi-track.

When it allocates a case to the multi-track, the court will either:

(a) Give directions for the management of the case and set a timetable for the steps to be taken between the giving of directions and the trial, or
(b) Fix a case management conference or a pre-trial review, or both, and give such other directions relating to the management of the case as it sees fit.

The court will fix the trial date or the period in which the trial is to take place as soon as practicable and will notify the parties of the date or period and specify the date by which the parties must file a pre-trial checklist.

6.5.3.1 Directions on allocation to the multi-track

Practice Direction 29.4 encourages the court to tailor its directions to the needs of the case and the steps which the parties have already taken to prepare the case of which it is aware. In particular, it will have regard to the extent to which Practice Direction (Pre-Action Conduct) or any pre-action protocol has or (as the case may be) has not been complied with. The court's primary concern is to ensure that the issues between the parties are identified and that the necessary evidence is prepared and disclosed.

The court will consider whether it is desirable or necessary to hold a case management conference immediately, or whether it is appropriate instead to give directions on its own initiative. Rule 29.4 provides that parties must endeavour to agree on appropriate directions for the management of the proceedings and requires the agreed directions or proposals to be submitted to the court within a specified time period.

The parties can agree on directions themselves without the need for a hearing and the matters to be dealt with are broadly in line with those applicable to fast-track cases. However, if the court does not approve the agreed directions filed by the parties but decides that it will give directions of its own initiative without fixing a case management conference, it will take them into account in deciding what directions to give.

Under para 4.10 of PD 29, where the court is to give directions on its own initiative without holding a case management conference and it is not aware of any steps taken by the parties other than the exchange of statements of case, its general approach will be as follows:

(1) To give directions for the filing and service of any further information required to clarify either party's case
(2) To direct standard disclosure between the parties
(3) To direct the disclosure of witness statements by way of simultaneous exchange
(4) To give directions for a single joint expert on any appropriate issue unless there is a good reason not to do so
(5) To direct disclosure of experts' reports by way of simultaneous exchange on those issues where a single joint expert is not directed
(6) If experts' reports are not agreed, to direct a discussion between experts for the purpose set out in r 35.12(1) and the preparation of a statement under r 35.12(3)
(7) To list a case management conference to take place after the date for compliance with those directions
(8) To specify a trial period, and
(9) In such cases as the court thinks appropriate, the court may give directions requiring the parties to consider ADR. Such directions may be, for example, in the following terms:

> The parties shall by [date] consider whether the case is capable of resolution by ADR. If any party considers that the case is unsuitable for resolution by ADR, that party shall be prepared to justify that decision at the conclusion of the trial, should the judge consider that such means of resolution were appropriate, when he is considering the appropriate costs order to make.

> The party considering the case unsuitable for ADR shall, not less than 28 days before the commencement of the trial, file with the court a witness statement without prejudice save as to costs, giving reasons upon which they rely for saying that the case was unsuitable.

To assist the parties in drafting a standard directions order, there is helpful guidance available on the justice.gov.uk website[3] which the parties can use to adapt and tailor them for their particular requirements.

6.5.3.2 Varying the case management timetable for multi-track cases

If a party wishes to vary the timetable set by the court, then he/she must apply under r 29.5(1) for:

(a) A case management conference
(b) A pre-trial review
(c) The return of a pre-trial checklist under rule 29.6
(d) The trial, or
(e) The trial period.

Rule 29.4 requires that the parties must endeavour to agree on appropriate directions for the management of the proceedings and submit agreed directions, or their respective proposals to the court at least seven days before any case management conference. Where the court approves agreed directions or issues its own directions, the parties will be so notified by the court and the case management conference will be vacated. Note that r 2.11 allows the parties to vary a date by written agreement except where the rules provide otherwise or the court orders otherwise.

6.6 The case management conference and costs

Another staging post in the lifetime of a case proceeding through the civil court system on the multi-track is the case management conference. This hearing which all parties and, if they are represented their legal representatives must attend, will be presided over by a district judge (county court) or a master (Royal Courts of Justice).

6.6.1 The case management conference

The overarching matters that the court should consider at the case management conference which will have a bearing on the future conduct of the case will include the following:

(1) Reviewing the steps which the parties have taken in the preparation of the case and in particular their compliance with any directions that the court may have given

3 www.justice.gov.uk/courts/procedure-rules/civil/standard-directions.

(2) Deciding and giving directions about the steps which are to be taken to secure the progress of the claim in accordance with the overriding objective, and
(3) Ensuring as far as it can that all agreements that can be reached between the parties about the matters in issue and the conduct of the claim are made and recorded.

The specific topics the court will consider at a case management conference are likely to include:

(a) Whether the claimant has made clear the claim he is bringing, in particular the amount he is claiming, so that the other party can understand the case he has to meet
(b) Whether any amendments are required to the claim, a statement of case, or any other document
(c) What disclosure of documents, if any, is necessary
(d) What expert evidence is reasonably required and how and when that evidence should be obtained and disclosed
(e) What factual evidence should be disclosed
(f) What arrangements should be made about the giving of clarification or further information and the putting of questions to experts, and
(g) Whether it will be just and will save costs to order a split trial or the trial of one or more preliminary issues.

In all cases, the court will set a timetable for the steps it decides are necessary to be taken. These steps may include the holding of a case management conference or a pre-trial review, and the court will be alert to perform its duty to fix a trial date or period as soon as it can.

Where expert evidence is concerned, it should be noted that under PD 29 para 5.5(1) and (2), the court will not at this stage give permission to use such expert evidence unless it can identify each expert by name or field in its order and say whether the expert's evidence is to be given orally or by the use of the expert's report. A party who obtains expert evidence before obtaining a direction about it does so at his own risk as to costs, except where he obtained the evidence in compliance with a pre-action protocol.

A party may make an application for a specific order relating to a direction which would not routinely be made at the case management conference if they think that application will be opposed. In which case, the party seeking the order should serve the application on the other party in good time before the case management conference and indicate how long it is likely to take to consider the issues raised.

6.6.2 Case summary

CPR Part 29 5.6 requires the parties to consider if a case summary would assist the court at the case management conference (see also Chapter 10 and the trial preparations). If it is considered that a case summary would be helpful, the parties must ensure that it should:

(a) Be designed to assist the court to understand and deal with the questions before it
(b) Set out a brief chronology of the claim, the issues of fact which are agreed or in dispute and the evidence needed to decide them
(c) Not normally exceed 500 words in length, and
(d) Be prepared by the claimant and agreed with the other parties if possible.

The case summary may assist the judge in making the appropriate directions and also consider what other steps ought to be taken, including what experts should be allowed to attend trial to give oral evidence and whether the case should be stayed to enable the parties to attempt ADR, perhaps mediation.

The justice.gov.uk website provides some helpful guidance on case management conferences.[4]

6.6.3 Variation of directions

Under Rule 29.5 a party must apply to the court if he/she wishes to vary the date which the court has fixed for:

- A case management conference
- A pre-trial review
- The return of a pre-trial checklist under rule 29.6
- The trial, or
- The trial period.

Practice Direction 6.3 (1) allows a party who is dissatisfied with a direction given or other order made by the court to make an application to the court for it to reconsider its decision.

6.6.4 Failure to comply with case management directions

Where a party fails to comply with a direction given by the court any other party may, without delay, warn the other party that it is his/her intention to apply for an order or that the other party must do so or for a sanction to be imposed or both of these.

The court may take any delay into account when it decides whether to make an order imposing a sanction or to grant relief from a sanction imposed by the rules or any other practice direction.

The court will not allow a failure to comply with directions to lead to the postponement of the trial unless the circumstances are exceptional and without a very good

4 www.justice.gov.uk/courts/procedure-rules/civil/standard-directions/general/case-management.

reason. For instance, the failure of a party to comply on time with directions previously given will not be treated as a good reason. The court will always exercise its powers in a manner that enables the case to come on for trial on the date or within the period previously set.

6.6.5 Costs management

As part of the overriding objective which requires the court to deal with cases, not only justly, but also at proportionate cost, CPR 3.13 requires that all parties except litigants in person must, in the following circumstances, file and exchange costs budgets in preparation for a case management conference:

(a) Where the stated value of the claim on the claim form is less than £50,000, with their directions questionnaires, or
(b) In any other case, not later than 21 days before the first case management conference.

All other parties, (other than litigants in person), must file an agreed budget discussion report no later than seven days before the first case management conference.

6.6.6 Costs budgets

Unless the court otherwise orders, a costs budget must be provided in a standard precedent format. Precedent H is helpfully annexed to PD 3E and available to download from the justice.gov.uk website.[5] In cases where a party's total costs (incurred and estimated) do not exceed £25,000 or the value of the claim as stated on the claim form is less than £50,000, the parties must only use the first page of Precedent H.

The budget should set out a detailed breakdown of costs already incurred and those estimated to be incurred based on the work involved in the future phases of the case in dealing with those matters displayed in the directions questionnaire. These will include work associated with witnesses of fact, expert witnesses, disclosure of evidence, pre-trial preparation (including pre-trial review), together with any anticipated costs associated with attempts to settle the case through ADR as well as the anticipated costs of the trial itself.

6.7 Non-compliance with orders, sanctions, and relief

6.7.1 Non-compliance with an order

As well as being able to exercise its case management powers for statements of case, the court does have the power under r 3.4(2) to strike out a party's case for failure to comply with a rule, practice direction, or court order.

5 www.justice.gov.uk/courts/procedure-rules/civil/rules/part03/practice-direction-3e-costs-management.

6.7.2 Court's power to make order of its own initiative

The increased case management powers include the ability of the court under r 3.3 to exercise its powers on an application of a party or of its own initiative (see Chapter 7 for the procedure under Part 23 for making an application). We have seen that this can be done when a party fails to return their directions questionnaire. Where the court proposes to make an order of its own initiative:

(a) It may give any person likely to be affected by the order an opportunity to make representations, and
(b) Where it does so it must specify the time by and the manner in which the representations must be made.

The court may make an order of its own initiative, without hearing the parties or giving them an opportunity to make representations, although a party affected by the order may apply to have it set aside, varied, or stayed, and the order must contain a statement of the right to make such an application.

If the court strikes out a statement of case or dismisses an application on its own initiative (including an application for permission to appeal or for permission to apply for judicial review) and it considers that the claim or application is totally without merit, the court's order must record that fact, and the court must at the same time consider whether it is appropriate to make a civil restraint order.

6.7.3 Striking out a statement of case

The Practice Direction to Rule 3.4 illustrates the court's far-reaching powers of case management and explains that this rule enables the court to:

(a) Strike out the whole or part of a statement of case which discloses no reasonable grounds for bringing or defending a claim under r 3.4(2)(a), or
(b) Which is an abuse of the process of the court or otherwise likely to obstruct the just disposal of the proceedings under r 3.4(2)(b).

Rule 24.2 enables the court to give summary judgment against a claimant or defendant where that party has no real prospect of succeeding on his claim or defence. Both those powers may be exercised on an application by a party or on the court's own initiative.

The court is given wide-ranging powers including the ability to strike out a statement of case if it appears:

(a) That the statement of case discloses no reasonable grounds for bringing or defending the claim
(b) That the statement of case is an abuse of the court's process or is otherwise likely to obstruct the just disposal of the proceedings, or

(c) That there has been a failure to comply with a rule, practice direction, or court order.

Where such a 'striking out' order is made, the court may order the claimant to pay costs to the defendant; if before the claimant pays those costs, the claimant starts another claim against the same defendant, arising out of facts which are the same or substantially the same as those relating to the claim in which the statement of case was struck out, the court may, on the application of the defendant, stay that other claim until the costs of the first claim have been paid. The court's order must record the fact that in the court's view the claimant's statement of case is totally without merit and the court must at the same time consider whether it is appropriate to make a civil restraint order.

Examples of where the court can strike out the statement of case are provided in Practice Direction 3A.

Where a claim is struck out for failing to disclose facts indicating what the claim is about, for example, 'Money owed £5000', or where the particulars are incoherent and make no sense, or those which contain a coherent set of facts but those facts, even if true, do not disclose any legally recognisable claim against the defendant.

In the case of a defence, the court may strike it out if it consists of a bare denial or otherwise sets out no coherent statement of facts, or the facts it sets out, while coherent, would not even if true amount in law to a defence to the claim.

Example

The Squeers defence in the personal injury claim brought by Madeline Bray is served, but the defence consists of a bare denial that Squeers was responsible for the accident. The defendant has therefore failed to comply with r 16.5 CPR 1998 (see Chapter 5). The district judge when performing his/her case management powers under Part 3 may make an order that unless the defendant files and serves a full defence setting out the full reasons for denying liability for the claimant's accident within seven days of service of the order, the defence will be struck out.

In the example provided, if the defendant fails to comply with the order to serve a full defence including details of the reasons for denying liability, the claimant can enter judgment in default for an unspecified sum with damages to be assessed at a separate hearing (see Chapter 5). The defendant can however apply under r 3.6 to set aside the judgment and if he intends to do so, must issue his application within 14 days after judgment was entered and served.

Case example

The first important post-Woolf decision demonstrating the court's far-reaching case management powers was illustrated by the case of *Biguzzi v Rank Leisure* [1999] EWCA Civ 1972. The case was struck out (for abuse of process) but reinstated because prejudice (through delays) or chance of a fair trial was not perceived to be present. The Court of Appeal (including Lord Woolf himself no less!) held that there was nothing prejudicial in allowing the case to go forward to trial and furthermore considered that both litigants had in fact been guilty of delays. Whilst the case illustrates the importance of compliance with the CPR, it also shows that there are other ways that the court can exercise its powers other than striking out, and the decision is a recognition of the importance and adherence to the overriding principle to 'the deal with civil cases justly and fairly'.

The court will strike out a case where there are sufficient grounds to do so. For instance, where a party has caused unreasonable delay or failed to comply with an order and that failure or non-compliance has meant that a fair trial would not be possible, striking out would be justified in order to uphold the principles of the overriding objective.

6.7.4 Other sanctions

Other than the striking out sanction, the court can impose sanctions on a party that has not complied with the CPR. Other options include:

a) Costs

It is not uncommon for the court to impose a costs sanction on the party in default. In such situations, the court will order the defaulting party to pay the costs occasioned by the delay on an indemnity basis (see Chapter 13). The court will make a summary assessment of those costs and may require the defaulting party to pay immediately.

If the court considers that the default was due to the party's legal representative's 'negligent, unreasonable, or improper behaviour', then the court may impose what is called a 'wasted costs order'.

See Chapter 7 for the types of costs sanctions that can be imposed by the court and also, Chapter 13 generally for a more detailed consideration of costs.

b) Interest

In the alternative, the court can make orders concerning interest payable on any damages. If the party at fault is the claimant, then the court can reduce the amount of interest payable on his/her damages. Conversely, if the defendant is at fault, then the court can increase the amount of interest payable on his/her damages. See Chapter 10 for the procedure for orders concerning interest once judgment has been delivered.

c) Unless orders

Practice Direction 28 for fast-track cases (paras. 5.1 to 5.4), and Practice Direction 29 for multi-track (paras. 7.1 and 7.2) allow the court to impose an order on any party who fails to comply with a direction given by the court. This allows any other party to apply for an order that the defaulting party must comply with or for a sanction to be imposed or both of these.

The 'unless order' is in effect a suspended sanction and the court will make such an order that unless a party complies with a particular order or rule within a prescribed timeframe, his/her claim will be struck out (see the example provided requiring a defendant to file a full defence, which is in effect an 'unless order').

6.7.5 Relief from sanctions

Where a party has failed to comply with a rule, practice direction, or court order, any sanction for failure to comply imposed by the rule, practice direction, or court order has effect unless the party in default applies for and obtains relief from the sanction. Where the sanction is the payment of costs, the party in default may only obtain relief by appealing against the order for costs.

Where a rule, practice direction, or court order requires a party to do something within a specified time and specifies the consequence of failure to comply, the parties may agree in writing to extend the time for the step to be taken for up to a maximum of 28 days, provided always that any such extension does not put at risk any hearing date (r 3.8(4)).

6.7.6 Procedure

A party can apply under r 3.9(1)(1) for relief from any sanction imposed for a failure to comply with any rule, practice direction, or court order. Upon hearing the application, the court will consider all the circumstances of the case, so as to enable it to deal justly with the application, including the need

(a) For litigation to be conducted efficiently and at proportionate cost, and
(b) To enforce compliance with rules, practice directions and orders.

An application for relief must be supported by evidence.

An important case which now sets out the suggested approach that the court should take when considering such applications is *Denton v T H White Ltd* [2014] EWCA Civ 906, which involves the court considering:

(1) The seriousness and significance of the default
(2) The reason for it, and
(3) All the circumstances of the case, so that the court can deal with the application justly.

The case and its three-stage test nicely illustrate the application of the overriding objective, i.e., to deal with cases fairly, promptly, and at proportionate cost (see section 6.1).

Chapter 6 revision points

Case management and interim applications

- Case management and the overriding objective:
    - Allocation to track – to fast track or multi-track
    - The allocation (directions) questionnaire
- The case management conference:
    - Directions
    - The allocation questionnaire
    - Case summaries
    - Varying directions and non-compliance (consequences)
    - Costs management and costs budgets
- Non-compliance with orders, sanctions, and relief:
    - Consequences of non-compliance – court's powers, striking out
    - Sanctions – costs penalties, interest, and unless orders
    - Relief from sanctions

7 Interim applications

7.1 Chapter overview

This chapter will consider the procedure for making an application during the course of proceedings, where to make it, and what to include in an application as well as the evidence required to support an application. The chapter will also look at what service requirements apply and the role of consent applications.

There will also be consideration of particular applications, including the grounds and procedure for summary judgment, interim payments, interim injunctions, and the mandatory and discretionary grounds for setting aside judgment with the associated orders the court can make. Finally, the chapter will look at the possible interim costs orders and their effect, summary assessment, and fixed costs.

7.2 Introduction: interim applications

From time to time, it will be necessary during the course of proceedings for one or other of the parties to make an application to the court. An interim application is therefore one which is made after proceedings have been commenced and before the case comes to trial.

The rules governing interim applications are found in CPR Part 23, which provides the general rules about applications for court orders. Some of the circumstances where interim applications can be made have already been briefly considered in previous chapters; for example, an application by the claimant under CPR Part 7.6 to extend the period of time for service of proceedings beyond the four-month period following issue of the claim form; an application by the defendant under CPR Part 15 to extend the time for service of his/her defence; or under CPR Part 19 an application by the claimant to add or substitute a defendant to proceedings. There may also be the need for the parties to amend their statement of case and this can be done under CPR Part 17.1.

7.3 Procedure for making an application

An application must be made on the prescribed court form, namely Form N244 (see Figure 7.1) by the applicant. The party against whom the order is being sought is known as the respondent.

DOI: 10.4324/9781003218500-11

N244

Application notice

For help in completing this form please read the notes for guidance form N244Notes.

Find out how HM Courts and Tribunals Service uses personal information you give them when you fill in a form: https://www.gov.uk/government/organisations/hm-courts-and-tribunals-service/about/personal-information-charter

Name of court	**Claim no.**
Fee account no. (if applicable)	**Help with Fees – Ref. no.** (if applicable)
	H W F –				–			
Warrant no. (if applicable)	
Claimant's name (including ref.)	
Defendant's name (including ref.)	
Date	

1. What is your name or, if you are a legal representative, the name of your firm?

2. Are you a ☐ Claimant ☐ Defendant ☐ Legal Representative

   ☐ Other (please specify)

   If you are a legal representative whom do you represent?

3. What order are you asking the court to make and why?

4. Have you attached a draft of the order you are applying for? ☐ Yes ☐ No

5. How do you want to have this application dealt with? ☐ at a hearing ☐ without a hearing

   ☐ at a telephone hearing

6. How long do you think the hearing will last? ☐ Hours ☐ Minutes

   Is this time estimate agreed by all parties? ☐ Yes ☐ No

7. Give details of any fixed trial date or period

8. What level of Judge does your hearing need?

9. Who should be served with this application?

9a. Please give the service address, (other than details of the claimant or defendant) of any party named in question 9.

N244 Application notice (01.21) 1

Figure 7.1 Form N244 Application notice.

10. What information will you be relying on, in support of your application?

- ☐ the attached witness statement
- ☐ the statement of case
- ☐ the evidence set out in the box below

If necessary, please continue on a separate sheet.

2

Figure 7.1 Continued.

Statement of Truth

I understand that proceedings for contempt of court may be brought against anyone who makes, or causes to be made, a false statement in a document verified by a statement of truth without an honest belief in its truth.

☐ **I believe** that the facts stated in section 10 (and any continuation sheets) are true.

☐ **The Applicant believes** that the facts stated in section 10 (and any continuation sheets) are true. **I am authorised** by the applicant to sign this statement.

Signature

☐ Applicant

☐ Litigation friend (where applicant is a child or a Protected Party)

☐ Applicant's legal representative (as defined by CPR 2.3(1))

Date

Day Month Year

Full name

Name of applicant's legal representative's firm

If signing on behalf of firm or company give position or office held

3

Figure 7.1 Continued.

Applicant's address to which documents should be sent.

Building and street

Second line of address

Town or city

County (optional)

Postcode

If applicable

Phone number

Fax number

DX number

Your Ref.

Email

Figure 7.1 Continued.

7.3.1 Where to make an application

Rule 23.2(1) provides that an application must be made to the court or County Court hearing centre where the claim was started. However, if the case has been transferred to another court for trial, then the application must be made to the court or the County Court hearing centre to which the claim has been transferred or sent for trial.

7.3.2 What an application notice must include

Rule 23.6 requires that an application notice must state what order the applicant is seeking and, briefly, why the applicant is seeking the order. If the applicant wishes to rely on matters set out in his application notice as evidence, an application notice must be verified by a statement of truth in accordance with CPR Part 22. Figure 7.1 shows an application notice issued by the defendant.

7.3.3 Evidence in support of an application notice

The evidence required to support an application notice will vary depending on the nature of the application and what the applicant is seeking by way of an order. As we will see in section 7.4 there are certain applications which will require specific evidence.

As a general rule, the court will need to be satisfied that sufficient information and evidence have been provided before the order can be granted. It is usual for the applicant therefore to serve a witness statement with the application notice, although this is not a strict requirement as the form provides space for sufficient written evidence to be provided.

7.3.4 Service of the application notice

A copy of the application notice must be served as soon as practicable after it is filed; and, except where another time limit is specified or a practice direction applies, must be served at least three days before the hearing at which the court is to deal with the application. If a copy of the application notice is to be served by the court, the applicant must, when he files the application notice, file a copy of any written evidence in support.

When a copy of an application notice is served it must be accompanied by:

(a) A copy of any written evidence in support, and
(b) A copy of any draft order that the applicant has attached to his/her application.

7.3.5 Applications by consent

If the parties agree as to the terms of the order sought, then they can agree that the court should dispose of the application without a hearing. The court can also dispense with a hearing if it considers it to be appropriate. A letter from the parties will usually be sufficient.

7.3.6 Service of application where application made without notice

Most applications will need to be made on notice, giving the respondent warning of the order being sought by the applicant. However, under para 3 of PD 23A, an application may be made without serving an application notice in the following circumstances:

a) where there is exceptional urgency,
b) the overriding objective is best furthered by doing so,
c) by consent of all parties,
d) with the permission of the court,
e) where a date for a hearing has been fixed and a party wishes to make an application at that hearing but he/she does not have sufficient time to serve an application notice he/she should inform the other party and the court (if possible in writing) as soon as he can of the nature of the application and the reason for it. He/she should then make the application orally at the hearing, or
f) where a court order, rule or practice direction permit.

If an order is made after making an application without notice, a copy of the order and supporting evidence must be served on the respondent accompanied by a statement that he/she may submit an application to set aside or vary the order which should be lodged within seven days.

7.3.7 Telephone hearings and video conferences

Interim applications, along with allocation hearings, listing hearings, case management conferences, and pre-trial reviews (with a time estimate of less than one hour) are a category which will usually by default be dealt with by telephone or, if the technology is available, by video conference. The exceptions to the rule are where an application has been made without notice or where one of the parties is unrepresented.

It should be noted that where a document is required to be filed and served, the party or the designated legal representative must do so no later than 4.00 p.m. at least two days before the hearing of the interim application. If the court requires it, a case summary and draft order must be filed and served in multi-track cases and small and fast-track cases.

7.4 Purpose, procedure, and evidence required for particular applications

There are particular applications which require specific procedural steps and the most commonly made interim applications that fall within this category are listed in the following.

7.4.1 Summary judgment

Under CPR Part 24 it is possible for a party to make an application for summary judgment.

This is available to both the claimant and the defendant. The aim of this is to enable proceedings to be brought to an early conclusion without the time and expense involved in pursuing the case all the way to trial.

7.4.1.1 Grounds

The circumstances that will allow for an application for summary judgment are where the claimant does not have a valid claim, or the defendant does not have a valid defence. So, under r 24.2, the court may give summary judgment against a claimant or defendant on the whole of a claim or on a particular issue if:

(a) it considers that:
   (i) the claimant has no real prospect of succeeding on the claim or issue; or,
   (ii) that defendant has no real prospect of successfully defending the claim or issue; and,
(b) there is no other compelling reason why the case or issue should be disposed of at a trial.

Para 1.3 of Practice Direction 24 for the summary disposal of claims provides that an application for summary judgment under r 24.2 may be based on:

(1) a point of law (including a question of construction of a document),
(2) the evidence which can reasonably be expected to be available at trial or the lack of it, or,
(3) a combination of these.

Case example

A compelling reason for the purposes of rule 24.2(b) is illustrated in the case of *Secretary of State for Health v Norton Healthcare Ltd & Others* [2004] LTL, 25 February, in which the claimants alleged that the defendants operated an unlawful price-fixing cartel or under an anti-competition arrangement in supplying a particular drug. One of the defendants in the action applied for summary judgment on the basis that the case against them was legally and factually flawed. The application was dismissed on the grounds that the public interest involved in controlling pharmaceutical costs and the investigation of a possible cartel were sufficiently compelling reasons for a trial to take place. The case also raised issues of conspiracy between the parties and the court considered it only right that these issues be examined at trial too.

There are therefore clearly situations where the court will consider the case not to be suitable for striking out, because there are aspects of the case which cause it to fail in meeting the requirement under r 24.2(b), that there is no other compelling reason why the case or issue should be disposed of at a trial. The bar is therefore set high for interim applications for summary judgment to succeed.

7.4.1.2 Procedure

The court must be satisfied that sufficient proof exists for an application for summary disposal to be granted. The claimant and the defendant must prove to the court's satisfaction that the other party has no real prospect of success.

7.4.1.3 Application timing

The claimant may apply for summary judgment once the defendant has filed either an acknowledgement of service or a defence. The defendant may do so once the acknowledgement of service has been filed.

7.4.1.4 Costs

Where the claimant succeeds in an application for summary judgment for a fixed amount of money, it will be usual for the court to award fixed costs in accordance with Part 45 and this will vary depending on the nature and value of the claim. Where a claim for an unspecified sum is concerned, the successful claimant will be awarded costs of the application and the amount of those, and the claimant's overall costs of the case will be determined at an assessment of damages hearing when the damages to which the claimant is entitled will also be considered. Costs of interim applications generally are further dealt with in the following and costs in general in Chapter 13.

7.4.2 The court's powers to strike out

Under CPR Rule 3.4, the court has the power to strike out a statement of case. In this rule and in r 3.5, reference to a statement of case includes reference to part of a statement of case. The court may strike out a statement of case if it appears that;

(a) The statement of case discloses no reasonable grounds for bringing or defending the claim
(b) The statement of case is an abuse of the court's process or is otherwise likely to obstruct the just disposal of the proceedings, or
(c) There has been a failure to comply with a rule, practice direction, or court order.

When the court strikes out a statement of case it may make any consequential order it considers appropriate.

Practice Direction 3A 1.4 provides guidance about the types of cases where the court may conclude that particulars of claim (whether contained in a claim form or filed separately) fall within r 3.4(2)(a), which allows the court to strike it out because the statement of case discloses no reasonable grounds for bringing or defending the claim:

(a) those which set out no facts indicating what the claim is about, for example 'Money owed £5000',

(b) those which are incoherent and make no sense,
(c) those which contain a coherent set of facts but those facts, even if true, do not disclose any legally recognisable claim against the defendant.

A claim may fall within r 3.4(2)(b) which allows the court to strike out the statement of case because it is vexatious, scurrilous, or obviously ill-founded.

If the judge decides that the document falls within r 3.4(2)(a) or (b), he/she may on his/her own initiative make an order striking it out. Where he/she does so he/she may extend the time for the defendant to file a proper defence. A defence may fall within r 3.4(2)(a) where:

(1) it consists of a bare denial or otherwise sets out no coherent statement of facts, or,
(2) the facts it sets out, while coherent, would not even if true amount in law to a defence to the claim.

7.4.3 Interim payments

Under CPR Part 25 it is possible to make an application for an interim remedy, one of which is an application for an interim payment. Rule 25.1 provides the procedure for an application for an interim payment. An interim payment is essentially an advance payment on account of any damages likely to be awarded in the action to provide relief from financial hardship. Such applications are not uncommon for personal injury claims and unless the defendant's insurance company agrees to make a voluntary interim payment, an application can be made, but only where certain conditions are met.

Rule 25.7(1) provides that the court may only make an order for an interim payment where any of the following conditions are satisfied:

(a) the defendant against whom the order is sought has admitted liability to pay damages or some other sum of money to the claimant;
(b) the claimant has obtained judgment against that defendant for damages to be assessed or for a sum of money (other than costs) to be assessed;
(c) it is satisfied that, if the claim went to trial, the claimant would obtain judgment for a substantial amount of money (other than costs) against the defendant from whom he is seeking an order for an interim payment whether or not that defendant is the only defendant or one of a number of defendants to the claim;
(d) the following conditions are satisfied:
    (i) the claimant is seeking an order for possession of land (whether or not any other order is also sought); and
    (ii) the court is satisfied that, if the case went to trial, the defendant would be held liable (even if the claim for possession fails) to pay the claimant a sum of money for the defendant's occupation and use of the land while the claim for possession was pending; or,

(e) in a claim in which there are two or more defendants, and the order is sought against any one or more of those defendants, the following conditions are satisfied:
   (i) the court is satisfied that, if the claim went to trial, the claimant would obtain judgment for a substantial amount of money (other than costs) against at least one of the defendants (but the court cannot determine which); and
   (ii) all the defendants are either:
      - a defendant that is insured in respect of the claim;
      - a defendant whose liability will be met by an insurer under section 151 of the Road Traffic Act 1988 or an insurer acting under the Motor Insurers Bureau Agreement, or the Motor Insurers Bureau where it is acting itself; or
      - a defendant that is a public body.

7.4.3.1 Procedure and evidence

An application for an interim payment must be supported by evidence and served no later than 14 days before the hearing. PD 25B para 2.1 requires that the evidence must deal with the following matters:

(a) the sum of money sought by way of an interim payment,
(b) the items or matters in respect of which the interim payment is sought,
(c) the sum of money for which final judgment is likely to be given,
(d) the reasons for believing that the conditions set out in rule 25.7 are satisfied,
(e) any other relevant matters,
(f) in claims for personal injuries, details of special damages and past and future loss, and,
(g) in a claim under the Fatal Accidents Act 1976, details of the person(s) on whose behalf the claim is made and the nature of the claim.

There is no requirement for the applicant to show any real need for an interim payment and, by the same token, the respondent cannot plead poverty if opposing the application. It is for the applicant to prove the grounds of the application on the civil standard of proof, that being on the balance of probabilities. It is not uncommon for an application for an interim payment to be accompanied by an application for summary judgment (see earlier).

If the court orders that an interim payment should be made, then it can under PD 25B para 3 order that the respondent pay by instalments, whereupon the order should set out the following:

- the total amount of the payment,
- the amount of each instalment,
- the number of instalments and the date on which each is to be paid, and
- to whom the payment should be made.

If the case proceeds to trial, the trial judge will not be told of any interim payments or their amount. If at trial the claimant succeeds and is awarded an amount greater than the interim payment already received, then the damages award will be reduced by the amount of the interim payment received. If at trial the court awards a sum less than the amount of the interim payment already received, then the claimant will be required to repay the excess with interest on the overpaid amount from the date when the interim payment was made.

7.4.4 Interim injunctions

Another interim remedy available by making an application under CPR Part 25 is for an injunction. This is a civil remedy which is available under Part 25.1(1)(a), to prevent someone from taking certain action (a prohibitory injunction) or requiring action to be taken (a mandatory injunction). If granted, the interim injunction will only remain in force until the application is considered at a further hearing or trial.

7.4.4.1 Procedure and evidence

Practice Direction 25A provides the procedural guidance for an application for an interim injunction. The application notice must state the nature of the order being sought, the date, time, and place of the hearing, and must be served no later than three days before the hearing. Whenever possible, a draft of the order sought should be filed with the application notice.

An application for an interim payment must be supported by evidence, and PD 25A para 3.2 requires that the application for an interim injunction must, unless the court requires an affidavit, be supported by evidence set out in either:

- a witness statement, or
- a statement of case provided that it is verified by a statement of truth, or
- the application provided that it is verified by a statement of truth.

The evidence must set out the facts on which the applicant relies for the claim being made against the respondent, including all material facts of which the court should be made aware. Where an application is made without notice to the respondent, the evidence must also set out why notice was not given.

7.4.4.2 Urgent applications and applications without notice

Such applications can be made before the claim form is issued. We are, however, concerned with those urgent applications where there is no requirement to give notice to the respondent following the commencement of proceedings and before trial. These applications are normally dealt with at a court hearing, but cases of extreme urgency may be dealt with by telephone.

Under PD 25A 4.3 the procedure for an urgent application for an injunction without notice requires that:

(1) the application notice, evidence in support and a draft order should be filed with the court two hours before the hearing wherever possible,
(2) if an application is made before the application notice has been issued, a draft order should be provided at the hearing, and the application notice and evidence in support must be filed with the court on the same or next working day or as ordered by the court, and
(3) except in cases where secrecy is essential, the applicant should take steps to notify the respondent informally of the application.

7.4.5 Orders for injunctions

Under PD 25A 5.1, any order for an injunction, unless the court orders otherwise, must contain:

(1) an undertaking by the applicant to the court to pay any damages which the respondent sustains which the court considers the applicant should pay.
(2) if made without notice to any other party, an undertaking by the applicant to the court to serve on the respondent the application notice, evidence in support and any order made as soon as practicable,
(3) if made without notice to any other party, a return date for a further hearing at which the other party can be present,
(4) if made before filing the application notice, an undertaking to file and pay the appropriate fee on the same or next working day, and
(5) if made before issue of a claim form –
    (a) an undertaking to issue and pay the appropriate fee on the same or next working day, or
    (b) directions for the commencement of the claim.

It should be noted that when the court makes an order for an injunction, it ought to consider whether to require the applicant to provide an undertaking to pay any damages sustained by a person other than the respondent, including another party to the proceedings or any other person who may suffer loss as a consequence of the order.

7.4.6 Setting aside judgment in default

Rule 13 provides the procedural requirements for an interim application for setting aside default judgment on mandatory and discretionary grounds.

7.4.6.1 Mandatory grounds

Under r 13.2 the court must set aside a judgment wrongly entered before the defendant's deadline for either filing an acknowledgement of service, or expiry of the deadline for filing a defence. The court is also obliged to set aside a default judgment which has been entered after the whole of the claim was satisfied before judgment was entered.

7.4.6.2 Discretionary grounds

Rule 13.3(1) provides that in any other case, the court may set aside or vary a judgment entered if:

(a) the defendant has a real prospect of successfully defending the claim; or
(b) it appears to the court that there is some other good reason why –
    (i) the judgment should be set aside or varied; or
    (ii) the defendant should be allowed to defend the claim.

Under r 13.3(1), in considering whether the defendant has a real prospect of successfully defending the claim, the same test as that applicable to applications for summary judgment under r 24.2 applies (see section 7.4).

In considering whether to set aside or vary a judgment entered in default, the court, however, under r 13.3(2) will have regard to whether the person seeking to set aside the judgment made an application to do so promptly. This demonstrates the application of the overriding objective and the importance that the court must place when exercising its case management powers in order to deal with cases fairly and expeditiously (see Chapter 6 and case management in section 6.1). The message here, however, is that the applicant must not delay in making his/her interim application to set aside judgment.

After it has considered the grounds in rules 13.3(1)(a) and (b) and 13.3(2), the court will also apply the three-stage approach set out in the case of *Denton* (see section 6.5 and relief from sanctions).

7.4.7 The possible orders the court can make

Upon hearing the application to set aside judgment, the court has three options:

(a) Set aside the default judgment
(b) Set aside judgment with conditions
(c) Refuse to set aside judgment.

If an order under (a) is made, then it is usual for the court to give directions for the future management of the case. If under (b) a conditional order is made, it is usual for the court to allow judgment to be set aside, but on the condition that the defendant pays into court a sum of money that he/she can reasonably afford.

7.4.7.1 Costs

The court will be required to consider what appropriate costs order to make following the outcome of the application to set aside judgment. The costs order will depend on the circumstances and the nature of the order made, and the following are some examples of the possible outcomes and the likely costs orders that the court could make:

(a) Where judgment is set aside on mandatory grounds, then it is usual for the claimant to pay the defendant's costs of the application for having entered judgment wrongly

(b) If the court has used its discretion to set aside judgment on the basis that the defendant has shown a good reason for default, then the court is likely to consider that neither party was at fault and make an order that costs be in the case (meaning that the costs of the application will usually be paid by losing party at trial)
(c) Where the defendant has only demonstrated a discretionary ground of a defence with a good case and reasonable prospects of success at trial the defendant will be considered to have been at fault and the usual order will be for the defendant to pay the claimant's costs
(d) If a conditional order is made, then it is probably because the defendant has made an application to set aside the judgment late and will be penalised for doing so by being ordered to pay the claimant's costs of the application.

7.5 Interim costs generally

Every interim application will involve the parties incurring some expense. The applicant will prepare an application usually supported by a witness statement and the defendant will usually prepare and serve a witness statement in response. At the end of the application the judge must consider the question of costs, i.e., who should pay the costs of the application. This is sometimes referred to as 'pay as you go litigation' and the general rule that the winner pays the loser's costs applies.

7.5.1 Possible orders

The court has the power to make different costs orders at the end of an interim application. The most common costs orders are provided by PD 44, para 4.2 and are set out in Table 7.1.

The court has the power to make an order about costs at any stage in a case, but if there is no mention of costs at the hearing, then the general rule is that none are payable. It is important therefore that the judge makes some kind of costs order.

7.5.1.1 Summary assessment

If the court makes an order in favour of one of the parties, either, for example, claimant's costs, claimant's costs thrown away, or defendant's costs of and caused by, then the court will make a summary assessment at that stage of the proceedings of costs of the party in whose favour the costs have been awarded. To enable the judge to consider the issue of costs of the interim application, the parties must file a statement of costs no later than 24 hours before the hearing.

7.5.1.2 Fixed costs

Rather than assessing costs summarily and making one of the orders set out in Table 7.1, the court will on occasion order fixed costs (see, e.g., summary judgment). CPR Part 45 sets out the circumstances where fixed costs can be granted and the amount which can be awarded to the party awarded fixed costs (see further Chapter 13).

Table 7.1 Costs orders which the court will commonly make in proceedings before trial

Term	Effect
Costs Costs in any event	The party in whose favour the order is made is entitled to that party's costs in respect of the part of the proceedings to which the order relates, whatever other costs orders are made in the proceedings
Costs in the case Costs in the application	The party in whose favour the court makes an order for costs at the end of the proceedings is entitled to that party's costs of the part of the proceedings to which the order relates
Costs reserved	The decision about costs is deferred to a later occasion, but if no later order is made the costs will be costs in the case
Claimant's/ defendant's costs in the case/application	If the party in whose favour the costs order is made is awarded costs at the end of the proceedings, that party is entitled to that party's costs of the part of the proceedings to which the order relates. If any other party is awarded costs at the end of the proceedings, the party in whose favour the final costs order is made is not liable to pay the costs of any other party in respect of the part of the proceedings to which the order relates
Costs thrown away	Where, for example, a judgment or order is set aside, the party in whose favour the costs order is made is entitled to the costs which have been incurred as a consequence. This includes the costs of: • Preparing for and attending any hearing at which the judgment or order which has been set aside was made • Preparing for and attending any hearing to set aside the judgment or order in question • Preparing for and attending any hearing at which the court orders the proceedings or the part in question to be adjourned • Any steps taken to enforce a judgment or order which has subsequently been set aside
Costs of and caused by	Where, for example, the court makes this order on an application to amend a statement of case, the party in whose favour the costs order is made is entitled to the costs of preparing for and attending the application and the costs of any consequential amendment to his own statement of case
No order as to costs Each party to pay own costs	Each party is to bear that party's own costs of the part of the proceedings to which the order relates whatever costs order the court makes at the end of the proceedings

Chapter 7 revision points

Interim applications

- Procedure for making an application
  - Where to make the application, what to include, and evidence in support
  - Service requirements
  - Consent applications
- Particular applications
  - Summary judgment – grounds and procedure
  - The court's power to strike out – on its own motion
  - Interim payments – grounds, procedure, evidence, and possible orders
  - Setting aside judgment – mandatory and discretionary grounds and possible orders
  - Interim costs orders – those possible and their effect, summary assessment, and fixed costs

Multiple-choice questions for Part 4

1. A has issued a claim for the recovery of a debt amounting to £12,750. B has filed a defence disputing all aspects of the claim. As part of the court's case management responsibilities, directions questionnaires have been sent to both parties. A has filed his completed directions questionnaire; however, B has not complied with the court's requirement to do so within 14 days.

*Which one of the following **best** explains what now can be done procedurally?*

A. The court will now serve a notice on the defendant explaining that failure to file the completed directions questionnaire within seven days will mean that its defence is struck out and judgment will be entered for the claimant.
B. The claim will automatically be struck out by the court using its case management powers and judgment will be entered for the claimant.
C. Because the claim is more than £10,000, but less than £25,000, the court will automatically allocate the to the fast track and then make its own directions about the future conduct of the case.
D. A will be able to make an interim application to the court asking the court to strike out the defendant's defence with judgment to be entered in his favour.
E. The court will now serve a notice of proposed allocation requiring the defendant B to file its directions questionnaire by a specified date; failure to do so will then enable the court to serve a notice on the defendant B, requiring compliance within seven days.

2. In a claim for damages for personal injury, the defendant has filed and served a defence which provides a bare denial of the liability and no more.

*Which one of the following **best** explains the procedural step that can now be taken?*

A. The court will automatically strike out the defendant's statement of case.
B. The claimant can make an application for summary judgment.
C. Procedurally, the claimant must wait for the case to be listed for a case management conference before making any applications.
D. The claimant can make an application for default judgment.
E. The claimant can make an application for summary judgment, but not until allocation questionnaires have been filed with the court.

PART

5

The evidence needed and disclosure steps required in commencing, responding to, progressing, or defending a claim

8 Evidence

8.1 Chapter overview

This chapter provides an overview of evidence and its use within civil proceedings, which are governed by the Civil Evidence Acts. This will firstly involve consideration of the burden and standard of proof and then move on to deal with the importance of evidential relevance, hearsay, and admissibility.

The chapter will then consider expert evidence, the expert's duty, and the court's power to restrict the use of expert evidence. The rules requiring experts' discussions, the use of written joint statements, and the circumstances where single joint experts are used will also be covered. Finally, the chapter will look at the format and structure of witness statements, witness summaries, and the format and structure of affidavits.

8.2 Introduction: evidence

In order for parties to a civil action involving the enforcement of a private or civil right to either successfully pursue or defend their case, it will be frequently necessary for them to produce supportive evidence to establish the facts relating to issues important to the case. In order to establish the ingredients of the cause of action, the burden of proof lies with the party making the allegations. The ingredients of the cause of action must be proved to the required standard of proof, which for civil cases is on the preponderance of evidence test, or in other words, on the balance of probabilities. This essentially means that the court will be satisfied a fact or event occurred if it considers that, on consideration of all the evidence, the fact or event was more likely than not to occur. The Civil Evidence Acts 1972 and 1995 are the guiding legislation for the use of evidence in civil proceedings.

In civil proceedings, the general rule is that evidence will be admissible if it is relevant. This rule applies unless:

- The evidence falls within an exclusionary rule prescribed by law, or
- The court exercises its discretion to exclude the evidence.

The rules of civil evidence are found in Parts 32 and 33 CPR 1988 and whilst they do not affect the law relating to the admissibility of civil evidence, the court's discretion

DOI: 10.4324/9781003218500-13

on what evidence can be produced is achieved by the application of its case management powers. The power of the court to control evidence is covered by r 32.1, which states that:

(1) The court may control the evidence by giving directions as to:
   (a) the issues on which it requires evidence;
   (b) the nature of the evidence which it requires to decide those issues; and
   (c) the way in which the evidence is to be placed before the court.
(2) The court may use its power under this rule to exclude evidence that would otherwise be admissible.
(3) The court may limit cross-examination.

Under r 32.2(3) the court has additional powers to control the evidence by giving directions, which:

(a) identify or limit the issues to which factual evidence may be directed;
(b) identify the witnesses who may be called or whose evidence may be read; or
(c) limit the length or format of witness statements.

In exercising its court management powers in relation to the regulation and admissibility of evidence, the court will at all times have regard to the overriding objective in r 1.1. At the directions stage, the court can therefore consider what issues remain relevant and as a consequence what evidence can be used. It is not unusual for the court to provide the parties with a list of issues which should be considered at trial.

8.3 Relevance, hearsay, and admissibility

8.3.1 Relevance

When presenting evidence before the court, for it to be admissible it will need to be relevant. In order to establish relevance, the party presenting the evidence or seeking to rely upon it must be able to show that the evidence concerned has an effect upon the probability of proving a matter relevant to the case; it does not have to actually prove or disprove a fact in issue.

8.3.2 Hearsay

Hearsay evidence is defined by s 1(2) of the Civil Evidence Act 1995 as being 'a statement made, otherwise than by a person while giving oral evidence in proceedings, which is tendered as evidence of the matters stated'.

The hearsay statement must constitute admissible evidence and must be relevant (see the preceding and following). It must also be an individual's own perception and not form any kind of expert opinion (see the following). Under s 5 of the Civil Evidence Act 1995, hearsay is not admissible if the maker of the statement is not a competent witness, for example, if they are too young, of unsound mind, or lack understanding.

Case example

The decision in *Breslin & Others v Murphy & Daly* [2013] NIQB 15 is helpful when considering the admissibility of hearsay evidence. Gillen J set out the test for the admissibility of hearsay evidence on civil cases as follows:

1) Relevance – namely that the material to be adduced was potentially probative of an issue in the action, i.e., if irrelevant it should not be admitted in the first place
2) Significance of the evidence – the strength of the argument for admitting the evidence will always depend primarily on the judge's assessment of its potential significance, assuming it to be true, in the context of the case as a whole
3) The overriding purpose must always be to promote the ends of justice by a trial process fair to all parties

8.3.2.1 Notice of intention to rely on hearsay evidence

Under s1 of the Civil Evidence Act 1995 evidence in civil proceedings shall not be excluded on the ground that it is hearsay and if a party wishes to adduce such evidence, he/she must prepare a notice of proposal to adduce hearsay evidence. The rules relating to the use of hearsay evidence are dealt with in Part 33 of the CPR 1988, which states that:

(1) Where a party intends to rely on hearsay evidence at trial and either –
  (a) that evidence is to be given by a witness giving oral evidence; or
  (b) that evidence is contained in a witness statement of a person who is not being called to give oral evidence;
  that party complies with section 2(1)(a) of the Civil Evidence Act 19951 serving a witness statement on the other parties in accordance with the court's order.
(2) Where paragraph (1)(b) applies, the party intending to rely on the hearsay evidence must, when he serves the witness statement –
  (a) inform the other parties that the witness is not being called to give oral evidence; and
  (b) give the reason why the witness will not be called.
(3) In all other cases where a party intends to rely on hearsay evidence at trial, that party complies with section 2(1)(a) of the Civil Evidence Act 1995 by serving a notice on the other parties which –
  (a) identifies the hearsay evidence;
  (b) states that the party serving the notice proposes to rely on the hearsay evidence at trial; and
  (c) gives the reason why the witness will not be called.
(4) The party proposing to rely on the hearsay evidence must –
  (a) serve the notice no later than the latest date for serving witness statements; and

(b) if the hearsay evidence is to be in a document, supply a copy to any party who requests him to do so.

8.3.2.2 Weight of hearsay evidence

Considerations relevant to weighing hearsay evidence are dealt with in s1 of the Civil Evidence Act 1995, which provides that:

(1) In estimating the weight (if any) to be given to hearsay evidence in civil proceedings the court shall have regard to any circumstances from which any inference can reasonably be drawn as to the reliability or otherwise of the evidence.
(2) Regard may be had, in particular, to the following –
   (a) whether it would have been reasonable and practicable for the party by whom the evidence was adduced to have produced the maker of the original statement as a witness;
   (b) whether the original statement was made contemporaneously with the occurrence or existence of the matters stated;
   (c) whether the evidence involves multiple hearsay;
   (d) whether any person involved had any motive to conceal or misrepresent matters;
   (e) whether the original statement was an edited account, or was made in collaboration with another or for a particular purpose;
   (f) whether the circumstances in which the evidence is adduced as hearsay are such as to suggest an attempt to prevent proper evaluation of its weight.

8.3.3 Admissibility

Evidence will generally be admissible if it is relevant to the issues involved in the case and is not excluded by the Civil Evidence Acts or any other relevant law which may be applicable. In some circumstances, exclusionary rules apply which may make the evidence inadmissible due to matters of public policy or some particular specified conditions or safeguards. If evidence is considered to be inadmissible, then the party seeking to rely upon it may be denied the opportunity to do so if the court rules it inadmissible. Matters relating to the inadmissibility of evidence are most commonly considered by the judge at trial, rather than at an interim or preliminary hearing.

8.4 The burden and standard of proof

8.4.1 The burden of proof

The general approach is that 'he who asserts must prove'. In other words, the legal burden of proof in civil disputes lies with the party asserting a proposition, not the party denying it. The person with the legal burden of proof seeking a remedy in the civil courts therefore bears the evidential burden or onus of proof. To satisfy the burden of proof the party with the burden of proof must prove the alleged fact to the standard required by the applicable standard of proof.

8.4.2 The standard of proof

The standard of proof in civil cases is 'on the balance of probabilities'. The court will need to be satisfied that an event was more likely to have occurred than not. This is summarised concisely by Lord Hoffman in *Re H (Minors) (Sexual Abuse: Standard of Proof)* [1996] AC 563, when he said that 'there is only one civil standard of proof and that is proof that the fact in issue more probably occurred than not'.

8.5 Opinion evidence

The general rule is that opinion evidence is not admissible. However, there are certain circumstances where evidence of a witness's opinion, although challenged, might be admissible under s.3(2) of the Civil Evidence Act 1972, which provides that:

> where a person is called as a witness in any civil proceedings, a statement of opinion by him on any relevant matter on which he is not qualified to give expert evidence, if made as a way of conveying relevant facts personally perceived by him, is admissible as evidence of what he perceived.

The other situation where opinion evidence can be admissible concerns expert witnesses, and s.3(1) of the Civil Evidence Act 1972, provides that:

> where a person is called as a witness in any civil proceedings, his opinion on any relevant matter on which he is qualified to give expert evidence shall be admissible in evidence.

The primary function of an expert witness is to assist the court in reaching its decision by providing independent expert/technical analysis and opinion on an issue or issues which are relevant to the case.

8.6 Expert evidence

The use of experts in civil proceedings is governed by Part 35 of the CPR and r 35 defines an 'expert witness' as a person who has been instructed to give or prepare expert evidence for the purpose of proceedings.

The admissibility of expert opinion evidence is governed by s.3(1) Civil Evidence Act 1972, which provides that, 'where a person is called as a witness in any civil proceedings, his opinion on any relevant matter on which he is qualified to give expert evidence shall be admissible in evidence'.

The Civil Justice Council's General Guidance on the Instruction of Evidence in Civil Claims can be found on the Courts and Tribunals Judiciary website.[1] This guid-

1 www.judiciary.uk/wp-content/uploads/2014/08/experts-guidance-cjc-aug-2014-amended-dec-8.pdf.

ance document provides helpful information about the duties of experts and their appointment.

8.6.1 Duties of experts

It is important to understand that an expert's overriding duty is to the court and that duty extends to assisting the court on matters only within their expertise. Most importantly, this duty overrides any obligation to the person from whom experts have received instructions or by whom they are paid (r 35.3). This means that the expert must present his/her expert opinion with objectivity and impartiality.

8.6.2 The court's power to restrict expert evidence

Judicial case management extends to the regulation of expert evidence. In fact, under r 35.1 judges are under a duty to restrict expert evidence to that which is reasonably required to resolve the proceedings.

The court's power to restrict expert evidence is extended by r 35.4, which states that:

(1) No party may call an expert or put in evidence an expert's report without the court's permission.
(2) When parties apply for permission, they must provide an estimate of the costs of the proposed expert evidence and identify –
  (a) the field in which expert evidence is required and the issues which the expert evidence will address; and
  (b) where practicable, the name of the proposed expert.
(3) If permission is granted it shall be in relation only to the expert named or the field identified under paragraph (2). The order granting permission may specify the issues which the expert evidence should address.

Permission to allow expert evidence will usually be given at the directions stage of proceedings. In Chapter 6 we considered the contents of the directions questionnaire. This includes the requirement for the parties to provide the information in r 35.4. Remember that the court can, through its powers to give directions under its own initiative (para 4.10 of PD 29), give specific directions about expert evidence (see Chapter 6).

The court will also consider whether it is necessary for experts to give oral evidence at trial. It is usual in fast-track cases for the parties to rely on the expert's written report rather than requiring them to give oral evidence. This is probably more about the application of the overriding objective and the requirement to save expense and deal with cases at proportionate cost than anything else; attendance of expert witnesses at court is expensive.

8.6.3 Instructing an expert witness

It is a requirement under r 35.10(4) that the instructions provided by a party's solicitor to an expert witness shall not be privileged against disclosure. But the court will not, in relation to those instructions, order disclosure of any specific document or permit any questioning in court, other than by the party who instructed the expert, unless it is satisfied that there are reasonable grounds to consider the statement of instructions to be inaccurate or incomplete.

The issue of privilege in relation to an expert's written instructions should, however, be considered in the light of Practice Direction 35, para 5, which states that cross-examination of experts on the contents of their instructions will not be allowed unless the court permits it (or unless the party who gave the instructions consents). Before it gives permission, the court must be satisfied that there are reasonable grounds to consider that the statement in the report of the substance of the instructions is inaccurate or incomplete. If the court is so satisfied, it will allow the cross-examination where it appears to be in the interests of justice.

It is of course the right of any party to proceedings to waive privilege should they wish, and it is not uncommon for the letter of instruction to the expert to be attached to the report. After experts' reports have been exchanged in accordance with any directions order given, it is not unusual for a party to send the other party's report to their expert for comment.

An example of a letter of instruction to a medical expert appears in Figure 8.1.

8.6.4 Form and contents of expert evidence

8.6.4.1 Form

Rule 35.5 requires that any expert evidence should be given in writing unless the court directs otherwise. The court will not direct an expert to attend a hearing to give oral evidence in those claims being dealt with on the small-claims track or the fast track unless it is necessary to do so in the interests of justice.

8.6.4.2 Content

Rule 35.10 provides guidance on the matters which the expert witness should deal with. As such the contents of an expert's report should deal with the following matters as provided by paras. 3.1 and 3.2 to Practice Direction 35:

(1) give details of the expert's qualifications;
(2) give details of any literature or other material which has been relied on in making the report;
(3) contain a statement setting out the substance of all facts and instructions which are material to the opinions expressed in the report or upon which those opinions are based;
(4) make clear which of the facts stated in the report are within the expert's own knowledge;
(5) say who carried out any examination, measurement, test or experiment which the expert has used for the report, give the qualifications of that person, and say

Mr V. R. Crummles
247 Harley St
London W1G 6AQ

Our Ref: 040898/RD/Y/402
10th July 2022

Dear Sir,

Re: Client: Madeline Bray

We are instructed by the above named born on **2nd May 1963** of **25 Mulberry Terrace, Melbourne, Staffs.** in connection with a claim for damages for personal injury and loss arising out of an accident which occurred on **13th December 2021.**

We would be grateful if you would kindly examine our client and provide us with a full and detailed report dealing with any relevant pre-accident medical history, the injuries sustained, treatment received and resent condition, the likely effects upon capacity for work, together with a prognosis.

It is central to our assessment of the nature of our client's injuries to establish the extent and duration of any continuing disability. Accordingly, in the prognosis section we would ask you to specifically comment on any areas of continuing complaint or disability or impact on daily living. If there is ongoing disability you should comment on the level of suffering or inconvenience caused and, if you are in in a position to do so, give your view as to when or if the complaint or disability is likely to resolve.

The Law Society and BMA have agreed a checklist of information which should be contained in a comprehensive expert medical report. If you would like to have a copy of this before preparing your report, please let us know.

Please send out client an appointment for this purpose, and should you be able to offer a cancellation appointment, again please contact our client direct. We confirm that we will be responsible foryour reasonable fees.

In order to comply with the Court Rules, we would eb grateful if you could insert in your report above your signature a statement that the contents of your report are true to the best of your knowledge and belief.

In order to avoid further correspondence, we can confirm that on the evidence we have, there is no reason to suspect that we will be pursuing a claim against the hospital or its staff.

We look forward to receiving your report within 6 weeks. If you will not be able to prepare your report within this timeframe, please let us know upon receipt of these instructions.

When acknowledging these instructions, it would assist if you could provide an estimate as to the likely timescale for the provision of your report and also an indication of your fee.

Yours faithfully,

Figure 8.1 Letter of instruction (medical expert).

whether or not the test or experiment has been carried out under the expert's supervision;

(6) where there is a range of opinion on the matters dealt with in the report –
  (a) summarise the range of opinions; and
  (b) give reasons for the expert's own opinion;

(7) contain a summary of the conclusions reached;

(8) if the expert is not able to give an opinion without qualification, state the qualification; and

(9) contain a statement that the expert –
  (a) understands their duty to the court, and has complied with that duty; and
  (b) is aware of the requirements of Part 35, this practice direction and the Guidance for the Instruction of Experts in Civil Claims 2014.

An expert's report must be verified by a statement of truth in the following form:

> I confirm that I have made clear which facts and matters referred to in this report are within my own knowledge and which are not. Those that are within my own knowledge I confirm to be true. The opinions I have expressed represent my true and complete professional opinions on the matters to which they refer.
>
> I understand that proceedings for contempt of court may be brought against anyone who makes, or causes to be made, a false statement in a document verified by a statement of truth without an honest belief in its truth.

8.6.5 Discussion between experts

Whilst not mandatory, it is not uncommon for the court to require the respective parties' expert witnesses to have a 'without prejudice' discussion about their reports. Rule 35.12 provides the guidance for such discussions, the purpose of which is twofold:

(1) To identify and discuss the expert issues in the proceedings, and
(2) Where possible, to reach an agreed opinion on those issues.

The court may specify the issues which the experts must discuss, and the general idea is for the experts to narrow and reduce the number of contentious issues between them. Practice Direction 35, para 9.2 suggests that the experts should try to identify:

(i) the extent of the agreement between them;
(ii) the points of and short reasons for any disagreement;
(iii) action, if any, which may be taken to resolve any outstanding points of disagreement; and
(iv) any further material issues not raised and the extent to which these issues are agreed.

Where the experts are to meet, the parties must discuss and if possible, agree on whether an agenda is necessary, and if so, attempt to agree on one that helps the experts to focus on the issues which need to be discussed. The agenda must not be in the form of leading questions or hostile in tone (PD, para 9.3).

8.6.5.1 Written joint statements

Following a discussion between the experts, the court may, under r 35 12(3), direct that they must prepare a statement for the court setting out those issues on which they agree and disagree, with a summary of their reasons for disagreeing.

Individual copies of the statements must be signed by the experts at the conclusion of the discussion, or as soon thereafter as practicable, and in any event within seven days. Copies of the statements must be provided to the parties no later than 14 days after signing (PD, para 9.6).

Experts must give their own opinions to assist the court and do not require the authority of the parties to sign a joint statement (PD, para 9.7). If an expert significantly alters an opinion, the joint statement must include a note or addendum by that expert explaining the change of opinion (PD, para 9.7).

It should be noted that under rules 35.12(4) and (5), the content of the discussion between the experts shall not be referred to at the trial unless the parties agree and where experts reach an agreement on an issue during their discussions, the agreement shall not bind the parties unless the parties expressly agree to be bound by the agreement.

8.6.5.2 Single joint experts

A 'single joint expert' as defined by r 35.2(2) is an expert instructed to prepare a report for the court on behalf of two or more of the parties (including the claimant) to the proceedings. The use of the single joint expert is the general approach in fast-track cases unless the court believes that there is a good reason not to do so (para 3.9 of PD 28).

The court's case management regarding expert witnesses extends to its power to direct that evidence should be given by a single joint expert. Under r 35.7 therefore the court may require that:

(1) Where two or more parties wish to submit expert evidence on a particular issue, the court may direct that the evidence on that issue is to be given by a single joint expert.
(2) Where the parties who wish to submit the evidence ('the relevant parties') cannot agree who should be the single joint expert, the court may –
    (a) select the expert from a list prepared or identified by the relevant parties; or
    (b) direct that the expert be selected in such other manner as the court may direct.

Practice Direction 35, para 7 provides helpful guidance for the use of single joint experts and states that when considering whether to give permission for the parties to rely on expert evidence and whether that evidence should be from a single joint expert, the court will take into account all the circumstances, in particular, whether:

(a) it is proportionate to have separate experts for each party on a particular issue with reference to –
    (i) the amount in dispute;
    (ii) the importance to the parties; and
    (iii) the complexity of the issue;
(b) the instruction of a single joint expert is likely to assist the parties and the court to resolve the issue more speedily and in a more cost-effective way than separately instructed experts;
(c) expert evidence is to be given on the issue of liability, causation or quantum;

(d) the expert evidence falls within a substantially established area of knowledge which is unlikely to be in dispute or there is likely to be a range of expert opinion;
(e) a party has already instructed an expert on the issue in question and whether or not that was done in compliance with any practice direction or relevant pre-action protocol;
(f) questions put in accordance with rule 35.6 are likely to remove the need for the other party to instruct an expert if one party has already instructed an expert;
(g) questions put to a single joint expert may not conclusively deal with all issues that may require testing prior to trial;
(h) a conference may be required with the legal representatives, experts and other witnesses which may make instruction of a single joint expert impractical; and
(i) a claim to privilege makes the instruction of any expert as a single joint expert inappropriate.

8.6.5.3 Consequences of failure to disclose expert's report

Under r 35.13 a party who fails to disclose an expert's report may not use the report at the trial or call the expert to give evidence orally unless the court gives permission.

8.7 Witness evidence

The general rule relating to evidence found in r 32.2(1) is that any fact which needs to be proved by the evidence of witnesses is to be proved at trial by their oral evidence given in public and at any other hearing by their evidence in writing. This is subject to any provision to the contrary contained in these Rules or elsewhere, to any order of the court. The court rules also provide that a witness may give evidence through a video link or by other means.

The Practice Direction to Part 32 provides that evidence at a hearing other than the trial should normally be given by witness statement. However, a witness may give evidence by affidavit if he/she wishes to do so (see the following) and they must be used as evidence in the following instances:

(1) where sworn evidence is required by an enactment, rule, order or practice direction, and
(2) in any application for a search order, a freezing injunction, or an order requiring an occupier to permit another to enter his land.

If a party believes that sworn evidence is required by a court in another jurisdiction for any purpose connected with the proceedings, he/she may apply to the court for a direction that evidence shall be given only by affidavit on any pre-trial applications.

The court may give a direction under r 32.15 that evidence shall be given by affidavit instead of or in addition to a witness statement or statement of case:

(1) on its own initiative, or
(2) after any party has applied to the court for such a direction.

An affidavit, where referred to in the Civil Procedure Rules or a Practice Direction, also means an affirmation unless the context requires otherwise.

Statements of case and application notices may also be used as evidence provided that their contents have been verified by a statement of truth.

8.7.1 Witness statements: form and structure

Practice Directions 17 to 20 of r 32 deal with the form and structure of witness statements.

8.7.2 Heading

By para 17.1 the witness statement should be headed with the title of the proceedings. The following should be clearly written at the top right-hand corner of the first page:

(1) the party on whose behalf it is made,
(2) the initials and surname of the witness,
(3) the number of the statement in relation to that witness,
(4) the identifying initials and number of each exhibit referred to,
(5) the date the statement was made, and
(6) the date of any translation.

8.7.3 Body of the witness statement

Paragraph 18.1 provides that the witness statement must, if practicable, be in the intended witness's own words and must in any event be drafted in their own language; the statement should be expressed in the first person and should also state:

(1) the full name of the witness,
(2) his place of residence or, if he is making the statement in his professional, business or other occupational capacity, the address at which he works, the position he holds and the name of his firm or employer,
(3) his occupation, or if he has none, his description,
(4) the fact that he is a party to the proceedings or is the employee of such a party if it be the case, and
(5) the process by which it has been prepared, for example, face-to-face, over the telephone, and/or through an interpreter.

A witness statement must indicate which of the statements in it are made from the witness's own knowledge and which are matters of information or belief. The witness must also confirm the source for any matters of information or belief (PD 32 para 18.2).

8.7.4 Exhibits

If an exhibit is used in conjunction with a witness statement it should be verified and identified by the witness and remain separate from the witness statement (PD 32 para 18.3). Where a witness refers to an exhibit or exhibits, he/she should state 'I refer to the (description of exhibit) marked …' (PD 32 para 18.4).

8.7.5 Statement of truth

Because a witness statement is the equivalent of the oral evidence that a witness would, if called, give in evidence at trial, it must include a statement by the intended witness in their own language that they believe the facts in it are true (PD 32 para 20.1).

To verify a witness statement the statement of truth must comply with the suggested wording as required by PD 22 para 2.2 and PD 32 para 20.2, which is as follows:

> I believe that the facts stated in this witness statement are true. I understand that proceedings for contempt of court may be brought against anyone who makes, or causes to be made, a false statement in a document verified by a statement of truth without an honest belief in its truth.

8.7.6 Consequences of false statements

The person making the statement must sign the statement of truth and under r 32.14, proceedings for contempt of court may be brought against a person who makes or causes to be made a false statement in a document, prepared in anticipation of or during proceedings and verified by a statement of truth, without an honest belief in its truth.

8.7.7 Using witness statements at trial

If a party has served a witness statement and he/she intends to rely on the evidence of the witness who made the statement at trial, the party must call the witness to give oral evidence, unless the court orders otherwise or he puts the statement in as hearsay evidence (see earlier).

Where a witness is called to give oral evidence, his/her witness statement shall stand as his evidence in chief unless the court orders otherwise. Under r 32.5(3) a witness giving oral evidence at trial may with the permission of the court amplify his witness statement and give evidence in relation to new matters which have arisen since the witness statement was served on the other parties. However, the court will only give permission for this if it considers that there is a good reason not to confine the evidence of the witness to the contents of his/her witness statement.

8.7.8 Other party's use of a witness statement

If a party who has served a witness statement decides not to call the witness to give evidence at trial or put the witness statement in as hearsay evidence, any other party may put the witness statement in as hearsay evidence (r 32.5(5)).

8.7.9 Witness summaries

It is occasionally difficult to persuade a witness to attend court to give supportive evidence, particularly if they feel that there will be adverse consequences if they do give evidence. The court rules do allow for witnesses to be compelled to attend court (see Chapter 10), but there is no knowing what the party will actually say at trial, as no witness statement will have been exchanged. In those circumstances the court's permission will be required if the witness is to give oral evidence at trial. So, a party who is required to serve a witness statement for use at trial, but is unable to obtain one, may apply, without notice, for permission to serve a witness summary instead.

The procedure for the use of witness summaries is contained in r 32.9, which provides that a witness summary is a summary of the evidence, if known, which would otherwise be included in a witness statement, or if the evidence is not known, the matters about which the party serving the witness summary proposes to question the witness. Unless the court orders otherwise, a witness summary must include the name and address of the intended witness and should be served within the period in which a witness statement would have had to be served.

Where a party serves a witness summary, as far as it is practicable to do so, rules 32.4 (requirement to serve witness statements for use at trial), 32.5(3) (amplifying witness statements), and 32.8 (form of witness statement) apply to the summary.

Example

In the *Bray v Squeers* case, Madeline Bray, who is suing Squeers for damages for personal injury arising from a tripping accident, would like to call upon a contractor who was working at Dotheboys Farm Shop on the day of her accident. The contractor, Harry Sliderskew, was present when Mrs Bray tripped/slipped on the uneven, broken concrete step outside the entrance to the farm shop, and could potentially give reliable evidence about its poor state of repair. Mr Sliderskew is a regular contractor of Squeers and, being concerned that he may not get further business from the farm, has declined to give a statement.

Madeline Bray's solicitors will be able to apply to the court without notice for permission to serve a witness summary. The witness summary should include the following matters:

(a) The evidence that otherwise would appear in Harry Sliderskew's witness statement
(b) If the claimant Madeline Bray does not know what evidence Harry Sliderskew will give, the areas upon which she proposes to question him, and
(c) Harry Sliderskew's name and address.

It is worth considering the circumstances where the court would not grant an application under r 32.9 for permission to serve a witness statement. This is considered in the following case example.

Case example

The words of Justice Kerr in his judgment given in *Morley (t/a Morley Estates) v The Royal Bank of Scotland Plc* [2019] EWHC 2865 (Ch) provide some helpful guidance:

> The wording of the rule (r 32.9) does not refer to a 'refusal' to provide a statement. Inability to obtain one can arise for other reasons, such as illness, ignorance of the witness's whereabouts, absence from the jurisdiction, confidentiality obligations, and so forth.
>
> On the plain wording of the rule, CPR 32.9(1)(a), and applying ordinary principles of causation, a person is, in my judgment, 'unable to obtain' a statement if the court is satisfied on the balance of probabilities that had a request been made to the witnesses to provide a statement the request would have been turned down.

It is important that a witness statement or a witness summary for use at trial is served on the other party. If either a witness statement or a witness summary is not served in respect of an intended witness within the time specified by the court, then the witness may not be called to give oral evidence unless the court gives permission (r 32.10).

8.7.10 Affidavits: form and structure

An affidavit is a sworn statement of evidence meaning that it must be sworn before an independent solicitor (not connected with the case) or another person authorised to administer oaths. Affidavit evidence is dealt with under r 32.15 which provides that:

(1) Evidence must be given by affidavit instead of or in addition to a witness statement if this is required by the court, a provision contained in any other rule, a practice direction or any other enactment.
(2) Nothing in the Rules prevents a witness giving evidence by affidavit at a hearing other than the trial if he chooses to do so in a case where paragraph (1) does not apply, but the party putting forward the affidavit may not recover the additional cost of making it from any other party unless the court orders otherwise.

Practice Directions 3 to 6 of r 32 deal with the form and structure of affidavits.

8.7.10.1 Heading

The affidavit should be headed with the title of the proceedings and in the top right-hand corner of the first page (and on the back sheet) the following should be clearly written:

(1) the party on whose behalf it is made,
(2) the initials and surname of the deponent,
(3) the number of the affidavit in relation to that deponent,
(4) the identifying initials and number of each exhibit referred to, and
(5) the date sworn.

8.7.10.2 Body of the affidavit

Paragraph 4.1 provides that the affidavit must, if practicable, be in the deponent's own words, the affidavit should be expressed in the first person, and the deponent should:

(1) commence 'I (full name) of (address) state on oath ...',
(2) if giving evidence in his professional, business or other occupational capacity, give the address at which he/she works in (1) above, the position he holds and the name of his firm or employer,
(3) give his/her occupation or, if he/she has none, his description, and
(4) state if he/she is a party to the proceedings or employed by a party to the proceedings, if it be the case.

An affidavit must indicate which of the statements in it are made from the deponent's own knowledge and which are matters of information or belief, and the source for any matters of information or belief (PD 32 para 4.2).

8.7.10.3 Exhibits

If an exhibit is used in conjunction with an affidavit, the deponent should state: 'there is now shown to me marked "..." the (description of exhibit)' (PD 32 para 4.3(1)), and if the deponent makes more than one affidavit (to which there are exhibits) in the same proceedings, the numbering of the exhibits should run consecutively throughout and not start again with each affidavit (PD 32 para 4.3(2)).

8.7.10.4 Jurat

The jurat of an affidavit is a statement set out at the end of the document which authenticates the affidavit and must, under para 5.2:

(1) be signed by all deponents,
(2) be completed and signed by the person before whom the affidavit was sworn whose name and qualification must be printed beneath his signature,
(3) contain the full address of the person before whom the affidavit was sworn, and
(4) follow immediately on from the text and not be put on a separate page.

There are some circumstances where the Rules require that an affidavit is used in support of the application rather than a witness statement, for instance where applications for freezing injunctions are being made.

Chapter 8 revision points

Evidence

- Relevance, hearsay, and admissibility:
  - Relevance – evidence that has an effect on the probability of proving a matter relevant to the case
  - Hearsay – a statement made, otherwise than by a person while giving oral evidence in proceedings, which is tendered as evidence of the matters stated
  - Admissibility – if it is relevant to the issues involved in the case and is not excluded by the Civil Evidence Acts or any other relevant law it will be admissible evidence
- Burden and standard of proof:
  - Burden – the person with the legal burden of proof seeking a remedy in the civil courts bears the evidential burden or onus of proof
  - Standard – the standard of proof in civil cases is 'on the balance of probabilities'
- Expert evidence:
  - Duty – the expert's duty is to assist the court
  - Restricting expert evidence – the court can allow or disallow expert evidence
  - Experts' discussions – the court can require the respective parties' expert witnesses to have a 'without prejudice' discussion
  - Written joint statements – following the experts' discussion these can be ordered by the court
  - Single joint experts – the court can order this, often to save time and cost (required in fast-track cases)
- Expert evidence:
  - The format and structure of witness statements
  - Witness summaries – used where witnesses cannot attend court
- The format and structure of affidavits

9 Disclosure and inspection

9.1 Chapter overview

In this chapter, we will consider the exchange of information and evidence concerning the case, through the formal disclosure process. This will include the nature and extent of standard disclosure of documents, the inspection of documents, the different types of privilege which can be used during disclosure, and the without prejudice nature of correspondence for the purposes of the disclosure process.

The procedural aspects including disclosure directions and the disclosure report required by the rules will also be considered. The chapter will also look at particular types of applications in relation to the disclosure process including pre-action disclosure and disclosure against third parties.

9.2 Introduction: disclosure and inspection

Whilst we have seen that during the pre-action protocol period the parties are encouraged to exchange information about the dispute to allow them to understand each other's position, so as to enable them to make informed decisions about settlement and how to proceed (see Chapter 2), there is no requirement to disclose information in documents that may be harmful to a party's case. This requirement changes once court proceedings are commenced and the culture of disclosure in the civil justice system of England and Wales can be described as one of openness.

The rules relating to disclosure and inspection of documents to be relied upon in civil proceedings are found in Part 31 CPR 1988 and apply to all claims except a claim on the small claims track. The duty of each party regarding the disclosure process during the course of civil proceedings extends to documents which exist or have existed (r 31.2) whether or not they are favourable. The exception to this rule applies to those documents to which legal professional privilege attaches (see the following). Rule 31.4 defines a document as 'anything in which information of any description is recorded', and 'copy', in relation to a document, means anything onto which information recorded in the document has been copied, by whatever means, and whether directly or indirectly.

The purpose of disclosure is to enable the parties to evaluate the strengths of their respective case before trial, to avoid unwelcome last-minute surprises and to

DOI: 10.4324/9781003218500-14

promote settlement where possible. The procedure for fast-track and multi-track claims requires each party to file and serve on each other a list of those documents that have a bearing on the case and thereafter each party has the right to inspect the other side's documents if they wish. Claims on the small claims track will usually require the parties to file and serve on every other party copies of all documents to be relied upon no later than 14 days before the final hearing.

9.3 The disclosure report

For all multi-track claims, other than those which include a claim for personal injuries, r 31.5(3) requires the parties to file and serve a report verified by a statement of truth not less than 14 days before the first case management conference. The disclosure report should be in Form N263 (see the following) and must include the following matters relating to the disclosure of documents:

(a) A brief description of what documents exist or may exist that are or may be relevant to the matters in issue in the case
(b) A description of where and with whom those documents are or may be located
(c) In the case of electronic documents, a description of how those documents are stored
(d) An estimate of the broad range of costs that could be involved in giving standard disclosure in the case, including the costs of searching for and disclosing any electronically stored documents
(e) Confirmation of which of the directions are to be sought (see the following on disclosure directions and obligations).

Not less than seven days before the first case management conference, and on any other occasion as the court may direct, the parties must, at a meeting or by telephone, discuss and seek to agree on a proposal in relation to disclosure that meets the overriding objective.

9.3.1 Disclosure directions

Rule 31.5 provides that the parties must, at least seven days before the first case management conference and on any other occasion as the court may direct, have a meeting or a telephone discussion, with a view to trying to agree on a proposal in relation to disclosure that meets the overriding objective (see Chapter 2). Rule 31.5(7) enables the court at the case management conference to make an order in relation to disclosure which:

(a) dispenses with disclosure;
(b) requires a party to disclose the documents on which it relies, and at the same time request any specific disclosure it requires from any other party;
(c) directs that disclosure to be given by each party on an issue by issue basis;

(d) requires each party to disclose any documents which it is reasonable to suppose may contain information which enables that party to advance its own case or to damage that of any other party, or which leads to an enquiry which has either of those consequences;
(e) requires a party give standard disclosure;
(f) the court considers appropriate in relation to disclosure.

Disclosure report

Name of court	Claim No.

To be completed by, or on behalf of,

who is [1st][2nd][3rd][ ][Claimant][Defendant]
[Part 20 claimant] in this claim

1. Please decribe in the table below (or in a separate document filed with this report), using the number 1, 2 etc., all documents which exist or may exist and which may be relevant to the issues in the case and in respect of each such document, where and with whom it may be found, and in the case of electronic documents how the same are stored.

No.	Document description	Where it may be found	(if an electronic document) how it is stored

Note: If an Electronic documents questionnaire (Form N264) has been exchanged, it must be filed with this report.

2. Please state in the box below the broad range of costs that could be involved in giving standard disclosure in this case, including the costs of searching for and disclosing any electronically stored documents.

3. To the extent that this is not already dealt with in Section D4 of your Directions Questionnaire, please state in the boxes below your proposed directions for disclosure to include what particular scope and form of disclosure and related directions you propose for yourself and the other parties by reference to CPR 31.5 (6) and (7) and if not standard the broad range of costs for disclosure.

If not standard, broad range of costs	Form of disclosure (CPR 31.5 (6))

Other disclosure directions (CPR 31.5 (7))

I believe that the facts stated in this Disclosure Report are true.

Signature

[Legal Representative for the][1st][2nd][3rd][ ]
[Claimant][Defendant][Part 20 claimant]

Date
/ /

Your name and full postal address

Postcode

If applicable	
Telephone no.	
Fax no.	
DX no.	
Your ref.	

E-mail

N263 Disclosure report (04.13)

Figure 9.1 Form N263 disclosure report.

9.3.2 Disclosure obligations

Rule 31.5(8) enables the court at any point to give directions as to how disclosure is to be given, and in particular:

(a) what searches are to be undertaken, of where, for what, in respect of which time periods and by whom and the extent of any search for electronically stored documents;
(b) whether lists of documents are required;
(c) how and when the disclosure is to be given
(d) in what format documents are to be disclosed (and whether any identification is required);
(e) what is required in relation to documents that once existed but no longer exist; and,
(f) whether disclosure shall take place in stages.

9.4 Electronic disclosure

9.4.1 Electronic documents

We live in the 'digital age' and many documents relevant to a case will exist in electronic format. The parties are under a duty to the court to preserve documents in an electronic format that might be relevant to the dispute. The following general principles apply to a search for electronic documents (PD 31B, para 6):

(1) electronic documents should be managed efficiently in order to minimise the cost incurred;
(2) technology should be used in order to ensure that document management activities are undertaken efficiently and effectively;
(3) disclosure should be given in a manner which gives effect to the overriding objective;
(4) electronic documents should generally be made available for inspection in a form which allows the party receiving the documents the same ability to access, search, review and display the documents as the party giving disclosure; and
(5) disclosure of electronic documents which are of no relevance to the proceedings may place an excessive burden in time and cost on the party to whom disclosure is given.

Guidance for discussions between the parties before the first case management conference in relation to the use of technology and disclosure is provided in paragraphs 8 and 9 of PD 31B. Such requirements include creating lists of documents to be disclosed, giving disclosure by providing documents and information regarding documents in electronic format, and presenting documents and other material to the court at the trial (PD 31B para 8).

Before the first case management conference, therefore, the parties and their legal representatives must discuss the disclosure of electronic documents. In some cases (for example heavy and complex cases) it may be appropriate to begin discussions before proceedings are commenced. The discussions should include (where appropriate) the following matters (PD 31B para 9):

(1) the categories of electronic documents within the parties' control, the computer systems, electronic devices, and media on which any relevant documents may be held, storage systems and document retention policies;
(2) the scope of the reasonable search for electronic documents required by r 31.7;
(3) the tools and techniques (if any) which should be considered to reduce the burden and cost of disclosure of electronic documents, including:
    (a) limiting disclosure of documents or certain categories of documents to particular date ranges, to particular custodians of documents, or to particular types of documents;
    (b) the use of agreed Keyword Searches;
    (c) the use of agreed software tools;
    (d) the methods to be used to identify duplicate documents;
    (e) the use of data sampling;
    (f) the methods to be used to identify privileged documents and other non-disclosable documents, to redact documents (where redaction is appropriate), and for dealing with privileged or other documents which have been inadvertently disclosed; and
    (g) the use of a staged approach to the disclosure of electronic documents.

The parties must also discuss matters relating to the preservation of electronic documents, with a view to preventing the loss of such documents before the trial. The methods by which the exchange of data relating to electronic documents in an agreed electronic format using agreed fields should be decided upon, and so too the formats in which electronic documents are to be provided on inspection. The parties should also consider whether it would be appropriate to use the services of a neutral electronic repository for the storage of electronic documents. The costs associated with the disclosure process for electronic documents must also be considered and addressed at this stage.

In some cases, the parties may find it helpful to exchange an electronic documents questionnaire in order to provide information to each other in relation to the scope, extent, and most suitable format for disclosure of electronic documents in the proceedings.

9.5 Standard disclosure

9.5.1 The requirements of standard disclosure

Practice Direction 31A requires that the normal order for disclosure will be an order that the parties give standard disclosure. Standard disclosure is defined by r 31.6 and requires a party to disclose only:

(a) the documents on which he relies; and
(b) the documents which:
    (i) adversely affect his own case;

(ii) adversely affect another party's case; or
(iii) support another party's case; and

(c) the documents which he is required to disclose by a relevant practice direction.

In order to give standard disclosure, the disclosing party must make a reasonable search for documents falling within the paragraphs of r 31.6 (para 1.2 of PD 31A) and having made the search the disclosing party must usually make a list of the documents of whose existence the party is aware that fall within those paragraphs and which are or have been in the party's control (para 1.2 of PD 31A). The obligations imposed by an order for standard disclosure may be dispensed with or limited either by the court or by written agreement between the parties. Any such written agreement should be lodged with the court (para 1.4 of PD 31A).

9.5.1.1 Duty to search

Rule 31.7 states that when giving standard disclosure, a party is required to make a reasonable search for documents falling within r 31.6(b) or (c) above, and r 31.7(2) outlines the factors relevant in deciding the reasonableness of a search, which will include the following:

(a) the number of documents involved;
(b) the nature and complexity of the proceedings;
(c) the ease and expense of retrieval of any particular document; and
(d) the significance of any document which is likely to be located during the search.

If a party has not searched for a category or class of document on the grounds that to do so would be unreasonable, he/she must state this in the disclosure statement identifying the category and class of the document(s).

9.5.1.2 The search for documents

Practice Direction 31A, para 3.1 provides guidance on the extent of the search which must be made for documents which relate to the issues in the case which remain in dispute. This will depend upon the circumstances of the case including, in particular, the factors referred to in rule 31.7(2) discussed earlier. The parties should bear in mind the overriding principle of proportionality (see r 1.1(2)(c) in Chapter 2). It may, for example, be reasonable to decide not to search for documents coming into existence before some particular date, to limit the search to documents in some particular place or places, or to documents falling into particular categories.

9.5.1.3 Duty of disclosure

The duty to disclose documents is limited to those documents which are or have been in a party's control (r 31.8). For this purpose, a party has or has had a document in his control if:

(a) it is or was in his/her physical possession;
(b) he/she has or has had a right to possession of it; or
(c) he/she has or has had a right to inspect or take copies of it.

9.5.1.4 *Right of inspection of a disclosed document*

Under r.31.3 a party to whom a document has been disclosed has the right to inspect that document, except where:

(a) the document is no longer in the control of the party who disclosed it;
(b) the party disclosing the document has a right or a duty to withhold inspection of it, or
(c) a party considers that it would be disproportionate to the issues in the case to permit inspection of documents within a category or class of document disclosed under rule. If this exception is to be claimed, then the party claiming it should state as such in his/her disclosure report.

Rule 31.15 provides that where a party has a right to inspect a document, that party must give the party who disclosed the document written notice of his/her wish to inspect it and the party who disclosed the document must permit inspection not more than seven days after the date on which he/she received the notice. In practical terms, the inspection can take place at the offices of the solicitors representing the party who disclosed the document. Alternatively, that party may request a copy of the document and, if he/she also undertakes to pay reasonable copying costs, the party who disclosed the document must supply him/her with a copy not more than seven days after the date on which he received the request.

9.5.2 Procedure for standard disclosure

Where an order for standard disclosure has been made, the parties are required to serve their lists of documents in a standard format. Although the parties can agree to disclose documents without making a list, they are encouraged to use Practice Form N265, a copy of which appears in Figure 9.2.

The list of documents must identify the documents in a convenient order and manner and as concisely as possible. Rule 31.10 (4) provides that the list must indicate those documents in respect of which the party claims a right or duty to withhold inspection, those documents which are no longer in the party's control, and what has happened to those documents.

Practice Direction 31A, para 3.2 provides guidance on how to set out the list. This suggests that it will normally be necessary to list the documents to be provided in date order, to number them consecutively and to give each a concise description (e.g., letter, claimant to defendant). Where there is a large number of documents all falling into a particular category, the Practice Direction suggests that the disclosing party may list those documents as a category rather than individually, e.g., 50 bank statements relating to account number __ at __ Bank, __20__ to __20__; or 35 letters passing between __ and __ between __20__ and __20__.

List of documents: standard disclosure

In the	
Claim No.	
Claimant (including ref)	
Defendant (including ref)	
Date	

Click here to clear all fields

Click here to print form

Notes

- The rules relating to standard disclosure are contained in Part 31 of the Civil Procedure Rules.
- Documents to be included under standard disclosure are contained in Rule 31.6
- A document has or will have been in your control if you have or have had possession, or a right of possession, of it or a right to inspect or take copies of it.

Disclosure Statement

I, the above named

☐ Claimant ☐ Defendant

☐ Party (if party making disclosure is a company, firm or other organisation identify here who the person making the disclosure statement is and why he is the appropriate person to make it)

state that I have carried out a reasonable and proportionate search to locate all the documents which I am required to disclose under the order made by the court on (date of order)

☐ I did not search for documents:-

☐ pre-dating

☐ located elsewhere than

☐ in categories other than

☐ for electronic documents

☐ I carried out a search for electronic documents contained on or created by the following:
(list what was searched and extent of search)

N265 Standard disclosure (10.05) HMCS

Figure 9.2 Form N265 list of documents.

9.5.2.1 The list of documents

The list of documents is divided into three parts. The first part requires the party to confirm those documents of which he/she has control of the documents numbered and listed here which the party does not object to the other party inspecting them/producing copies. The party should give a short description of each document

☐ I did not search for the following:-

☐ documents created before

documents contained on or created by the ☐ Claimant ☐ Defendant

☐ PCs ☐ portable data storage media
☐ databases ☐ servers
☐ back-up tapes ☐ off-site storage
☐ mobile phones ☐ laptops
☐ notebooks ☐ handheld devices
☐ PDA devices

documents contained on or created by the ☐ Claimant ☐ Defendant

☐ mail files ☐ document files
☐ calendar files ☐ web-based applications
☐ spreadsheet files ☐ graphic and presentation files

documents other than by reference to the following keyword(s)/concepts
(delete if your search was not confined to specific keywords or concepts)

I certify that I understand the duty of disclosure and to the best of my knowledge I have carried out that duty. I further certify that the list of documents set out in or attached to this form, is a complete list of all documents which are or have been in my control and which I am obliged under the order to disclose.

I understand that I must inform the court and the other parties immediately if any further document required to be disclosed by Rule 31.6 comes into my control at any time before the conclusion of the case.

☐ I have not permitted inspection of documents within the category or class of documents (as set out below) required to be disclosed under Rule 31(6)(b)or (c) on the grounds that to do so would be disproportionate to the issues in the case.

Signed **Date**

(Claimant)(Defendant)('s litigation friend)

Figure 9.2 Continued.

or bundle so that it can be identified, and say if it is kept elsewhere, i.e., with a bank or solicitor. The second part lists and numbers those documents the party has in their control, but which the party objects to the other party inspecting. The main reason for a party objecting to inspection is where the party claims privilege, perhaps because they are letters passing between the party and his/her legal representative.

List and number here, in a convenient order, the documents (or bundles of documents if of the same nature, e.g. invoices) in your control, which you do not object to being inspected. Give a short description of each document or bundle so that it can be identified, and say if it is kept elsewhere i.e. with a bank or solicitor	I have control of the documents numbered and listed here. I do not object to you inspecting them/producing copies.
List and number here, as above, the documents in your control which you object to being inspected. (Rule 31.19)	I have control of the documents numbered and listed here, but I object to you inspecting them:
Say what your objections are	I object to you inspecting these documents because:
List and number here, the documents you once had in your control, but which you no longer have. For each document listed, say when it was last in your control and where it is now.	I have had the documents numbered and listed below, but they are no longer in my control.

Figure 9.2 Continued.

In the third part of the list should appear those documents that the party has had but are no longer in their control. Here the party should, for each document listed, say when it was last in their control and where it is now.

9.5.2.2 Disclosure statement

The first part of the list of documents contains the disclosure statement, which the party must sign unless the parties specifically agree in writing to dispense with disclosure statements. A disclosure statement is required by r 31.10(5) and is a statement made by the party disclosing the documents which:

(a) sets out the extent of the search that has been made to locate documents which he/she is required to disclose;

(b) certifies that he/she understands the duty to disclose documents; and
(c) certifies that to the best of his/her knowledge he/she has carried out that duty.

If the party making the disclosure statement is a company, firm, association, or other organisation, the statement must also identify the person making the statement and explain why he/she is considered an appropriate person to make the statement. Whilst Part 22 of the Civil Procedure Rules allows the legal representative to sign the statement of truth, this is, however, only in relation to 'a statement of case, a response or an application'. There is no indication that this extends to a disclosure statement, although in practice the point is rarely taken, and it is generally accepted that a solicitor may sign the disclosure statement on behalf of their client with their express authority.

It should be noted that Rule 31.23 proceedings for contempt of court may be brought against a person if he/she makes or causes to be made a false disclosure statement, without an honest belief in its truth.

It should be noted that the duty of disclosure continues throughout the course of proceedings and until they are concluded (r 31.11). If documents to which that duty extends come to a party's notice at any time during the proceedings, he/she must immediately notify every other party. If a party wishes to rely on additional documents, then a supplemental list should be prepared and served on the other party. Should the other party object, then an application by the party wishing to rely on the additional documents should be made.

9.6 Privilege and without prejudice communications

We have seen that a party has a right to withhold inspection of documents which are considered to be privileged because they fall into one of three classes of privilege:

(a) Documents protected by legal professional privilege
(b) Documents which incriminate the party producing them
(c) Documents privileged on the grounds of public policy.

These categories of documents will be considered in turn.

9.6.1 Legal professional privilege

This applies to communications passing between a party and his/her legal advisers or between a party's legal advisers.

This is also described as 'legal privilege' and the documents falling into this category include correspondence between a solicitor and client or their agents, or between solicitor and/or client and a third party prepared for the purpose of or in contemplation of litigation.

The extent of this privilege applies to communications between a party and his legal representative's employee or agent and also to communications between a party and his legal representative in his service. It also applies to communications between the legal representative and a third party, which contains information provided by the client to the legal representative, which is covered by legal advice privilege and which the client has given the legal representative authority to disclose to the third party.

9.6.1.1 Communications passing between a legal representative and a third party

This is described as 'litigation privilege' and such communications are privileged from inspection if their sole purpose was to obtain legal advice in relation to existing or contemplated litigation and if:

(a) They come into existence after litigation is contemplated or commenced, and
(b) They are made with a view to litigation.

Experts' reports or witness statements would fall into this category if they were commissioned by a legal representative in preparation or contemplation of litigation.

9.6.1.2 Communications passing between a client and a third party

Litigation privilege would apply to such communications, for instance, those documents that have been produced for the sole purpose of obtaining legal advice in relation to existing or contemplated litigation. The test is to determine the 'dominant purpose' of the communication, and for privilege to attach to such documents, they must have been prepared by the party's legal representative in order to provide legal advice on the prospects of litigation success.

9.6.1.3 Documents which incriminate the party producing them

Although specifically relating to criminal proceedings, this issue may arise during the course of civil litigation. If documents come into existence that tend to incriminate either him/her or his/her spouse, that party is entitled to claim privilege in relation to the inspection of those documents.

9.6.1.4 Documents which are privileged on the grounds of public policy

If a document that is likely to be harmful to the public interest exists, it may be withheld from production on the grounds of public policy. Such documents might include those which relate to national security or sensitive records held by social services departments of a local authority.

9.6.1.5 Waiving privilege

Privilege belongs to the party and not his/her legal representative and may therefore be waived at any time by the party. In Chapter 8 dealing with evidence, we considered the special circumstances that apply to written communications between the legal representative and the expert witness, whose report a party proposes to rely upon at trial.

9.6.2 Without prejudice correspondence

Any genuine efforts through negotiation which take place between the parties or their respective legal representatives are considered to be 'without prejudice' or private for the purposes of the disclosure process. This means that correspondence that includes details of such negotiations, whilst being privileged, will satisfy the definition applicable to standard disclosure under r 31.6 and will not have to be disclosed. Such correspondence does not make it exempt from inspection. Without prejudice correspondence will often include an indication of both the strengths and weaknesses of a party's case and often include concessions. The only circumstances where such privileged correspondence might be exempt from inspection would be in a case where there are more than two parties (multi-party litigation).

9.7 Orders for specific disclosure

If a party considers that another party's disclosure is inadequate, Rule 31.12 enables that party to apply to the court for an order for specific disclosure or specific inspection. Such an order is an order that a party must do one or more of the following things (r 31.12(2)):

(a) disclose documents or classes of documents specified in the order;
(b) carry out a search to the extent stated in the order;
(c) disclose any documents located as a result of that search.

An order for specific inspection is an order that a party permit inspection of a document referred to in rule 31.3(2).

The party should request any documents which he/she considers should be disclosed in writing explaining fully why those documents should be disclosed. If the other party does not comply with the request, then Practice Direction 31A para 5 provides helpful guidance on making an application for specific disclosure.

9.7.1 Procedure

The application notice must specify the order that the applicant intends to ask the court to make and must be supported by evidence (see the preceding which describes the orders the court may make under r 31.12(2)). The grounds on which the order is sought may be set out in the application notice itself but if not set out there, the applicant must file a witness statement in support which clearly sets out the grounds.

In deciding whether or not to make an order for specific disclosure the court will take into account all the circumstances of the case and, in particular, the overriding objective (see Part 1 of the CPR in Chapter 2). But if the court concludes that the party from whom specific disclosure is sought has failed adequately to comply with the obligations imposed by an order for disclosure (whether by failing to make a sufficient search for documents or otherwise) the court will usually make such order as is necessary to ensure that those obligations are properly complied with.

It is also possible for a party to make an application for inspection of documents omitted from his/her disclosure statement on the grounds that to allow inspection would be disproportionate.

9.8 Pre-action and non-party disclosure

9.8.1 Disclosure before proceedings

In some circumstances, it may be necessary for a potential claimant to see documents which are in the possession of the potential defendant. If the potential defendant does not agree to disclose the document(s) requested, then the potential claimant can, under r 31.16, make an application for their disclosure.

9.8.1.1 Procedure

The application must be supported by evidence, usually a witness statement, and the court may make an order under this rule only where:

(a) the respondent is likely to be a party to subsequent proceedings;
(b) the applicant is also likely to be a party to those proceedings;
(c) if proceedings had started, the respondent's duty by way of standard disclosure, set out in r 31.6, would extend to the documents or classes of documents of which the applicant seeks disclosure; and
(d) disclosure before proceedings have started is desirable in order to:
  (i) dispose fairly of the anticipated proceedings;
  (ii) assist the dispute to be resolved without proceedings; or
  (iii) save costs.

If the application is granted, the order for pre-action disclosure should specify the documents or the classes of documents which the respondent must disclose and require him/her, when making disclosure, to specify any of those documents which are no longer in his/her control or, in respect of which he claims a right or duty to withhold inspection.

The order may require the respondent to indicate what has happened to any documents which are no longer in his/her control and specify the time and place for disclosure and inspection.

9.8.2 Non-party disclosure

Once proceedings have been commenced, it is possible for a party to make an application under r 31.17 for an application for disclosure by a person who is not a party to the proceedings.

9.8.2.1 Procedure

Such an application must be supported by evidence and the court may make an order under this rule only where:

(a) The documents of which disclosure is sought are likely to support the case of the applicant or adversely affect the case of one of the other parties to the proceedings, and
(c) Disclosure is necessary in order to dispose fairly of the claim or to save costs.

If the application is granted, the order for non-party disclosure must specify the documents or the classes of documents which the respondent must disclose and require the respondent, when making disclosure, to specify any of those documents which are no longer in his/her control, or in respect of which he/she claims a right or duty to withhold inspection. The order may require the respondent to indicate what has happened to any documents which are no longer in his control and specify the time and place for disclosure and inspection.

Chapter 9 revision points

Disclosure and inspection

- The purpose of disclosure is to:
  - Enable the parties to evaluate the strengths of their respective case
  - Avoid unwelcome last-minute surprises
  - Promote settlement where possible
- Standard disclosure of documents, including those documents:
  - To be relied upon
  - Which adversely affect a party's own case
  - Which adversely affect another party's case
  - Which support another party's case
  - Required to be disclosed by a relevant practice direction
- Inspection can be withheld due to privilege, which means:
  - Professional privilege
  - Documents which incriminate the party producing them
  - Documents privileged on the grounds of public policy
- Without prejudice correspondence is private for the purposes of the disclosure process and includes those:
  - Containing genuine efforts to negotiate

  - Which take place between the parties or their respective legal representatives
- Pre-action disclosure:
  - Grounds for application
  - Supportive evidence
- Third-party disclosure:
  - Grounds for application
- Supportive evidence

Multiple-choice questions for Part 5

1. In a claim for damages for personal injury arising from a road traffic accident, the claimant wishes to use the evidence of a witness who says that she saw the defendant speeding shortly before the accident. The case is listed for a three-day trial when the witness is abroad.

*Which one of the following is the **best** way to deal with the introduction of the evidence from this witness?*

A. Despite the fact that the witness says that she will be out of the country when the case has been listed for trial, the witness must be sent a witness summons requiring her to attend court to give oral evidence.
B. The claimant must ask the court to prepare a notice of proposal to adduce hearsay evidence.
C. The evidence of this witness is inadmissible as it is hearsay, and this will not be allowed by the court.
D. The claimant must prepare a notice of proposal to adduce hearsay evidence and arrange for it to be served on the defendant (its legal representatives).
E. The claimant will be required to ask the court's permission to adduce this evidence as it is hearsay.

2. A is the defendant in a contractual dispute. The case has been allocated to the fast track and directions have been given for trial which includes the requirement to exchange documents relevant to the case. A asks you as his solicitor whether a letter written to the proposed claimant prior to proceedings being commenced should be disclosed.

*Which one of the following is the **best** advice to give to your client?*

A. The letter does not have to be disclosed as it is considered to be written 'without prejudice'.
B. Legal professional privilege will attach to this letter despite the fact that it was written prior to the commencement of court proceedings and its existence therefore will not have to be disclosed.
C. Whilst the letter shows a genuine attempt to settle the claim, because it was written by your client and not by you it will not be treated as being 'without prejudice' and must be disclosed.
D. The letter does not have to be disclosed as it is likely to incriminate A if disclosure is ordered.
E. As the letter was written prior to the commencement of court proceedings it will not be considered to be 'without prejudice' and must be disclosed.

PART 6

Preparation of a case for a trial, the trial, and any post-trial steps

10 Trial

10.1 Chapter overview

The procedural steps in preparing a case for trial, including listing directions, trial arrangements, and the completion of the pre-trial checklists (listing questionnaires) for fast-track and multi-track cases, will be considered in this chapter. Other matters which need to be addressed at this stage of the proceedings, such as witness attendance at trial and the witness summons procedure, will be explained.

The chapter will go on to explain the typical civil trial procedure, followed by delivery of judgment, which will deal with both liability and quantum if the claim is founded in tort, as well as other aspects that a judge will be required to deal with as part of the judgment, such as interest and costs.

10.2 Introduction: preparing a case for trial

It is worth mentioning that of all the cases that are commenced in either the county court or the high court, it is only somewhere in the region of 4 per cent of those cases that actually come to trial and require a decision from a judge. Many are settled before trial, some are disposed of through judgment being entered, either by default or through a successful application for summary judgment, and some cases are simply discontinued; others are resolved through successful ADR outcomes including mediation. Settlement negotiations can continue up until the day of the trial and it is not uncommon for cases to settle at the doors of the court; these are commonly known as 'doorstep settlements'.

If the case is to proceed to either a fast-track or multi-track trial, parties who have legal representation will, through their solicitor or legal representative, usually retain the services of a barrister who is skilled in the art of advocacy and has trial experience. In those circumstances, it will be necessary for the parties' legal representative to draft a brief to counsel. An example brief to counsel in the *Madeline Bray v Arthur Squeers* case appears in Figure 10.2.

10.3 Pre-trial checklists and listing

As will have been seen in Chapter 6 which dealt with case management, the court will have given a timetable of directions to the parties following allocation of the case in

DOI: 10.4324/9781003218500-16

Listing questionnaire
(Pre-trial checklist)

Click here to clear all fields

Name of court	
Claim No.	
Last date for filing with court office	
Date(s) fixed for trial or trial period	

To be completed by, or on behalf of,

who is [1st][2nd][3rd][ ][Claimant][Defendant] [Part 20 claimant][Part 20 defendant] in this claim

This form must be **completed** and **returned** to the court no later than the date given above. If not, your statement of case may be struck out or some other sanction imposed.

If the claim has settled, or settles before the trial date, you must let the court know immediately.

Legal representatives only: If no costs management order has been made. You must **attach** estimates of costs incurred to date, and of your likely overall costs. In substantial cases, these should be provided in compliance with CPR.

For multi-track claims only, you must also **attach** a proposed timetable for the trial itself.

A Confirmation of compliance with directions

1. I confirm that I have complied with those directions already given which require action by me. ☐ Yes ☐ No

   If you are unable to give confirmation, state which directions you have still to comply with and the date by which this will be done.

Directions	Date

2. I believe that additional directions are necessary before the trial takes place. ☐ Yes ☐ No

   If Yes, you should attach an application and a draft order.

   Include in your application all directions needed to enable the claim ***to be tried on the date, or within the trial period, already fixed.*** *These should include any issues relating to experts and their evidence, and any orders needed in respect of directions still requiring action by any other party.*

3. Have you agreed the additional directions you are seeking with the other party(ies)? ☐ Yes ☐ No

B Witnesses

1. How many witnesses (including yourself) will be giving evidence on your behalf at the trial? *(Do not include experts - see Section C)* ☐

Continued over

N170 Listing questionnaire (Pre-trial checklist) (05.14)

 1 of 3

Figure 10.1 Listing questionnaire (pre-trial checklist).

Witnesses continued

2. If the trial date is not yet fixed, are there any days within the trial period you or your witnesses would wish to avoid if possible? *(Do not include experts - see Section C)*

Please give details

Name of witness	Dates to be avoided, if possible	Reason

Please specify any special facilities or arrangements needed at court for the party or any witness (e.g. witness with a disability).

3. Will you be providing an interpreter for any of your witnesses? ☐ Yes ☐ No

C Experts

You are reminded that you may not use an expert's report or have your expert give oral evidence unless the court has given permission. If you do not have permission, you must make an application (see section A2 above)

1. Please give the information requested for your expert(s)

Name	Field of expertise	Joint expert?	Is report agreed?	Has permission been given for oral evidence?
		☐ Yes ☐ No	☐ Yes ☐ No	☐ Yes ☐ No
		☐ Yes ☐ No	☐ Yes ☐ No	☐ Yes ☐ No
		☐ Yes ☐ No	☐ Yes ☐ No	☐ Yes ☐ No

2. Has there been discussion between experts? ☐ Yes ☐ No

3. Have the experts signed a joint statement? ☐ Yes ☐ No

4. If your expert is giving oral evidence and the trial date is not yet fixed, is there any day within the trial period which the expert would wish to avoid, if possible? ☐ Yes ☐ No

If Yes, please give details

Name	Dates to be avoided, if possible	Reason

2 of 3

Figure 10.1 Continued.

D Legal representation

1. Who will be presenting your case at the trial? ☐ You ☐ Solicitor ☐ Counsel

2. If the trial date is not yet fixed, is there any day within the trial period that the person presenting your case would wish to avoid, if possible? ☐ Yes ☐ No

   If Yes, please give details

Name	Dates to be avoided, if possible	Reason

E The trial

1. Has the estimate of the time needed for trial changed? ☐ Yes ☐ No

   If Yes, say how long you estimate the whole trial will take, including both parties' cross-examination and closing arguments ☐ days ☐ hours ☐ minutes

2. If different from original estimate have you agreed with the other party(ies) that this is now the **total** time needed? ☐ Yes ☐ No

3. Is the timetable for trial you have attached agreed with the other party(ies)? ☐ Yes ☐ No

Fast track cases only
The court will normally give you 3 weeks notice of the date fixed for a fast track trial unless, in exceptional circumstances, the court directs that shorter notice will be given.

Would you be prepared to accept shorter notice of the date fixed for trial? ☐ Yes ☐ No

F Document and fee checklist

Tick as appropriate

I attach to this questionnaire -

☐ An application and fee for additional directions ☐ A proposed timetable for trial

☐ A draft order ☐ An estimate of costs

☐ Listing fee **or** quote your Fee Account no. ☐

Signature

[Legal Representative for the]
[1st][2nd][3rd][ ]
[Claimant][Defendant][Part 20 claimant]

Date ☐☐/☐☐/☐☐☐☐

Your name and full postal address

Postcode ☐☐☐☐ ☐☐☐

If applicable	
Telephone no.	
Fax no.	
DX no.	
Your ref.	

E-mail

3 of 3

Figure 10.1 Continued.

fast-track cases, and at the case management conference stage for multi-track cases. The directions order will require the parties to complete a pre-trial checklist, the purpose of which is to check that they have complied with the directions given in the case so that the court can fix a date for trial. The procedure differs slightly between fast track (CPR Part 28) and multi-track (CPR Part 29) cases.

10.3.1 Pre-trial checklists (listing questionnaires) for fast-track cases

Rule 28.5 deals with the procedure for completing and filing pre-trial checklists for fast-track cases, and paragraph 6 of Practice Direction 28 suggests that Form N170 (see Figure 10.2) should be used. The usual procedure for trial preparation is as follows:

(1) The court will send the parties a pre-trial checklist (listing questionnaire) for completion and return by the date specified in the notice of allocation unless it considers that the claim can proceed to trial without the need for a pre-trial checklist
(2) The date specified for filing a pre-trial checklist will not be more than eight weeks before the trial date or the beginning of the trial period
(3) If no party files the completed pre-trial checklist by the date specified, the court will order that unless a completed pre-trial checklist is filed within seven days from service of that order, the claim, defence, and any counterclaim will be struck out without further order of the court.

Rule 28.5(4) allows the court to give directions in the following circumstances, where:

(a) a party files a completed pre-trial checklist, but another party does not;
(b) a party has failed to give all the information requested by the pre-trial checklist; or
(c) the court considers that a hearing is necessary to enable it to decide what directions to give in order to complete preparation of the case for trial.

The court will usually send Forms N170 and N171 (notice of the date for the return of the pre-trial checklist) to each party no later than two weeks before the date specified in the notice of allocation or in any later direction of the court for the return of the completed checklists. So as to avoid the court being given conflicting or incomplete information, the parties are encouraged to exchange their checklists before filing. Should either party fail to file a checklist, the court can order that unless a completed pre-trial checklist is filed within seven days, the claim, defence, and any counterclaim will be struck out without further order of the court. When a party files a pre-trial checklist, but another party does not do so, the court will normally give directions (see the following) which will usually confirm the trial date and provide for steps to be taken to prepare the case for trial.

10.3.1.1 Listing directions

Practice Direction 28, para 7 provides the guidance for directions at this stage of proceedings. The court must confirm the date and place and confirm a time estimate for the trial which will last for no longer than one day.

The parties are encouraged to agree on directions, which should deal with the following matters:

(a) Evidence
(b) A trial timetable and time estimate
(c) The preparation of an agreed trial bundle
(d) Any other matter needed to prepare the case for trial.

The court will consider any directions which the parties have agreed and may adjust/modify them or include such of these provisions as are appropriate, regardless of whether the parties have an agreement on the required directions.

On the question of expert evidence, you will recall from Chapter 8 that the case management provisions applicable to fast-track claims encourage the parties to avoid having to call expert witnesses and encourage the parties to arrange a 'without prejudice' meeting between the respective parties' experts. If neither a 'without prejudice' meeting nor another discussion between experts has taken place, the court may grant that permission conditionally on such a discussion taking place and a report being filed before the trial. A direction giving permission to use expert evidence will say whether it gives permission for oral evidence or reports or both and will name the experts concerned. The court will not make a direction giving permission for an expert to give oral evidence unless it believes it is necessary in the interests of justice to do so, taking into account the overriding objective, of course.

The timetable for the trial should include a time estimate for the following stages during the trial:

- Cross-examination of the claimant and defendant (their evidence-in-chief will be contained in their witness statements)
- The claimant's and defendant's evidence
- Submissions on behalf of each party
- The judge to consider and give the judgment and deal with costs.

The claimant is required to lodge an indexed bundle of documents (the trial bundle – see the following) contained in a ring binder and with each page clearly numbered. This should be done not more than seven days and not less than three days before the start of the trial. Included in the trial bundle should be a case summary not exceeding 250 words, outlining the matters still in issue, and referring where appropriate to the relevant documents. This is designed to help the judge in reading the papers before the trial. The parties are encouraged to agree, if possible, on the contents of the trial bundle and the case summary before the commencement of the trial.

10.3.2 Pre-trial checklists (listing questionnaires) for multi-track cases

Rule 29.6 deals with the procedure for completing and filing pre-trial checklists for multi-track track cases, para 8.1(1) of which suggests that the standard form N170 (also used for fast-track cases) should be used. The usual procedure as recommended by PD 29.6 is as follows:

(1) The court will send the parties a pre-trial check list (listing questionnaire) for completion and return by the date specified in directions given under rule 29.2(3) unless it considers that the claim can proceed to trial without the need for a pre-trial check list.
(2) Each party must file the completed pre-trial check list by the date specified by the court.
(3) If no party files the completed pre-trial checklist by the date specified, the court will order that unless a completed pre-trial checklist is filed within 7 days from service of that order, the claim, defence, and any counterclaim will be struck out without further order of the court.

Rule 29.6(4) allows the court to give directions in the following circumstances, where:

(a) a party files a completed pre-trial checklist, but another party does not;
(b) a party has failed to give all the information requested by the pre-trial checklist; or
(c) the court considers that a hearing is necessary to enable it to decide what directions to give in order to complete preparation of the case for trial.

Unless it dispenses with pre-trial checklists and orders an early trial on a fixed date, the court will specify the date for filing completed pre-trial checklists when it fixes the trial date or trial period. The court should ensure that the date for filing the completed pre-trial checklist will not be later than eight weeks before the trial date or the start of the trial period, and the court will have served the pre-trial checklists on the parties at least 14 days before that date. To avoid the court being given conflicting or incomplete information, the parties are encouraged to exchange copies of the checklists before they are filed. When all the checklists have been filed or when the time for filing them has expired and where a party has filed a checklist, but another party has not done so, the court file relating to the case will be placed before a judge in order for directions to be given in preparation for trial.

Where no party files a pre-trial checklist the court will order that unless a completed pre-trial checklist is filed within seven days, the claim, defence, and any counterclaim will be struck out without further order of the court. Where a party files a pre-trial checklist, but another party (the defaulting party) does not do so, the court will fix a hearing. Whether or not the defaulting party attends the hearing, the court will normally fix or confirm the trial date and give directions about the steps to be taken to prepare the case for trial.

At this stage, the court can, if it chooses to do so, require the parties to attend a pre-trial review. A pre-trial review will be held if the case is complex, or the trial is expected to be lengthy. The aim is to make sure the trial will proceed efficiently, and it is an opportunity for the judge to consider particular areas of dispute which may be identified in an effort to narrow the issues, as far as possible, between the parties.

A helpful timetable of the pre-trial steps required for a multi-track case is provided by the justice.gov.uk website[1] and is reproduced as Table 10.1.

10.4 Summoning witnesses

10.4.1 Evidence at trial

It is important that all the witnesses who the parties intend to call to give evidence at trial should be asked to provide dates of availability if the trial takes place and they be required to attend. The court will have been provided with these dates to avoid when the parties completed and filed their directions questionnaires, pre-trial checklist, and listing questionnaires. Once the trial date has been fixed by the court, all witnesses should be notified of the trial date and venue.

It is common practice to remind the witnesses of the trial date by serving them with a witness summons. Rule 34.2 deals with the procedure for issuing a witness summons, which is essentially a document issued by the court requiring a witness to attend court to

(a) Give evidence
(b) Produce documents to the court.

The rules provide that the relevant practice form which should be used for the witness summons is Form N20, and there must be a separate witness summons form completed for each witness. The witness summons may require a witness to produce documents to the court, either on the date fixed for a hearing or on any other date that the court may direct. Once completed with the details of the witness, the witness summons should be sent with the required fee to the court with a request that it be issued and then returned for service. A witness

1 Available at: www.justice.gov.uk/courts/procedure-rules/civil/standard-directions/general/trial-arrangements.

Table 10.1 Trial arrangements

Direction	Explanation
The trial will be listed as follows: The trial window is between [date] and [date] inclusive. The estimated length of trial is [... days].	Initially, a claim may be given a 'trial window' of several weeks, during which it is expected the trial will take place. The estimate of the length of the trial is provisional at this stage. If a party comes to believe that too much or too little time has been allowed, he must inform the court, giving reasons.
By [date] the parties must file with the court their availability for trial, preferably agreed and with a nominated single point of contact. They will be notified of the time and place of trial.	There may be periods when a party or a witness would not be able to come to court. The party must inform the court of this by the date stated. If he does not, it may be very difficult or impossible to change the trial date later. In arranging the trial date, the court office will work with the persons named as the 'single point of contact' for each party.
By 4.00 p.m. on [date] pre-trial checklists must be sent to the court.	Although the court will usually send out a pre-trial checklist to each party, they can use it to confirm that everything necessary has been done in readiness for the trial. Where this has gone wrong, the judge will probably give further directions. Parties can apply for particular directions to be given if they wish. Also, parties can use the form to say whether they will need special facilities for the trial (the second part of section B 2) and whether they will be bringing an interpreter (section B 3).
By 4.00 p.m. on [date] the parties are to apply to the Clerk of the Lists for an appointment to fix a date or period for trial Trial: judge alone, category A/B/C Trial window from [date] to [date] inclusive Time estimate [...] days The parties must file pre-trial checklists as directed by the Clerk of the Lists.	This direction is given only in claims proceeding in the Royal Courts of Justice in London.

(*Continued*)

Table 10.1 (Continued)

Direction	Explanation
There will be a pre-trial review four weeks before the trial window starts with a time estimate of 30 minutes. The pre-trial review will be conducted by telephone unless the court orders otherwise. The claimant must make the relevant arrangements in accordance with PD 23A.	A pre-trial review is held if the case is complex, or the trial is expected to be lengthy. The aim is to make sure the trial will proceed efficiently, with particular areas of dispute being identified and narrowed down as far as possible. Judges often take hearings by telephone, though less often when parties are unrepresented. The Practice Direction sets out what the party told to make the arrangements for the telephone conference call should do. Unrepresented parties are rarely expected to do this.
At least three clear days before the pre-trial review the claimant must file and send to the other party or parties preferably agreed and by email: • Draft directions • A chronology • A statement of the issues • A case summary • A trial timetable	The claimant, in cooperation with the other party or parties, must help the judge by suggesting the directions that are thought to be needed. Describe the directions you think the judge should give. It is better not to try drafting a directions order without qualified help. A chronology is a list, with dates and in date order, of the events leading up to the claim. A statement of the issues identifies the matters on which the parties disagree, briefly describing the position taken by each of the parties on each matter. A case summary is a concise but complete overview of the whole case. For a trial expected to last several days or more, a timetable describing in what order and roughly when different parts of it will happen is helpful, e.g., in organising witnesses' attendance. These documents should be discussed among the parties so that agreed versions can be given to the judge if possible.

(Continued)

Table 10.1 (Continued)

Direction	Explanation
Not more than seven nor less than three clear days before the trial, the claimant must file at court and serve an indexed and paginated bundle of documents, which complies with the requirements of Rule 39.5 and PD 39A. The parties must endeavour to agree on the contents of the bundle before it is filed. The bundle will include: • A case summary • A chronology • A trial timetable	The trial bundle becomes the working folder from which the judge and everyone else involved in the trial will work. While one party (usually, as here, the claimant) is given the job of preparing it, he/she must do so in consultation with the other parties. The Practice Direction referred to sets out the detailed requirements in paragraph 3. The pages of the bundle must all be numbered, and an index provided identifying each item and showing its (first) page number so that everyone using the bundle at the trial can find what they want quickly and easily. Enough copies of the bundle must be prepared and brought to the trial so that there are sufficient for all participants.
The parties must file with the court and exchange skeleton arguments at least three days before the trial by email.	A skeleton argument sets out how as a matter of law a party's case is justified. If you are unrepresented, you will probably need the help of a lawyer to prepare this. If you do not have access to email, then you should tell the court that you will have to send this document in paper form.

summons should be served at least seven days before the date on which the witness is required to attend court.

Form N20 provides that the person serving (sending by first class post) the witness summons must certify that the summons is a true copy and confirm the date upon which it was served by him/her by posting to the witness (by inserting the name of the witness) at the address stated on the summons. Also enclosed with the witness summons should be either a postal order or a cheque for a reasonable sum to cover the witness's travel expenses and compensation for loss of time; PD 34A 3.2(2) states that this is a sum in respect of the period during which earnings or benefit are lost or such a lesser sum as it may be proved that the witness will lose as a result of his/her attendance at court in answer to the witness summons.

So as to ensure that a witness attends trial to give the evidence that the party hopes they will give, it is always safer to issue and serve a witness summons. A party must, however, obtain permission from the court if he/she wishes to:

(a) Have a summons issued less than seven days before the date of the trial
(b) Have a summons issued for a witness to attend court to give evidence or to produce documents on any date except the date fixed for the trial, or
(c) Have a summons issued for a witness to attend court to give evidence or to produce documents at any hearing except the trial.

In the event that a witness does not attend court, there is a greater chance that the trial judge will allow an adjournment of the trial if the evidence of the witness is considered critical to the case and in the interest of justice.

10.4.2 Briefing counsel

It is usual for a party who has legal representation to employ the services of a barrister (counsel) to present their case at trial. Barristers are skilled advocates, and they will need to be fully 'briefed' on the case so as to prepare for trial. It is therefore necessary to provide counsel with copies of all the relevant documents and a summary of the important aspects of the case which will include the pleadings, any documents obtained following inspection, and the evidence available from both sides. It is not uncommon to have a pre-trial conference with counsel. It is obviously desirable for the barrister who has been involved in the case previously; perhaps counsel has settled (drafted) the particulars of the claim and other legal documents (pleadings) for the purpose of litigation. In the event that the same barrister is not available for trial, then the brief should be drafted in such a way as to enable another barrister to take on the case and appear at trial.

A specimen brief to counsel in the *Bray v Squeers* case appears in Figure 10.2. In practical terms, a brief fee will need to be agreed upon with the counsel's instructing solicitor once the brief has been delivered to the counsel's chambers. For multi-track cases listed for more than one day, the brief fee will only include the first day of the trial and thereafter counsel will be entitled to a 'refresher' for each subsequent day of the trial. As a negotiating tactic, a legal representative for a claimant can legitimately say that unless the case is settled by a certain date, the brief will be delivered. This has an implication for the defendant if the case settles after the brief is delivered, as the claimant will be entitled to claim his/her reasonable costs including the brief fee. In a complex multi-track case conducted in the high court, a brief fee of £10,000 would not be unreasonable.

IN THE HUDDERSFIELD COUNTY COURT **CASE No: HD 003612**

BETWEEN:

Madeline Bray

-v-

Arthur Squeers t/a Dotheboys Farm

BRIEF TO COUNSEL TO APPEAR FOR THE CLAIMANT AT TRIAL ON WEDNESDAY 5TH FEBRUARY 2024

Counsel has herewith copies of the following:

1. Pleadings
   (a) Claim Form – 09.12.22
   (b) Particulars of Claim – 19.12.22
   (c) Defence – 09.01.23
   (d) Claimant's Response to Defendant's Part 18 Request for Further Information – 17.02.23
   (e) Notice of Trial
   (f) Notice of Intention to give Hearsay Evidence
   (g) Directions questionnaires and Pre-trial Checklists
   (h) Orders made during the action

2. Documents obtained from the Defendant on inspection

3. Claimant's documents in Part 1 of her list

4. Exchanged witness statements

5. Exchanged expert reports

6. Case Summary

7. Directions for trial

8. Proposed trial bundle index

9. Previous instructions to and advice from counsel

Instructing solicitors act on behalf of the Claimant MADELINE BRAY who has the benefit of legal expense insurance in order to pursue a claim for personal injury and loss arising out of a tripping accident which occurred on 13th December 2021.

Facts
Counsel will no doubt recall this case as he previously advised in writing, settled the Particulars of Claim and Response to Request for Further Information. For the facts of the case Counsel is however once again referred to the Particulars of Claim, the statements of Mrs Bray, her husband John Bray, and their daughter Louise Bray, and the Case Summary. Counsel recently advised on evidence, and it is Counsel's advice that there are more than reasonable prospects of Mrs Bray succeeding in her claim, i.e., she has at least a 51% chance of success.

Proceedings
Court proceedings were commenced in December 2022. A Defence was subsequently served, the case was allocated to the Fast Track and has now been listed for Trial on 5th February 2024 at 10.30am.

Figure 10.2 Brief to counsel.

Counsel should be aware that Louise Bray cannot attend Trial as she is out of the country. A Civil Evidence Act Notice has been served in respect of her evidence and the Defendants have no objection to her non-attendance.

Liability
Liability remains in dispute. The case is likely to turn on whether the Defendant has breached his duty under s.*2.2 of the Occupiers Liability Act 1957*, which imposes and obligation on the Defendant as occupier of the premises to ensure the safety of all lawful visitors to their premises. In failing to ensure that their premises were safe to all visitors, in particular in failing to warn of a potential hazard, presented by the uneven and obscurely curved step at the entrance to the Defendant's farm shop, the Defendant will be found liable for the Claimant's accident.

Quantum

(a) General Damages
Counsel should be aware that the report of Mr V. R. Crummles dated 25th August 2022 has been agreed and his oral evidence will therefore not be required at trial.

(b) Special Damages
A schedule of special damages has been prepared and served with the Particulars of Claim and these are not agreed. It will be apparent to Counsel that Mrs Bray's losses amount some £7,527, including a claim for loss of earnings in the sum of 5,375 (the main area of special damages in dispute). Note however, that the interest rate up to the date of trial will have to be calculated.

Counsel is therefore instructed to appear on behalf of the Claimant at trial on Wednesday 5th February 2024 at the Huddersfield County Court. Given that this is a fast track case, Counsel's instructing solicitor will not be attending himself, however Mr and Mrs Bray will be in attendance and have been asked to arrive at court by at least 10.00am.

Claimant's Part 36 Offer
Counsel will note that on 3rd March 2023, the Claimant made a Part 36 Offer to settle claim for £10,000, which offer has been rejected. The relevant period for acceptance having expired on 24th March 2023, the Defendant has been advised that potential additional interest, indemnity costs, and an additional sum payable under CPR Rule 36.17(4)(a)-(d) will be apply, should the Claimant obtain judgment at least as favourable as the offer made, as that awarded at trial.

If Counsel requires any further information or assistance, then he should not hesitate to contact his instructing solicitor, by letter, telephone, or email.

Figure 10.2 Continued.

10.5 Trial bundles

Before the trial commences, the parties are encouraged to agree on the documents that will be made available to the court at trial (PD 32, para 27.12). The court may in fact have given directions at an earlier stage (perhaps at the case management conference in a multi-track case) to this effect, and the usual order will require the claimant to file the trial bundle no later than seven days and not less than three days before the start of the trial.

Paragraph 27.5 of PD 32, which relates to the Miscellaneous Provisions Relating to Hearings, requires that unless the court orders otherwise, the trial bundle should include copies of the following documents:

(d) the claim form and all statements of case;
(e) a case summary and/or chronology where appropriate;
(f) requests for further information and responses to the requests;

(g) all witness statements to be relied on as evidence;
(h) any witness summaries;
(i) any notices of intention to rely on hearsay evidence under r 32.2;
(j) any notices of intention to rely on evidence (such as a plan, photograph etc.) under rule 33.6 which is not –
    (i) contained in a witness statement, affidavit or experts' report;
    (ii) being given orally at trial; and
    (iii) hearsay evidence under r 33.2;
(k) any medical reports and responses to them;
(l) any experts' reports and responses to them;
(m) any order giving directions as to the conduct of the trial; and
(n) any other necessary documents.

The parties should also agree, where possible, that the documents contained in the bundle are authentic even if not disclosed under Part 31, and that documents in the bundle may be treated as evidence of the facts stated in them even if a notice under the Civil Evidence Act 1995 has not been served. Where it is not possible to agree on the contents of the bundle, a summary of the points on which the parties are unable to agree should be included.

All the documents contained in bundles which have been agreed for use at a hearing shall be admissible at that hearing as evidence of their contents unless the court orders otherwise or a party gives written notice of objection to the admissibility of particular documents.

The party responsible for preparing the trial bundle should provide sufficient copies for all those requiring one; their own counsel, the 'other side', the judge, and the witness box.

Practice Direction 28 for fast-track cases recommends that the claimant should lodge an indexed bundle of documents contained in a ring binder and with each page clearly numbered at the court not more than seven days and not less than three days before the start of the trial.

10.5.1 Case summary

This is also known as the skeleton argument, probably because it is the 'bare bones' of each party's case and will be used at trial to assist the court, and particularly the judge, in understanding the basic details of each party's case. The case summary will include details of those issues not in dispute as well as the arguments that the parties propose to advance about those matters remaining in dispute. A case summary should include the following matters:

(a) A concise review of each party's submissions of fact with reference to the evidence
(b) A concise summary of the propositions of law relied upon (case law and statute)

Heading/Title of Proceedings

Case Summary

Issues in Dispute

Cross reference here to specific pleadings in the trial bundle, in particular the statement of case and the defence, including page and paragraph numbers (e.g., para 4, page 1 particulars of claim).

The Evidence Required to Deal with those Issues in Dispute

Cross reference here to specific evidence in the trial bundle, in particular witness statements and experts' reports, including page and paragraph numbers (e.g., the report of Mr V. R. Crummles para 7 page 3).

The Claimant

[Legal Issues]

Factual

Expert

The Defendant

[Legal Issues]

Factual

Expert

Figure 10.3 Case summary template.

(c) Numbered paragraphs and paginated (pages numbered)
(d) An indication as to which documents the judge should try to read prior to trial.

Each party's case summary should therefore outline the matters still in issue and refer where appropriate to the relevant documents included in the bundle for the assistance of the judge in reading the papers before the trial. Every effort should be made by the parties to restrict their case summaries to no more than 250 words. A typical case summary appears in Figure 10.3.

The parties are required to try to agree on the contents of the trial bundle and the case summary in advance of the trial.

10.6 Trial procedure

Whether or not the case is fast-track or multi-track, the trial of the case will take place in a trial centre. This may be a different venue from the court where the case has been managed. In the High Court, if the case is not being managed in the Royal Courts of Justice, the case will be heard at one of the District Registries in a city that has a trial centre.

Table 10.2 Trial timetable with time estimates

Timetable	Time estimate
Opening speeches	20 minutes
Cross-examination and re-examination of claimant's witnesses	90 minutes
Cross-examination and re-examination of defendant's witnesses	90 minutes
Defendant's closing submissions	15 minutes
Claimant's closing submissions	15 minutes
Judge's preparation and delivery of judgment	30 minutes
Summary assessment of costs	30 minutes

In fast-track cases, Practice Direction 28.8 provides that the trial will normally take place at the court where the case is being managed, but it may be moved to another court if it is appropriate, having regard to the needs of the parties and the availability of court resources. The judge will generally have read the papers in the trial bundle and may dispense with an opening address. The judge may confirm or vary any timetable given previously, or if none has been given set his/her own.

Under the provisions in Part 32, which you will recall from Chapter 8 deals with evidence, the court has the power to control what evidence is presented before the court at trial and to restrict cross-examination of witnesses if it considers it to be appropriate. Where a witness is called to give oral evidence, his/her witness statement shall stand as his/her evidence-in-chief unless the court orders otherwise. With the court's permission, the provisions of Part 32 allow a witness giving oral evidence at trial to amplify his/her witness statement, and also to give evidence in relation to new matters which have arisen since the witness statement was served on the other parties. It should also be noted that if a party who has served a witness statement does not either call the witness to give evidence at trial or put the witness statement in as hearsay evidence, any other party may put the witness statement in as hearsay evidence.

We have seen earlier that a timetable for a fast-track trial will have been agreed on by the parties and provided to the court; this will include time estimates for each stage of the trial proceedings, a typical example of which appears in Table 10.2.

At the conclusion of the trial, the judge will normally summarily assess the costs of the claim in accordance with r 44.6 and Section VI of Part 45 (fast-track trial costs). Costs will be dealt with in more detail in the following and in Chapter 13. Fast track trials are normally listed for one day, however, where a trial is not finished on the day for which it is listed, the rules enable a judge to require all parties to return the next court day to complete it.

10.6.1 Order of proceedings

The trial is an opportunity for the parties' advocates to display their skills of advocacy. Whilst in common-law jurisdictions the ultimate aim at trial is to discover the truth, it can be argued that the outcome of the trial will be based not only on the weight of evidence, but on the strength of the arguments presented to the judge. Remember, there is no jury present at the majority of civil trials, the exceptions being those cases concerning defamation, actions against the police involving false imprisonment, malicious prosecution, and cases alleging fraud. The party's advocate therefore has to convince the judge alone that their client's case is the stronger.

Advocacy is sometimes described as an art, but it is more of a skill because the key to good advocacy is sound preparation. It is for the advocate to get his/her points across in a coherent order. Learning the art of advocacy can be challenging, particularly the examination-in-chief of one's own witnesses. This is because an advocate cannot ask their own witnesses leading questions, i.e., those questions that prompt the witness or which pre-suppose an answer based on information the advocate is looking to be confirmed, which has otherwise yet to be proved. Such questions are not allowed by the claimant's advocate. The civil trial has a set procedure which assists the orderly presentation of the case and its defence.

10.6.1.1 Preliminary issues

Before the trial of the issues formally commences, the court may be required to consider some preliminary issues which either of the parties may raise, even at this late stage in the proceedings. These are matters which the trial judge may consider should have been raised at the pre-trial review. If there was no pre-trial review, then the judge may permit the parties to address him/her on these late issues.

Preliminary issues may, for example, include:

- Permission by either party to amend the statement of case or defence
- The introduction of additional evidence
- An application by either party to strike out an opponent's witness statement
- Variation of the timetable.

10.6.1.2 The claimant

The claimant's advocate has the right to begin as the burden of proof in civil cases will usually lie with the claimant.

10.6.1.2.1 Claimant's opening speech

The judge may allow the claimant's legal representative or barrister to make an opening speech. To assist the court, the claimant's advocate will draw attention to the case summary and/or skeleton argument filed with the trial bundle, indicating particularly the facts and the areas remaining in dispute, as the submission is designed to be brief and simply deal with the background to the case and the facts that remain in issue.

10.6.1.2.2 Evidence-in-chief

The claimant and the claimant's witnesses will then be required to give their evidence; this is known as evidence-in-chief and will usually, certainly for fast-track cases, be the witness statements which have been disclosed. The witness will be asked to confirm that the contents of their statement are correct and may only be required to amplify its contents if the judge considers it necessary to do so. This is to avoid the potential for the claimant's advocate to ask the witness leading questions.

10.6.1.2.3 Cross-examination

The defendant's advocate is then allowed to put questions to the claimant's witness; this is known as cross-examination and leading questions are allowed. The defendant's advocate will be required to put the defendant's case to the claimant's witness (and vice versa). The intention of the cross-examination by the defendant's advocate is to make the claimant's evidence appear less reliable.

In some instances, the cross-examination will be approached in such a way as to try to discredit the claimant's witness and make them appear less believable, and in this way bring about doubt regarding the reliability of their evidence. Such cross-examination tactics could include an attempt by the defendant's advocate to show that there are inconsistencies in the witness's story, or that the witness is mistaken about the circumstances of particular events.

The advocate may even raise a witness's previous convictions so as to discredit them. Cross-examination is often more subtly approached so as to lead the witness, when answering the questions, to present doubt to the court about the claimant's case.

10.6.1.2.4 Re-examination

The claimant's advocate will be allowed to put further questions to the claimant's witness once the defendant advocate's cross-examination has concluded. This might, for example, be an opportunity to restore the credibility of the witness whose character might have been damaged by the defendant's advocate's skilful cross-examination. This is also an opportunity to clear up any ambiguities or uncertainties with the evidence already given by this witness. The claimant's advocate certainly should not introduce any fresh topics which have not already been raised by the witness.

10.6.1.2.5 Hostile witnesses

On occasion, a witness called by one party may during the course of delivering their evidence, provide evidence that is considered to be unfavourable to the party by whom they have been called. This may occur during skilful cross-examination by the other party's advocate. Particularly damaging evidence may be considered 'hostile' to a party's case for whom the witness has been asked to give evidence. In such circumstances, the party who has called this now 'hostile' witness may ask permission of the trial judge for their advocate to cross-examine their own witness (contrary to the rule against cross-examination of one's own witness).

10.6.1.3 The defendant

To ensure 'equality of arms', in other words, to provide the same procedural rights to the defendant, the defendant will present his/her evidence in exactly the same way as the claimant.

10.6.1.4 Closing speeches

Once both parties have delivered their evidence, it is usual for the defendant's advocate to deliver a closing speech followed by the claimant.

10.7 The nature and effect of judgment

After the closing speeches, the judge will deliver his/her judgment. The judge will sometimes adjourn to the following day if the hour is late and sometimes may reserve judgment to a later date, in which case the parties will be told at a later date when the judgment will be delivered (read out).

10.7.1 The judgment

A judgment in an action for tort, for instance, will usually address the following matters:

(a) Liability – if the claimant has proved its cause of action, then liability will have been established and judgment will be entered
(b) Quantum – this is a value of the damages to which the claimant should be entitled. In a tortious claim (for instance a claim for damages arising from personal injury), the damages will have been unspecified at the outset of the claim and as such the judge will now be required to award a sum for each of the heads of damage: general damages and special damages
(c) Interest – the judge will be able to award interest on the damages awarded. The amount of which will have been worked out by the respective parties' advocates. Interest is dealt with in more detail in the following
(d) Costs – Rule 44.2(2)(a) provides the general rule that the unsuccessful party will be ordered to pay the costs of the successful party at trial. At the conclusion of a fast-track trial, the trial judge will not only make a costs order, but also assess the

amount payable. Costs are dealt with in more detail in Chapter 13. With a multi-track case, the trial judge will only make an order for costs determining who is to pay and the amount of those costs will be reserved for consideration by another judge (a costs judge) at an assessment of costs hearing at a later date, to determine the amount that the paying party should pay.

If there has been a Part 36 offer to settle the case made during the course of proceedings, the claimant should make an application for an order pursuant to r 36.17(4) and the defendant pursuant to r 36.17(3). See Chapter 5 for the costs consequences associated with Part 36 offers.

10.7.2 Interest

10.7.2.1 Interest up to the date of judgment

As long as a claim for interest is made in the particulars of the claim, then interest will normally be awarded by the trial judge, although it is discretionary. In the absence of any contractual provision which may have been agreed or in the case of commercial debt actions and the entitlement to interest under the provisions of the Late Payment of Commercial Debts (Interest) Act 1988, interest on damages will usually be awarded by the trial judge in his discretion under s.35A Supreme Court Act 1981, or under s.69 of the County Courts Act 1984, from the date of the loss up until the date of judgment.

10.7.2.2 Interest after judgment

Once judgment has been given, interest is payable on the award (the judgement debt) depending on where the claim was being conducted. In the High Court, under s.17 of the Judgments Act 1838, interest is payable at the rate of 8 per cent pa (unless there is a contractual entitlement to an increased sum). In the County Court, interest is payable at the rate of 8 per cent pa under the County Courts (Interest on Judgment Debts) Order 1991 (SI 1991/1184), provided the judgment was for at least £5,000 (or, if less, that the Late Payment of Commercial Debts (Interest) Act 1998 applies).

Whilst the claim for interest is mandatory, the trial judge does have the discretion to decide what rate of interest applies to the amount of the judgment debt.

10.7.3 The implication of judgment debts

10.7.3.1 The Register of Judgments Orders and Fines

Those who have a judgment debt will have this officially recorded in the Register of Judgments Orders and Fines. Unless the judgment debt is paid immediately the registration will last for six years and such a County Court Judgment or often commonly referred to as a 'CCJ' may well affect a judgment debtor's credit worthiness. The gov.uk website provides guidance for those with county court judgments for debt.[2]

2 Available at: www.gov.uk/county-court-judgments-ccj-for-debt/ccjs-and-your-credit-rating.

Chapter 10 revision points

Preparing for trial

- Pre-trial checklists (listing questionnaires) for fast-track and multi-track cases – standard form
- Witness attendance at trial – witness summons procedure
- Trial procedure:
  - Preliminary issues
  - Claimant's opening, followed by evidence-in-chief, then cross-examination and re-examination
  - Defendant follows same procedure
  - Closing speeches
- Judgment:
  - Liability
  - Quantum
  - Interest
  - Consideration of any Part 36 offers
  - Costs

11 Appeals

11.1 Chapter overview

This chapter will look at appeals and commence with applications for permission to appeal to the County Court and High Court. As permission to appeal is required in all cases, the test and grounds for appeal will be outlined. The procedure for an appeal, both from the appellant's and the respondent's perspective, will be covered, and procedural aspects of the hearing of the appeal, including the required documents, will be explained.

The chapter will also cover the special rules that apply to appeals to the Court of Appeal. It is important that appeals are made to the correct appeal centre and therefore the destination of appeals, and the court to which the appeal lies will be considered.

11.2 Introduction: appeals

In civil cases, appeals from the County Court, Court of Chancery, Queen's Bench, and Family Divisions of the High Court should be made to the Court of Appeal (Civil Division). From the Court of Appeal, appeals are made to the Supreme Court. Appeals from a master or a district judge should be made to a High Court judge and appeals from a High Court judge should be made to the Court of Appeal where three judges will sit to hear the appeal. The routes to be taken from one judge to another are covered by ss.55 to 57 Access to Justice Act 1999.

Those appeals within the County Court, appeals from the County Court, and appeals within the High Court to a judge of the High Court, must be brought in the appropriate appeal centre and all other notices (including any respondent's notice) and applications must be filed at that appeal centre. The venue for an appeal within the County Court will be determined by the designated civil judge and may be different from the appeal centre. CPR Part 52 deals with the procedure for civil appeals.

11.3 Permission

Permission to appeal is required in all cases except those appeals against committal orders, a refusal to grant habeus corpus, a secure accommodation order made under the s.25 Children Act 1989, or a decision made by a district judge, circuit judge, or

DOI: 10.4324/9781003218500-17

bankruptcy registrar in exercise of bankruptcy or insolvency jurisdiction. The general test for permission is whether the appeal is likely to have a more than reasonable prospect of success. Rule 52.6 provides the 'permission to appeal test' which essentially means:

- If the court considers that the appeal would have a real prospect of success, or alternatively
- If there is some other compelling reason for the appeal to be heard.

Applications for permission to appeal will normally be requested by a party's advocate at the hearing at which the order or judgment was made. If permission is refused or not sought, then the party intending to appeal must lodge an appeal notice with the court (see the following). Where the lower court refuses (or gives) permission to appeal, it should complete a form briefly explaining why permission was refused (or granted). In granting an order giving permission, the court may limit the issues to be heard and grant the order subject to specific conditions.

11.3.1 Applications for permission to appeal to the County Court and High Court

An application for permission to appeal may be made either to the lower court at the hearing at which the decision to be appealed was made or to the appeal court by way of an appeal notice. The party seeking to appeal the court's decision is known as the appellant. The appellant must file the appellant's notice at the appeal court within such period as the lower court may direct, usually 21 days after the date of the decision of the lower court which the appellant wishes to appeal. The appellant's notice of appeal must be served on each respondent no later than seven days (r 52.12). The respondent should then file a notice in response within 14 days of being served with the notice of appeal.

The parties may apply for an order to extend the time for filing the notice of appeal and the court may make an order granting or refusing an extension of time with or without a hearing. If an order is made without a hearing, any party seeking to set aside or vary the order may apply, within 14 days of service of the order, for a hearing.

11.4 Procedure for an appeal

11.4.1 The appellant's notice

Practice Direction 52 para 4.2 provides guidance on the appropriate form to use, and an appellant's notice should be in Form N161 or, in respect of a small claim, Form N164. These are the prescribed forms to use for all appeals up to the Court of Appeal. It must be filed and served in all cases and must be accompanied by the appropriate fee or, if appropriate, a fee remission application or certificate. Form N161 comprises 11 sections as follows:

(1) Details of the case the appellant is appealing against, including –
    - details of the appellant and respondent;

(2) Details of the appeal –
- from which court the appeal is being brought
- the name of the Judge whose decision is being appealed
- the date of the decision you wish to appeal against;

(3) Details of legal representation;
(4) Permission to appeal;
(5) Other information required for the appeal;
(6) Grounds of appeal;
(7) Arguments in support of grounds for appeal;
(8) Aarhus Convention Claim – for applications made under the Town & Country Planning Act 1990 or the Planning (Listed Buildings and Conservation Areas) Act 1990;
(9) What the appellant is asking the Appeal Court to do;
(10) Other applications, which may include –
- A stay of execution
- An extension of time for filing the appeal notice
- Any other order;

(11) Evidence in support –
Here the appellant should give reasons and evidence in support of his/her application set out in section 10.

Practice Direction 52 para 4.2 requires that the appellant must also file with the appellant's notice the following documents:

(a) three copies of the appellant's notice and one additional copy for each respondent;
(b) a copy of the sealed order under appeal;
(c) where an application was made to the lower court for permission to appeal, a copy of any order granting or refusing permission to appeal together with a copy of the reasons, if any, for allowing or refusing permission to appeal; and
(d) grounds of appeal, which must be set out on a separate sheet attached to the appellant's notice and must set out, in simple language, clearly and concisely, why the order of the lower court was wrong or unjust because of a serious procedural or other irregularity (r 52.21(3)).

11.4.2 Applications in the appeal

Any application to be made in the appeal (for example, for a stay of the order of the lower court, or for an extension of time) should be included within the appellant's notice. Any application for a transcript at public expense should be made within the appellant's notice.

11.4.3 The respondent's notice

The respondent should use Form N162, which is the prescribed form to use for all appeals up to the Court of Appeal. Rule 52.13 provides the procedure for the respondent's notice, and it includes the situation where a respondent seeks permission to appeal from the appeal court or wishes to ask the appeal court to uphold the decision of the lower court for reasons different from or additional to those given by the lower court. In all these circumstances, the respondent's notice must be filed within such period as may be directed by the lower court at the hearing at which the decision to be appealed was made or any adjournment of that hearing. Otherwise, where the court makes no direction, the respondent's notice should be filed within 14 days after the hearing and unless the appeal court orders otherwise, a respondent's notice must be served on the appellant and any other respondent as soon as practicable, and in any event not later than seven days after it is filed.

Form N162 comprises ten sections as follows:

(1) Details of the claim or case
(2) Details of the respondent (name and address)
(3) Time estimate for appeal hearing
(4) Details of the order(s) or part(s) of order(s) to be appealed
(5) Permission to file a respondent's appeal notice
(6) Grounds for appeal or for upholding the order
(7) Arguments in support of grounds
(8) Details of the decisions which the respondent is asking the appeal court to make
(9) Other applications
(10) Supporting documents.

If the respondent's skeleton argument is not included in section 7 it should either be attached, or the respondent should confirm that it is to follow within 21 days.

11.4.4 Skeleton arguments

The purpose of a skeleton argument is to assist the court by providing a brief and concise summary of the areas of controversy in the case. It will also set out the arguments upon which a party intends to rely. Standard form N163 should be used and PD 52 para 5.1(2) provides that a skeleton argument must:

- be concise;
- both define and confine the areas of controversy;
- be set out in numbered paragraphs;
- be cross-referenced to any relevant document in the bundle;
- be self-contained and not incorporate by reference material from previous skeleton arguments;
- not include extensive quotations from documents or authorities;
- identify any documents to be relied on.

The obvious function of skeleton arguments is to assist the court on any application for permission to appeal and on the hearing of the appeal. Where it is necessary to refer to an authority, a skeleton argument must:

(a) State the proposition of law the authority demonstrates, and
(b) Identify the parts of the authority that support the proposition.

If more than one authority is cited in support of a given proposition, the skeleton argument must briefly state why.

Skeleton arguments are required from all parties to the appeal, both appellants and respondents and even those without legal representation. The appellant and respondent should ideally file their skeleton arguments at the same time as filing their respective notices (there is space to do so on the prescribed court forms); in any event, they should be filed as soon as possible and well before the hearing of the appeal, to enable the court to make any administrative arrangements and case management decisions about the hearing of the appeal.

11.4.5 Hearing of the appeal

As soon as practicable, but in any event within 35 days of the filing of the appellant's notice, the appellant must file an appeal bundle which must contain only those documents relevant to the appeal. The appeal bundle must be paginated and indexed (r 52 6.3.)

The following documents relevant to the appeal (as required by r 52 6.4) should be included in the appeal bundle:

(a) A copy of the appellant's notice
(b) A copy of any respondent's notice
(c) A copy of any appellant's or respondent's skeleton argument
(d) A copy of the order under appeal
(e) A copy of the order of the lower court granting or refusing permission to appeal together with a copy of the judge's reasons, if any, for granting or refusing permission
(f) A copy of any order allocating the case to a track
(g) A transcript of the judgment of the lower court or other record of reasons (except in appeals in cases which were allocated to the small claims track and subject to any order of the court).

The following documents should also be considered for inclusion in the appeal bundle but should be included only where relevant to the appeal:

(a) Statements of case
(b) Application notices
(c) Other orders made in the case
(d) A chronology of relevant events
(e) Witness statements made in support of any application made in the appellant's notice

(f) Other witness statements
(g) Any other documents which any party considers would assist the appeal court.

Rule 52.21 provides that every appeal will be limited to a review of the decision of the lower court unless a practice direction makes different provision for a particular category of appeal, or the court considers that in the circumstances of an individual appeal it would be in the interests of justice to hold a re-hearing. Unless it orders otherwise, the appeal court will not receive oral evidence, evidence which was not before the lower court. The appeal court will allow an appeal where the decision of the lower court was either wrong or unjust because of a serious procedural or other irregularity in the proceedings in the lower court. At the hearing of the appeal, a party may not rely on a matter not contained in that party's appeal notice unless the court gives permission. In arriving at its decision, the appeal court may draw any inference of fact that it considers justified on the evidence.

11.4.6 Leapfrog appeals

In rare cases, it is possible to appeal a decision of the lower courts (the County Court and the High Court) direct to the Court of Appeal under the provisions of section 57 of the Access to Justice Act 1999 or to the Supreme Court pursuant to section 13 of the Administration of Justice Act 1969. A 'leapfrog appeal' is also possible from the High Court to the Supreme Court but would only be permitted in circumstances where the High Court is bound by a previous Supreme Court or House of Lords decision, and the party appealing the decision would not be able to succeed in the Court of Appeal (because lower courts cannot overturn the decision of higher courts).

A 'leapfrog appeal' from the High Court to the Supreme Court may be made if:

(a) All parties consent
(b) The judge grants a certificate, but only if the case involves a point of law of general public importance concerning either the construction of a statutory instrument or a matter already fully considered by the Court of Appeal or the Supreme Court, and
(c) The Supreme Court grants leave.

The 'leapfrog appeal' is sometimes considered appropriate in order to save time and costs where an issue would be much better dealt with by a more superior court. The court's case management powers which it to grant permission for a 'leapfrog appeal', are derived from s.57 of the Access to Justice Act 1999, which permits such appeals from district judges, masters, and circuit judges direct to the Court of Appeal. The procedure also allows the Master of the Rolls to make an order leapfrogging to the Court of Appeal, an appeal which would otherwise be heard in the county court or the High Court.

11.4.7 Second appeals

Special rules apply to those appeals that have already been heard in the County Court or High Court. Matters relating to such 'second appeals' are covered by sections 55 to 57 Access to Justice Act 1999. The lower courts have no jurisdiction to grant such permission and therefore and if either party wishes to pursue a second appeal, they must seek and obtain permission from the Court of Appeal.

Rule 52.7 deals with the matters relating to the requirement for permission to appeal a decision of the County Court, the family court, or the High Court to the Court of Appeal, which was itself made on appeal, or a decision of the Upper Tribunal which was made on appeal from a decision of the First-Tier Tribunal on a point of law, where the Upper Tribunal has refused permission to appeal to the Court of Appeal. The Court of Appeal will only grant permission if the following criteria are satisfied:

(a) The appeal would have a reasonable prospect of success
(b) The appeal would raise an important point of principle or practice
(c) Some other compelling reason exists for the Court of Appeal to hear it.

Even if the criteria are met, the court should have regard for other matters such as whether it is fair and reasonable to allow the appeal; hence the Court of Appeal should have regard for the application of the overriding objective.

11.4.8 The appeal court's decision

It is important to note that the appeal court has all the powers of the lower court. The appeal court therefore has the power to:

(a) Affirm, set aside, or vary any order or judgment made or given by the lower court
(b) Refer any claim or issue for determination by the lower court
(c) Order a new trial or hearing
(d) Make orders for the payment of interest
(e) Make a costs order.

Remember that in some specific types of cases, civil trials can have a jury. In an appeal from a claim tried with a jury, the Court of Appeal may, instead of ordering a new trial, either make an order for damages or vary an award of damages made by the jury.

11.5 Destination of appeals

Practice Direction 52.2.1 requires that all appeals within the County Court, appeals from the County Court, and appeals within the High Court to a judge of the High Court must be brought in the appropriate appeal centre and all other notices (including any respondent's notice) and applications must be filed at that appeal centre.

Table 11.1 The court to which the appeal lies

Court	Deciding judge	Decision under appeal	Destination
County	District judge	Any, other than a decision in non-insolvency proceedings brought pursuant to the Companies Acts	Circuit judge (County Court)
		A decision in non-insolvency proceedings brought pursuant to the Companies Acts	High Court judge or registrar
	Circuit judge	Any	High Court judge
High	Master, registrar, or district judge	Any	High Court judge
	High Court judge	Any	Court of Appeal
Intellectual Property Enterprise Court	District judge	Any	Enterprise judge
	Enterprise judge	Any	Court of Appeal

The venue for an appeal within the County Court will be determined by the designated civil judge and may be different from the appeal centre. Table 11.1 provides helpful guidance on which court in which the appeal lies.

Appeals to the High Court may be transferred between appeal centres by a direction given by the President of the King's Bench Division or the Chancellor of the High Court or their respective nominee. A party seeking to transfer the appeal to an Appeal Centre other than the one in which it was filed may seek to do so by letter addressed to the President of the King's Bench Division or the Chancellor of the High Court as appropriate.

11.6 Grounds for appeals

The grounds of appeal are set out in r 52.21 and any appellant must identify as concisely as possible the respects in which the judgment of the court below is:

(a) Wrong, or
(b) Unjust because of a serious procedural or other irregularity.

The reasons why the decision under appeal is wrong or unjust must be confined to the skeleton argument and must not be included in the grounds of appeal in the prescribed form.

11.7 Appealing to the Court of Appeal: special provisions

The Court of Appeal civil division has jurisdiction to hear appeals from the High Court and the County Court. It also hears references from the Upper Tribunal, Employment Tribunal, Immigration Appeal Tribunal, Lands Tribunal, and the Social Security Commissioners. The head of the Court of Appeal civil division is the Master of the Rolls.

Essentially, the procedure, including the use of prescribed forms and skeleton arguments, for appealing to the Court of Appeal is the same as for appeals to the lower courts, although there are special provisions under r 52.23 which cover the assignment of appeals to the Court of Appeal; namely, where the court from or to which an appeal is made or from which permission to appeal is sought considers that:

(a) An appeal which is to be heard by the County Court or the High Court would raise an important point of principle or practice, or
(b) There is some other compelling reason for the Court of Appeal to hear it.

In this case, the relevant court may order the appeal to be transferred to the Court of Appeal. The Master of the Rolls has the separate statutory power to direct that an appeal which would be heard by the County Court or the High Court should be heard instead by the Court of Appeal (see section 57 of the Access to Justice Act 1994.) The Master of the Rolls or the Court of Appeal may return an appeal to the court in which the original appeal was or would have been brought. It is fair and reasonable to allow the appeal; hence the Court of Appeal should have regard for the application of the overriding objective.

11.7.1 Reopening final appeals

Under r 52.30, the Court of Appeal or the High Court will not reopen a final determination of any appeal unless:

(a) It is necessary to do so in order to avoid real injustice
(b) The circumstances are exceptional and make it appropriate to reopen the appeal, and
(c) There is no alternative effective remedy.

Permission is needed to make an application under this rule to reopen a final determination of an appeal even in cases where under r 52.3(1) permission was not needed for the original appeal. There is no right to an oral hearing of an application for permission unless, exceptionally, the judge so directs. The judge must not grant permission without directing the application to be served on the other party to the original appeal and giving that party an opportunity to make representations. There is no right of appeal or review from the decision of the judge on the application for permission, which is final.

Chapter 11 revision points

Appeals

- Permission to appeal is required in all cases; the test is:
  - Relevance – the court considers that the appeal would have a real prospect of success, or alternatively
  - If there is some other compelling reason for the appeal to be heard
- Grounds for appeal:
  - The judgment of the court below is wrong, or
  - Unjust because of a serious procedural or other irregularity
- Procedure for an appeal:
  - The appellant's notice – the 11 points
  - Plus – three copies of the appellant's notice, sealed order under appeal, copy of any order granting or refusing permission to appeal, grounds for appeal
  - The respondent's notice – the ten points
  - Skeleton arguments
- Hearing of the appeal – the required documents

12 Enforcement

12.1 Chapter overview

In this chapter we will look at the steps that can be taken after judgment has been obtained, to enforce a money judgment in the event that the judgment debtor fails to honour the judgment debt. This will include the judgment creditor's choice of enforcement process. The circumstances where there is a need to obtain information from the judgment debtor and the application procedure to obtain an order for information will be considered first.

The chapter will then consider the main methods of enforcement, including taking control of goods, third-party debt orders, attachment of earnings, and a brief explanation of the procedure involved for each method. Finally, the application process and procedure and the supportive evidence required for the enforcement of foreign judgments will be addressed, before outlining the requirements for registering a foreign judgment.

12.2 Introduction: enforcement

Once a judgment has been obtained against an opponent, the party against whom judgment has been obtained will be required to honour the judgment within the timeframe required in the judgment order, usually 28 days. There are circumstances, however, where judgment is not honoured, and in this chapter, we will focus mainly on the enforcement of money judgments. Judgments are not enforced automatically by the court and once judgment has been obtained, whether it be by default, summary judgment, or after judgment is given after a trial, there are a number of ways to enforce the judgment which are available to the successful party. Post-judgment, the successful party will be known as the judgment creditor for the purposes of enforcement. From the judgment creditor's perspective, it is important to ensure that the losing party, or judgment debtor as he/she will now be called at this stage, can be traced, in order that enforcement proceedings can be commenced in the event that the judgment debt remains unpaid.

Information about the judgment debtor's personal circumstances will be required. For example, a last known address and place of work would be really useful. It may be that the services of an enquiry agent will have been used at some stage to determine as much useful information about the judgment debtor including details of

DOI: 10.4324/9781003218500-18

his/her means. A bankruptcy search may have been carried out against an individual or a company search made against a company before proceedings were commenced. The results of these searches will have revealed details of the judgment debtor's solvency. Now that judgment has been obtained, these searches should be renewed and updated. All this information should ideally have been established before taking the decision to commence proceedings, of course, as there is little point in pursuing a claim against a defendant who has limited or no means to satisfy a judgment. The judgment creditor can also apply to the court for an order to obtain information from the judgment debtor (see the following).

Once sufficient information has been established about the judgment debtor, should payment of the judgment debt remain unforthcoming, the appropriate method of enforcement will need to be chosen. The methods of enforcement available for money judgments are considered in the following.

12.3 Obtaining information from the judgment debtor

The rules governing the procedure for applications for obtaining information from a judgment debtor (formerly known as oral examinations) are found in CPR Part 71, and these rules provide for a judgment debtor to be required to attend court to provide information to a court officer, for the purpose of enabling a judgment creditor to enforce a judgment or order against him/her.

A judgment creditor may therefore apply for an order requiring a judgment debtor; or if a judgment debtor is a company or other corporation, an officer of that organisation, to attend court to provide information about the judgment debtor's means; or any other matter about which information is needed to enforce a judgment or order.

12.3.1 Procedure for making an application for an order to obtain information

An application for an order to obtain information may be made without notice and must be issued in the court or County Court hearing centre which made the judgment or order that the judgment creditor is looking to enforce. The Practice Direction to Rule 71 provides the guidance for such an application to be made under r 71.2(1). The application must be made by filing an application notice in Practice Form N316 if the application is to question an individual judgment debtor or N316A if the application is to question an officer of a company or other corporation.

Practice Direction 71 para 1 requires that the application notice must include the following matters:

(1) the name and address of the judgment debtor;
(2) the identity of the judgment or order which the judgment creditor is seeking to enforce must be;

(3) if the application is to enforce a judgment or order for the payment of money, the amount presently owed by the judgment debtor under the judgment or order should be clearly stated;
(4) if the judgment debtor is a company or other corporation, the name and address of the officer of that body whom the judgment creditor wishes to be ordered to attend court, and his position in the company should be clearly stated;
(5) if the judgment creditor wishes the questioning to be conducted before a judge, this should be stated, and reasons given;
(6) if the judgment creditor wishes the judgment debtor (or other person to be questioned) to be ordered to produce specific documents at court, those documents should be identified; and,
(7) if the application is to enforce a judgment or order which is not for the payment of money, the matters about which the judgment creditor wishes the judgment debtor (or officer of the judgment debtor) to be questioned should be identified.

The order will provide for the judgment debtor (or other person to be questioned) to attend the County Court hearing centre serving the address where the judgment debtor resides or carries on business, unless a judge decides otherwise. The order will provide for questioning to take place before a judge only if the judge considering the request decides that there are compelling reasons to make such an order (r 71 2). The judgment debtor will be warned by the court that if they do not attend the information hearing, they will be in contempt of court and may be imprisoned.

The order must be served personally on the judgment debtor at least 14 days before the information hearing and the judgment creditor's enquiry agent should swear an affidavit to that effect and file it with the court at least two days before the hearing. The judgment debtor will be entitled to claim reasonable travelling expenses for attending the hearing.

12.3.1.1 The information hearing

The court officer will ask a standard series of questions, as set out in the forms in Appendixes A and B to PD 71. The form in Appendix A will be used if the person being questioned is the judgment debtor, and the form in Appendix B will be used if the person is an officer of a company or other corporation.

The judgment creditor or his representative may either attend court and ask questions himself or request the court officer to ask additional questions by attaching a list of proposed additional questions to his application notice. At the hearing the court officer will be responsible for the following:

(1) Making a written record of the evidence given, unless the proceedings are tape-recorded
(2) At the end of the questioning, reading the record of evidence to the person being questioned and asking him/her to sign it, and
(3) If the person refuses to sign it, noting that refusal on the record of evidence.

If the judgment debtor fails to attend the information hearing or attends but refuses to take the oath, affirm, answer any questions, or sign the record of evidence provided, a committal order may be made against him/her.

12.4 Interest on judgment debts

A judgment creditor can claim interest on a judgment debt and any claim for interest High Court judgments must be included in any application or request to issue enforcement proceedings in relation to that judgment details.

12.4.1 High Court judgments

In the High Court interest does not stop accruing during enforcement proceedings and interest may be claimed on High Court judgment debts under s.17 of the Judgments Act 1838. The current rate of interest is 8 per cent pa.

12.4.2 County Court judgments

Interest may be claimed on County Court judgment debts under s.74 County Courts Acts 1984. Interest of 8 per cent pa can be claimed and on judgment debts of £5,000 or more. The County Courts (Interest on Judgment Debts) Order 1991 specifies when interest may be claimed on the County Court judgment debts.

If a judgment creditor wishes to claim interest on a judgment debt, a claim for interest must be included in any application or request to issue enforcement proceedings in relation to that judgment details. The claim for interest should include the following:

(1) The amount of interest claimed and the sum on which it is claimed
(2) The dates from and to which interest has accrued, and
(3) The rate of interest which has been applied, and where more than one rate of interest has been applied, the relevant dates and rates.

It should be noted that, unlike High Court judgment debts, even where interest is payable on a County Court judgment debt, it ceases to be payable once the judgment creditor commences enforcement proceedings in the County Court, unless, however, those proceedings fail to produce any payment from the judgment debtor.

12.5 Methods of enforcement

Rule 70.2 specifies the methods of enforcement that a judgment creditor may use to enforce a judgment or order for the payment of money. The following enforcement options are commonly available:

(1) A writ of control or warrant of control (see Parts 83 and 84)
(2) A third-party debt order (see Part 72)

(3) A charging order, stop order, or stop notice (see Part 73)
(4) An attachment of earnings order in the County Court (see Part 89).

12.5.1 Taking control of goods

This is a method of enforcement that enables the judgment debtor's goods to be seized by an enforcement agent (a bailiff in the County Court and a High Court enforcement officer in the High Court) and then sold at auction, the proceeds of which will be used to pay the judgment debt, costs, and costs of enforcement. Any surplus proceeds of sale will be returned to the judgment debtor. For judgment debts of more than £600, but less than £5,000, the judgment creditor can choose whether to issue proceedings for this method of enforcement in either the County Court or the High Court. An agreement regulated under the Consumer Credit Act 1974 can only be enforced in the County Court and the £5,000 upper limit does not apply. Parts 83 and 84 deal with matters relating to taking control of goods.

12.5.1.1 County Court procedure – warrant of control

For a request for a warrant of control, the judgment creditor should use prescribed Form 323, and the procedure is as follows:

(1) The judgment creditor completes the form for request of warrant of control
(2) The judgment creditor files the form of request with the County Court hearing centre which serves the area where the judgment debtor's goods are to be seized, together with the appropriate fee
(3) The warrant is executed by the County Court enforcement agent for the district where the judgment debtor resides or carries on business.

12.5.1.2 High Court procedure – writ of control

Before a writ of control can be applied for, a 'certificate of judgment' is required. This has the case details and confirms how much the judgment creditor is owed. To request this, prescribed Form N293A, a combined certificate of judgment to enforce the judgment by a writ of control, should be completed which should state the following:

- The date of judgment and the amount the order was made for, including any additional costs allowed by the court since judgment, and
- The total of any interest that has accrued on the judgment, and if appropriate, the daily rate.

To request for a writ of control, the judgment creditor should then use prescribed Form 53, and the procedure is as follows:

(1) The judgment creditor completes the form for request of writ of control
(2) The judgment creditor files the form of request with the court office, together with the judgment, certificate of judgment
(3) The court seals the writ and returns one copy of it to the judgment creditor

(4) The judgment creditor sends the sealed copy of the writ of control to the High Court enforcement officer for the county where the debtor resides or carries on business, to be executed.

12.5.1.3 Mode of entry – enforcement agents

It is important to note that bailiffs and High Court enforcement officers should only enter a judgment debtor's dwelling with their permission and should not gain entry to a house by force. The only exception here concerns business premises (if no living accommodation is attached) and the enforcement agent can then only break into those business premises if there is a genuine belief that the debtor's goods are inside. Enforcement agents are also not permitted to enter the debtor's premises if only children under 16 or vulnerable people (with disabilities, for example) are present, between the hours of 9.00 p.m. and 6.00 a.m., or through anything except the door.

12.5.1.4 Items exempt from seizure

The enforcement agent can only take goods which belong to the debtor or are jointly owned. For example, the enforcement agent cannot take goods that the judgment debtor can prove belong exclusively to the debtor's partner. Any goods which the enforcement agent takes must be likely to fetch money at auction and enforcement agents will not remove goods if they think that they will not fetch enough to pay something towards the warrant after the costs of removing and selling them at auction have been paid.

Enforcement officers cannot seize the following:

- Items which the debtor needs for his/her job or business, such as tradesman's tools or books
- Essential household items which the debtor and his/her family need such as clothing or bedding
- Items which are leased, rented, or on hire purchase agreements, or
- Goods which may have already been seized by enforcement agents acting under another warrant
- Cars which are bought on hire purchase, or
- Equipment which does not belong to a business (for example, office furniture, machinery, and vehicles may be leased).

12.5.1.5 Suspending a warrant

The judgment debtor can, upon payment of a fee, request that the court suspends the warrant of control by using prescribed Form N245. The court will send a copy of the judgment debtor's application to suspend the warrant and form N2456A (the judgment creditor's reply to the debtor's application to suspend the warrant). The judgment creditor may:

- Agree to the warrant being suspended and accept the debtor's offer of payment
- Agree to the suspension but think that the debtor could pay more than he or she has offered, or
- Not agree to the warrant being suspended.

If the judgment creditor agrees to the suspension but not the debtor's offer, a court officer will look at the information given on the judgment debtor's application and decide how much the judgment debtor can afford to pay. The court will send an order to the judgment debtor telling him/her how much to pay and when. You can ask for a district judge to decide what would be a fair rate for the debtor to pay.

If the judgment debtor still does not accept the amount required to pay, he/she may, within 16 days, then write to the court saying why they object to the court officer's decision and give reasons. The judgment debtor will then be required to attend court, and if at the hearing the warrant is suspended but the debtor does not pay as he/she said (or as ordered), the judgment debtor can use proscribed Form N445 (request for reissuing warrant) to ask the court to issue the warrant again. This is called 'reissuing the warrant'.

12.5.2 Third-party debt order

If the judgment debtor is owed money by a third party, then a third-party debt order may be a viable method of enforcement for the judgment creditor. In those circumstances, an order can be obtained requiring the party owing money to the judgment debtor to be ordered to pay the judgment creditor the amount of the judgment debt and costs direct. A bank or building society account are potential targets for the third-party debt order. At the information hearing, details of such holding accounts or, for instance, trade debts owed to a sole trader or business will have been disclosed.

12.5.2.1 Procedure

The application should be issued in the County Court that made the judgment order to be enforced or in the event of a County Court Money Centre judgment, the application should be filed in the County Court hearing centre for the district where the judgment debtor resides or carries on business. Rule 72.2 provides the procedure for making an application for a third-party debt order. An application by a judgment creditor under r 71.2(1) must be made by filing an application notice in Practice Form N316 if the application is to question an individual judgment debtor or N316A if the application is to question an officer of a company or other corporation.

The application notice must include the following matters:

(1) The name and address of the judgment debtor
(2) The judgment or order which the judgment creditor is seeking to enforce should be identified
(3) If the application is to enforce a judgment or order for the payment of money, the amount presently owed by the judgment debtor under the judgment or order should be stated
(4) If the judgment debtor is a company or other corporation, the application should state:
    (a) The name and address of the officer of that body whom the judgment creditor wishes to be ordered to attend court, and
    (b) His/her position in the company

(5) If the judgment creditor wishes the questioning to be conducted before a judge, state this and give his reasons
(6) If the judgment creditor wishes the judgment debtor (or other person to be questioned) to be ordered to produce specific documents at court, identify those documents, and
(7) If the application is to enforce a judgment or order which is not for the payment of money, identify the matters about which the judgment creditor wishes the judgment debtor (or officer of the judgment debtor) to be questioned.

12.5.2.2 The hearing

The hearing will take place before a judge and once the court has heard the application judgment creditor's application for a third-party money order, the judge may make an order (a 'final third party debt order') requiring a third party to pay to the judgment creditor:

(1) The amount of any debt due or accruing due to the judgment debtor from the third party, or
(2) So much of that debt as is sufficient to satisfy the judgment debt and the judgment creditor's costs of the application.

The court will not make a third-party debt order without first making an 'interim third-party debt order'. The judge will also fix a hearing for the final third-party debt order, which will not be less than 28 days after the interim order was made.

The interim debt order should then be served on the third party at least 21 days before the hearing of the final order, and on the judgment debtor within seven days of service on the third party.

12.5.2.3 Obligations of third parties served with interim order

The effect on the bank or building society account will be to freeze it up to the amount outstanding under the judgment order. Rule 72.6 requires that a bank or building society served with an interim third-party debt order must take the following steps:

(1) carry out a search to identify all accounts held with it by the judgment debtor.
(2) must disclose to the court and the creditor within 7 days of being served with the order, in respect of each account held by the judgment debtor –
    (a) the number of the account;
    (b) whether the account is in credit; and
    (c) if the account is in credit:
        (i) whether the balance of the account is sufficient to cover the amount specified in the order;
        (ii) the amount of the balance at the date it was served with the order, if it is less than the amount specified in the order; and

(iii) whether the bank or building society asserts any right to the money in the account, whether pursuant to a right of set-off or otherwise, and if so giving details of the grounds for that assertion.

If the judgment debtor does not hold an account with the bank or building society, or the bank or building society is unable to comply with the order for any other reason (for example, because it has more than one account holder whose details match the information contained in the order and cannot identify which account the order applies to), the bank or building society must inform the court and the judgment creditor of that fact within seven days of being served with the order.

Any third party other than a bank or building society served with an interim third-party debt order must notify the court and the judgment creditor in writing within seven days of being served with the order if he claims not to owe any money to the judgment debtor or to owe less than the amount specified in the order.

Once the final third-party debt order is made, the money in the account which has been frozen must be paid over by the third party to the judgment creditor.

In circumstances where the judgment debtor or his/her family is likely to suffer hardship in meeting ordinary living expenses as a result of the third-party debt order being made, the judgment debtor can apply under r 72.7 for an order permitting the bank or building society to make payment out of the account. This is known as a hardship payment order. Any application for a hardship payment order should be supported by evidence filed by a judgment debtor which should include documentary evidence, for example (if appropriate), bank statements, wage slips, and mortgage statements, to prove his financial position and need for the payment.

12.5.3 Charging order

The judgment creditor may be able to obtain a charge on the judgment creditor's beneficial interest in an asset or security. The most common target for a charging order is land, and this is what we will focus on here. Once a charging order is granted, the judgment creditor will become a secured creditor subject to any prior mortgages attached to the land in question.

12.5.3.1 Procedure

The procedure for an application for a charging order is to be found in r 73 and may be made without notice. Where an application for a charging order is to be made to the County Court, it must be made to the County Court Money Claims Centre unless the application is for a charging order over an interest in a fund in court.

An application for a charging order must be made by filing an application notice in Practice Form N379 if the application relates to land (Form N380 should be used if the application relates to securities). The application notice must contain the following information:

(1) The name and address of the judgment debtor
(2) Details of the judgment or order sought to be enforced
(3) The amount of money remaining due under the judgment or order
(4) If the judgment debt is payable by instalments:
(a) Whether the order was made on or after 1 October 2012, and
(b) The amount of any instalments which have fallen due and remain unpaid
(5) If the judgment creditor knows of the existence of any other creditors of the judgment debtor, their names and (if known) their addresses
(6) Identification of the asset or assets which it is intended to charge including, where applicable, the title number under which any land upon which it is sought to impose a charge is registered
(7) Details of the judgment debtor's interest in the asset, and
(8) The names and addresses of the persons on whom an interim charging order must be served.

Where an application for a charging order is made to the County Court Money Claims Centre for a charging order on the judgment debtor's interest in land, the application will initially be dealt with without a hearing; the judge may make an interim charging order, the effect of which will be to impose a charge over the judgment debtor's interest in the land to which the application relates.

The court may at this stage consider it appropriate to transfer the application to the judgment debtor's home court for the fixing of a hearing to consider whether to make a final charging order. If this is done the court will serve upon all persons concerned including the judgment debtor (see the following for full list), the notice of the hearing together with the interim charging order, the application notice, and any documents filed in support of it on the judgment creditor, within 21 days of the interim order being made.

The persons to be served with the interim charging order are:

- The judgment debtor
- If the order relates to an interest in land, any co-owner
- The judgment debtor's spouse or civil partner (if known)
- Such other creditors as are identified in the application notice or as the court directs
- If the order relates to an interest under a trust, on such of the trustees as the court directs.

The interim order should at this stage be registered against the land in question and if at the final hearing of the application for the charging order such an order is made, that too should be registered.

In using its discretion to grant a charging order, the court will consider the position of others including other creditors of the judgment debtor, any trustees of the land and any others with beneficial entitlements to the property in question.

12.5.3.2 Enforcement of charging order by sale

Rule 73.10C allows a judgment creditor to commence proceedings to enforce the sale of the land against which the charging order attaches. The County Court has jurisdiction to determine a claim for the enforcement of a charging order if the amount owing under the charge does not exceed the County Court limit, currently £5,000. Otherwise, the application should be directed to the High Court Chancery Division. In either case, the application for an order for sale should be made by commencing a Part 8 claim.

A copy of the charging order must be filed with the claim form. Once the application has been considered, the court may then order the sale of the property to enforce the charging order.

Making an order for sale is a draconian measure and the decision is not taken lightly by the court as the effect of sale proceedings may well cause the judgment debtor and his/her family to be rendered homeless.

12.5.4 An attachment of earnings order

An attachment of earnings order is appropriate where the judgment creditor knows that the judgment debtor is employed and the identity of the employer. Such an order if granted requires the judgment debtor's employer to make regular deductions from the judgment debtor's earnings and pay them into court. The regime for this method of enforcement is governed by the Attachment of Earnings Act 1971 and the High Court has no jurisdiction for such applications. If therefore judgment was obtained in the High Court, the proceedings will have to be transferred to the County Court in order for this method of enforcement to be pursued.

12.5.4.1 Procedure

The procedure for an application for a charging order is to be found in Rule 89. An application for an attachment of earnings order must include a certificate of the amount of money remaining due under the judgment or order and that the whole or part of any instalment due remains unpaid.

An application for an attachment of earnings order must include a certificate of the amount of money remaining due under the judgment or order and that the whole or part of any instalment due remains unpaid.

The judgment creditor must complete prescribed Form N337 and together with this, the court must serve the judgment debtor with Form N56 (the 'reply form'). The notice of application must include an instruction to the debtor to complete and file the reply form within eight days after service, and that instruction constitutes a requirement under section 14(4) of the 1971 Act. Within eight days after service of the documents, the debtor must file a completed reply form and on receipt of a reply from the debtor, the court officer must send a copy of the reply to the creditor.

12.5.5 Insolvency

Strictly speaking, this is not a method of enforcement. However, the threat of insolvency can often be the incentive needed for the judgment debtor to honour the judgment debt.

12.5.6 Bankruptcy

If the debt is £5,000 or more, the judgment creditor might consider petitioning for bankruptcy, the first stage of which is for the judgment creditor to complete and serve a statutory demand on the judgment debtor using a prescribed form. After 21 days have elapsed, if the judgement debtor has still not paid the judgment debt, the judgment creditor may file a bankruptcy petition supported by an affidavit. The court will fix a date for the bankruptcy hearing, 14 days prior to which the judgment debtor should be served with the bankruptcy petition. At the hearing, the judgment creditor will be required to prove that the judgment debt remains outstanding, and if satisfied the court will then make the bankruptcy order, whereupon all the judgment debtor's assets will vest in the trustee in bankruptcy.

12.5.7 Winding up

If the judgment debtor is a company and if the debt is £750 or more, the judgment creditor might consider applying to the court for a winding-up petition against the company. If successful, the winding up petition will have the following effect:

- The company assets are sold
- Any legal disputes are settled
- The judgment creditor collects the money owed
- Funds are paid to the judgment creditor and any other creditors.

12.6 Enforcement of foreign judgments

There are a variety of provisions that enable the courts of England and Wales to recognise and enforce foreign judgments, including those under the Administration of Justice Act 1920, the Foreign Judgments (Reciprocal Enforcement) Act 1933, and the Civil Jurisdiction and Judgments Act 1982.

In the absence of any further agreement on jurisdiction and enforcement of judgments, it remains necessary to apply domestic law to enforce a judgment from a court of one of the member states of the European Union (EU) or one of the European Free Trade Association (EFTA) states (Iceland, Liechtenstein, Norway, and Switzerland) in England and Wales. This means that common law rules relating to recognition and enforcement of judgments apply:

- Where the originating jurisdictions do not have applicable treaties in place with the UK, or
- In the absence of any applicable UK statute.

Example

If a German citizen obtains judgment in Germany against a US citizen, the German citizen will be entitled to register the German judgment in England if the American defendant has assets in England. In these circumstances, the German court will have assumed jurisdiction because of the German nationality of the claimant

Part 74 deals with the procedure for the enforcement of foreign judgments, applications for which must be made to the High Court and may be made without notice. An application for registration of a judgment under the 1920, 1933, or 1982 Act (mentioned earlier) must be supported by written evidence exhibiting the following:

(1) The judgment or a verified or certified or otherwise authenticated copy of it, and
(2) Where the judgment is not in English, a translation of it into English:
    (a) Certified by a notary public or other qualified person, or
    (b) Accompanied by written evidence confirming that the translation is accurate.

The written evidence in support of the application must state the following:

(1) The name of the judgment creditor and his/her address for service within the jurisdiction
(2) The name of the judgment debtor and his address or place of business, if known
(3) The grounds on which the judgment creditor is entitled to enforce the judgment
(4) In the case of a money judgment, the amount in respect of which it remains unsatisfied, and
(5) Where interest is recoverable on the judgment under the law of the state of origin:
    (a) The amount of interest which has accrued up to the date of the application, or
    (b) The rate of interest, the date from which it is recoverable, and the date on which it ceases to accrue.

There are also specific requirements regarding written evidence in support of an application under the 1920 Act and 1982 Acts (see r 74.4).

12.6.1 Registering a foreign judgment

An order granting permission to register a judgment ('a registration order') must be drawn up by the judgment creditor and served on the judgment debtor. The judgment debtor may be served with the registration order out of the jurisdiction without the permission of the court.

A registration order must state the following:

(1) The full particulars of the judgment registered
(2) The name of the judgment creditor and his/her address for service within the jurisdiction
(3) The right of the judgment debtor:
  (a) In the case of registration following an application under the 1920 or the 1933 Act, to apply to have the registration set aside
  (b) In the case of registration following an application under the 1982 Act, to appeal against the registration order
(5) The period within which such an application or appeal may be made, and
(6) That no measures of enforcement will be taken before the end of that period, other than measures ordered by the court to preserve the property of the judgment debtor.

Chapter 12 revision points

Enforcement

- Choice of enforcement process – obtaining information from the judgment debtor:
  - Order to obtain information – application procedure
  - The information hearing – questioning the judgment debtor
- Interest on judgment debts:
  - County Court – current rate is 8 per cent
  - High Court – current rate is 8 per ceent
- Methods of enforcement:
  - Taking control of goods – County Court (warrant of control), High Court (writ of control)
  - Third-party debt order
  - Attachment of earnings
  - Insolvency, bankruptcy, and winding up
- Enforcement of foreign judgments
  - Recognition and enforcement provisions
  - Application process and supportive evidence
  - Registering a foreign judgment

Multiple-choice questions for Part 6

1. When preparing a case for trial the case summary, also known as the skeleton argument, will include details of those issues not in dispute as well as the arguments which the parties propose to advance about those matters remaining in dispute; it should include a number of other important matters to assist the trial judge.

*Which one of the following is **not best** included in a case summary when preparing the case for trial?*

A. A concise summary of the propositions of law relied upon (case law and statute).
B. An indication as to which documents the judge should try to read prior to trial.
C. A concise summary of the costs incurred in the case and an estimate of those to be incurred.
D. Numbered paragraphs and pagination (page numbers).
E. A concise review of each party's submissions of fact with reference to the evidence.

2. You represent a defendant insurer in a personal injury claim in the High Court. At trial, the judge refused to allow the evidence of a witness due to procedural irregularities. The judge ruled against the defendant and the claimant was awarded a large sum in damages and costs. The defendant believes that had the judge allowed the evidence, which was ruled out, the outcome of the trial would have been different.

*Which one of the following **best** explains what now can be done procedurally?*

A. There are grounds for appeal to the King's Bench Divisional Court on the basis that the decision of the judge in ruling out the defendant's evidence was unjust because of a serious procedural irregularity.
B. There are grounds for appeal to the Court of Appeal as the decision of the judge in ruling out the defendant's evidence was unjust because of a serious procedural irregularity.
C. There are no grounds for appeal as the judge's decision was not unjust because there was no procedural irregularity.
D. There are grounds for a leapfrog appeal to the Supreme Court due to a particular and specific point of law concerning the judge's ruling about the defendant's evidence.
E. There are no grounds for appeal as the judge's decision was not unjust because there was no error in law.

3. A is an electrical wholesaler who is owed £10,250 by B for electrical goods which he supplied to B (a sole trader) at B's request. The various invoices are now at least 90 days overdue and some substantially more than this. Despite constant promises to settle the debt, B has failed to pay a penny. B is in financial difficulty, there has been a downturn in his business, and he is currently trading at a loss, but awaiting a payment of about £12,500 from C, a regular customer. A is unaware of B's precarious financial position but commences proceedings and obtains judgment in default for the full amount of the debt together with interest and costs to be paid within 28 days.

*Which one of the following **best** explains the steps that A should take if B has not paid the judgment debt within the prescribed time period?*

A. A should enforce the judgment debt by using a warrant of execution to seize goods to the value of the judgment debt.
B. A should enforce the judgment debt by applying for an attachment of earnings order.
C. A should enforce the judgment debt by applying for a charging order over B's property.
D. A should apply for B to be made bankrupt.
E. A should enforce the judgment debt by applying for a third-party debt order.

PART 7

Procedures and processes relevant to costs involved in dispute resolution

13 Costs

13.1 Chapter overview

In this final chapter, we will look at costs, the indemnity principle, and the importance of costs management and budgeting, before considering the basis of assessment and the inter-partes costs orders that can be made, both interim before trial, and the final costs orders that the judge will make at trial.

The chapter will also look at the principle of qualified one-way costs shifting, which is applicable to claims involving damages arising from personal injury or death, and what this means. The chapter will also take a somewhat detailed look at the possible costs consequences of Part 36 offers, before considering the procedure for applying for an order for security for costs.

13.2 Introduction: costs

Where litigation costs are concerned, it is important to note that there is a distinction between solicitor and client costs, and the costs that may be awarded between the parties as a result of litigation. Rule 44.3(2)(a) CPR 1998 provides that as a general rule the unsuccessful party will pay the successful party's cost of the proceedings, but only an amount in costs that the successful party is liable to pay to his or her legal representatives (this is known as the indemnity principle). The court will often be required to assess what is reasonable (unless the parties can reach an agreement) and it is usual that the successful party will never recover all of the costs it has incurred with its solicitor. The unsuccessful party will therefore only have to pay the successful party what the court considers to be reasonable or what has been agreed between the parties.

Rule 44.1(1)(iv) defines 'costs' as including fees, charges, disbursements, expenses, remuneration, reimbursement allowed to a litigant in person, and any fee or reward charged by a lay representative for acting on behalf of a party in proceedings allocated to the small-claims track.

When considering the question of costs associated with litigation, it is worth being reminded of the overriding objective which requires the parties and their legal representatives to ensure that they deal with a case justly and at proportionate cost.

DOI: 10.4324/9781003218500-20

Part 44 provides the general rules about costs and when awarding costs, the court will apply its discretion under r 44.2 as to:

(1) Whether costs are payable by one party to another
(2) The amount of those costs, and
(3) When they are to be paid.

When making an order for costs, the general rule is that the unsuccessful party will be ordered to pay the costs of the successful party, but the court has the power to make a different order. In exercising its discretion and deciding what order (if any) to make about costs, the court will have regard to all the circumstances, which include:

(1) The conduct of all the parties
(2) Whether a party has succeeded on part of its case, even if that party has not been wholly successful, and
(3) Any admissible offer to settle made by a party which is drawn to the court's attention, and which is not an offer to which costs consequences under Part 36 apply.

The conduct of the parties includes conduct before, as well as during, the proceedings and in particular the extent to which the parties followed the Practice Direction – Pre-Action Conduct or any relevant pre-action protocol. The court will also consider the following:

(1) Whether it was reasonable for a party to raise, pursue, or contest a particular allegation or issue
(2) The manner in which a party has pursued or defended its case or a particular allegation or issue, and
(3) Whether a claimant who has succeeded in the claim, in whole or in part, exaggerated its claim.

The court has a range of options when making a costs order. The orders that the court may make include an order that a party must pay:

(1) A proportion of another party's costs
(2) A stated amount in respect of another party's costs
(3) Costs from or until a certain date only
(4) Costs incurred before proceedings have begun
(5) Costs relating to particular steps taken in the proceedings
(6) Costs relating only to a distinct part of the proceedings, and
(7) Interest on costs from or until a certain date, including a date before judgment.

Where the court orders a party to pay costs subject to detailed assessment, it will order that party to pay a reasonable sum on account of costs, unless there is good reason not to do so.

13.3 Costs management and budgeting

Costs management forms part of the court's case management responsibilities which includes the power to influence and control the future costs of a case. The court is therefore able to manage both the steps to be taken and the costs to be incurred by the parties to any proceedings in furtherance of the overriding objective. This is assisted by the parties providing costs budgets.

13.3.1 Costs budgets

Rule 3.12(1) limits costs management to all multi-track cases commenced after 22 April 2014, where the amount of money claimed is less than £10 million. The requirements for filing and exchanging budgets and budget discussion reports are dealt with by the court's general case management powers under r 3.13, and provide that unless the court otherwise orders, all parties except litigants in person must file and exchange costs budgets in the following circumstances:

(1) Where the stated value of the claim on the claim form is less than £50,000, with their directions questionnaires, or
(2) In any other case, not later than 21 days before the first case management conference.

In the event that a party files and exchanges a costs budget, all other parties (who are not litigants in person), must file an agreed budget discussion report no later than seven days before the first case management conference.

13.3.1.1 Contents of the costs budget

Unless the court otherwise orders, a costs budget must be in the form of Precedent H annexed to Practice Direction 3E (see example in Figure 13.1). It must be in landscape format with an easily legible typeface. In cases where a party's total costs (incurred and estimated) do not exceed £25,000 or the value of the claim as stated on the claim form is less than £50,000, the parties must only use the first page of Precedent H.

As will be seen in Figure 13.1, the budget should provide a detailed breakdown of the costs and disbursements (those litigation expenses other than costs) already incurred in the case both pre-action and those associated with the issue of proceeding, as well as an estimate of the future costs to be incurred associated with the phases of litigation, including the case management conference, disclosure, exchange of witness statements/experts' reports, any pre-trial review, trial preparation, and the trial itself as well as any costs that may be incurred if ADR or settlement discussions are attempted.

The 'contingent cost' sections of form H should be used for anticipated costs which do not fall within the main categories set out in the form. Examples might be the trial of

Costs budget of [Claimant / Defendant] dated [ ] page 1

In the:	to be completed
Parties:	to be completed
Claim number:	to be completed

Work done / to be done	Incurred		Estimated		Total (£)
	Disbs (£)	Time costs (£)	Disbs (£)	Time costs (£)	
Pre-action costs	£0.00	£0.00			£0.00
Issue / statements of case	£0.00	£0.00	£0.00	£0.00	£0.00
CMC	£0.00	£0.00	£0.00	£0.00	£0.00
Disclosure	£0.00	£0.00	£0.00	£0.00	£0.00
Witness statements	£0.00	£0.00	£0.00	£0.00	£0.00
Expert reports	£0.00	£0.00	£0.00	£0.00	£0.00
PTR			£0.00	£0.00	£0.00
Trial preparation			£0.00	£0.00	£0.00
Trial			£0.00	£0.00	£0.00
ADR / Settlement discussions	£0.00	£0.00	£0.00	£0.00	£0.00
Contingent cost A: [explanation]			£0.00	£0.00	£0.00
Contingent cost B: [explanation]			£0.00	£0.00	£0.00
GRAND TOTAL (including both incurred costs and estimated costs)	£0.00	£0.00	£0.00	£0.00	**£0.00**

This estimate excludes VAT (if applicable), success fees and ATE insurance premiums (if applicable), costs of detailed assessment, costs of any appeals, costs of enforcing any judgment and [complete as appropriate]

Approved budget		£ -
Budget drafting	*1% of approved budget or £1,000*	£ -
Budget process	2%	£ -

Statement of Truth dated

This budget is a fair and accurate statement of incurred and estimated costs which it would be reasonable and proportionate for my client to incur in this litigation.

Signed

Position

Figure 13.1 Precedent H – costs budget.

preliminary issues, applications to amend, and applications for disclosure against third parties. Costs which are disputed (such as the need for a particular expert) should be set out in the appropriate phase of the budget and if necessary, marked as disputed. Only costs which are more likely than not to be incurred should be included.

13.3.1.2 Contents of the costs budget discussion report

Once the costs budget reports have been exchanged, the parties should complete a budget discussion report in the form of Precedent R (see example in Figure 13.2) and as mentioned earlier, this should be done no later than seven days before the first case management conference.

A budget discussion report must set out the following:

(1) Those figures which are agreed upon for each phase
(2) Those figures which are not agreed upon for each phase, and
(3) A brief summary of the grounds of dispute.

The final columns are for the judge to complete with details of the order made on budgeted costs and disbursements and any comments he/she wishes to make on the amounts allowed.

13.3.2 Costs management orders

Whilst the parties are encouraged to agree on their costs management reports where possible, if there is no agreement, the court will be required to exercise its case management powers. When reviewing budgeted costs, the court will not undertake a detailed assessment in advance, but rather will consider whether the budgeted costs fall within the range of reasonable and proportionate costs. The court may not therefore approve any costs incurred before the date of any budget, but may record its comments on those costs, and will take into account those costs when considering the reasonableness and proportionality of all subsequent costs.

If the court does not make a costs management order, Practice Direction 44, para 3.2 to 3.7 provide guidance in such a situation. If for instance there is a difference of 20 per cent or more between the costs claimed by a receiving party on detailed assessment and the costs shown in a budget filed by that party, the receiving party must provide a statement of the reasons for the difference with the bill of costs. The court may regard the difference between the costs claimed and the costs shown in the budget to be unreasonable or disproportionate, in which case the court will consider that the receiving party has not provided a satisfactory explanation for that difference and not allow the claim for the difference.

Furthermore, if the paying party claims to have reasonably relied on a budget filed by a receiving party or wishes to rely upon the costs shown in the budget in order to dispute the reasonableness or proportionality of the costs claimed, the paying party

Precedent R : Budget discussion report.								Budgeted costs for : C/D/etc			
Party:	C/D etc			X				CCMC Date	xx/xx/xxxx		
Court:	Name			Y							
Case Number	Number			Z							
	Incurred costs	Budgeted costs : claimed			Budgeted costs : offered			Paying party comments on offers made	Order	Judge's comments / sums allowed	
Phase		Claimed	Time £	Disbs £	Offered	Time £	Disbs £		Budgeted costs	Judge Time (hours)	Judge Disbs
Pre action costs	£0.00	na	na	na	na	na	na	na			
Issue / stm of case	£0.00	£0.00			£0.00				£0.00		
CMC	£0.00	£0.00			£0.00				£0.00		
Disclosure	£0.00	£0.00			£0.00				£0.00		
Witness stms	£0.00	£0.00			£0.00				£0.00		
Experts reports	£0.00	£0.00			£0.00				£0.00		
PTR	na	£0.00			£0.00				£0.00		
Trial preparation	na	£0.00			£0.00				£0.00		
Trial	na	£0.00			£0.00				£0.00		
ADR		£0.00			£0.00				£0.00		
A:	na	£0.00			£0.00				£0.00		
B:	na	£0.00			£0.00				£0.00		
Total budgeted costs	Incurred £0.00	Claimed £0.00	Time £ £0.00	Disbs £ £0.00	Offered £0.00	Time £ £0.00	Disbs £ £0.00		Budgeted £0.00		

	Claimed	Total of budgeted and incurred costs	Offered
Incurred	£0.00		£0.00
Budgeted costs claimed	£0.00		£0.00
GT	£0.00		£0.00

Post CCMC costs summary	
Incurred	£0.00
Budgeted sum ordered	£0.00
GT	£0.00

Figure 13.2 Precedent R – costs budget discussion report.

must serve a statement setting out the case regarding that party's points of dispute. Where the court considers that the paying party reasonably relied upon the budget, the court may restrict the amount of costs to those which are considered reasonable and notwithstanding that such sum is less than the amount of costs reasonably and proportionately incurred by the receiving party.

13.4 Basis of assessment

Rule 44.3(1) provides that where the court is to assess the amount of costs (whether by summary or detailed assessment) it will assess those costs on either the standard basis or on the indemnity basis, but the court will not in either case allow costs which have been unreasonably incurred or are unreasonable in amount. Under r 44.4(3), the court will also have regard for the following key factors:

(1) the conduct of all the parties, including in particular conduct before, as well as during, the proceedings; and the efforts made, if any, before and during the proceedings in order to try to resolve the dispute;
(2) the amount or value of any money or property involved;
(3) the importance of the matter to all the parties;
(4) the particular complexity of the matter or the difficulty or novelty of the questions raised;
(5) the skill, effort, specialised knowledge and responsibility involved;
(6) the time spent on the case;
(7) the place where and the circumstances in which work or any part of it was done; and,
(8) the receiving party's last approved or agreed budget.

13.4.1 The standard basis

This is the basis of assessment which is used unless the court orders otherwise. Where the court assesses costs on a standard basis, it will only allow costs which are proportionate to the matters in issue. Costs which are disproportionate in amount may be disallowed or reduced even if they were reasonably or necessarily incurred, and to resolve any doubt which it may have as to whether costs were reasonably and proportionately incurred or were reasonable and proportionate in amount, the court will make an order favourable to the paying party.

Under para 6.2 of PD 44, if costs are awarded on the standard basis, the court assessing those costs will disallow any costs:

(1) which it finds to have been unreasonably incurred;
(2) which it considers to be unreasonable in amount;
(3) which it considers to have been disproportionately incurred or to be disproportionate in amount, or
(4) about which it has doubts as to whether they were reasonably or proportionately incurred, or whether they are reasonable and proportionate in amount.

13.4.2 The indemnity basis

The court will only consider making an order for costs on an indemnity basis to mark its disapproval of a party's behaviour in relation to its involvement in litigation, an example of which might be where there has been consistent non-compliance with a court order by one party.

The court will make an award of costs that is greater than that usually awarded as standard and in doing so, will in effect be imposing a penalty on the paying party. Where the amount of costs is to be assessed on the indemnity basis, the court will resolve any doubt which it may have as to whether costs were reasonably incurred or were reasonable in amount in favour of the receiving party.

Where the court makes an order for costs on the indemnity basis, it will want to be sure that:

(1) The costs were reasonably incurred
(2) The costs were reasonable in amount.

Whether considering costs on either a standard or an indemnity basis, the court will want to be sure that the costs incurred are proportionate. The test for this as applied under r 44.3(5) will be whether the costs involved bear a reasonable relationship to the following matters:

(1) the sums in issue in the proceedings;
(2) the value of any non-monetary relief in issue in the proceedings;
(3) the complexity of the litigation;
(4) any additional work generated by the conduct of the paying party;
(5) any wider factors involved in the proceedings, such as reputation or public importance; and
(6) any additional work undertaken, or expense incurred due to the vulnerability of a party or any witness.

The main difference between the two bases of costs is that costs awarded on a standard basis will only be those which the court considers to have been reasonably incurred and are proportionate to the matters associated with the case. A case therefore where a legal representative's bill of costs amounts to some £100,000 in a fast-track case where the monetary value of the claim is only £15,000 is likely to be considered disproportionate.

13.5 Inter-partes costs orders (interim and final)

13.5.1 Interim inter-partes costs orders

There are certain costs orders that the court will commonly make in proceedings before trial. See Chapter 7 for the range of these costs orders, which are also displayed in tabular format in Chapter 7 setting out the general effect of these orders. The table is not an exhaustive list of the orders that the court may make, however.

13.5.2 Final costs orders

The judgment delivered by the judge will also deal with the question of costs. Where the court orders one party to pay the other party's costs (usually the winner will be awarded costs at trial), the court will either make a summary assessment of the costs there and then, or the judge may order that the costs be dealt with at a separate detailed assessment hearing to take place at a later date.

When making a final order for costs, the court will exercise its discretion and take into account a number of factors when deciding the amount payable. As a general rule, the party who has been unsuccessful at trial will be ordered to pay the winning party's costs, although the amount of those costs will depend on a number of factors, including whether the costs being claimed are considered reasonable and proportionate to the value of the claim and the extent to which the party ordered costs has won (for instance, there may be parts of the case in which the winning party was unsuccessful).

13.6 Non-party costs

It is possible for the court to make costs orders in favour of or against non-parties and rule 46 deals with this; in particular, r 46 2(1) states that where the court is considering whether to exercise its costs discretion, it may make a costs order in favour of or against a person who is not a party to proceedings. In those circumstances it must do the following:

(a) Ensure that the person is added as a party to the proceedings for the purposes of costs only, and
(b) Ensure that the person added must be given a reasonable opportunity to attend a hearing at which the court will consider the matter further.

13.7 Qualified one-way costs shifting

Qualified one-way costs shifting is a process that applies to claims involving those for damages arising from personal injury or death. It was introduced in April 2013 to deal with the situation where a claimant has been successful overall (perhaps at trial), but the defendant is entitled to recover some of its costs due to an interim costs order having been made in his/her favour, perhaps as a result of the claimant having failed to beat the defendant's Part 36 offer.

In these circumstances, r 44.14(1) provides that orders for costs made against a claimant may be enforced without the permission of the court but only to the extent that the aggregate amount in money terms of such orders does not exceed the aggregate amount in money terms of any orders for damages and interest made in favour of the claimant. Orders for costs made against a claimant may only be enforced after the proceedings have been concluded and the costs have been assessed or agreed upon.

Orders for costs made against the claimant may be enforced to the full extent of such orders without the permission of the court where the proceedings have been struck out on the following grounds:

(1) The claimant has disclosed no reasonable grounds for bringing the proceedings
(2) The proceedings are an abuse of the court's process, or
(3) The conduct of the claimant or a person acting on the claimant's behalf and with the claimant's knowledge of such conduct.

The court's permission will, however, be required for orders for costs made against the claimant where the claim is found, on the balance of probabilities, to be fundamentally dishonest.

13.8 Part 36 and other offers

We saw in Chapter 5 that an offer to settle made pursuant to CPR Part 36 is often considered to be a tactical step that arguably favours the defendant. This is because such an offer can put pressure on the claimant to accept it because they know that failure to do so, may give rise to an adverse costs order if at trial the claimant is awarded an amount less than or equal to the offer made by the defendant. The costs consequences following judgment are dealt with by Rule 36.17.

13.8.1 Costs consequences of acceptance of a Part 36 offer

The costs consequences will depend on when the Part 36 offer was accepted or the outcome of the trial, i.e., the amount of damages awarded by the judge if the claimant is successful.

13.8.1.1 Acceptance within the relevant period

Where a Part 36 offer is accepted within the relevant period (21 days after the Part 36 offer was made), the claimant will be entitled to the costs of the proceedings (including their recoverable pre-action costs) up to the date on which notice of acceptance was served on the defendant.

Where a defendant's Part 36 offer relates to part only of the claim, and at the time of serving notice of acceptance within the relevant period the claimant abandons the balance of the claim, the claimant will only be entitled to the costs of such part of the claim unless the court orders otherwise.

Where the claimant's Part 36 offer is accepted by the defendant within the relevant period, the claimant is entitled to his/her costs of the proceedings up to the date on which notice of acceptance is served on the claimant.

13.8.1.2 Acceptance outside the relevant period (late acceptance)

If the claimant accepts the defendant's Part 36 offer late, i.e., after the expiry of the relevant period as specified in the offer, and the parties cannot come to an agreement over payment of costs, the court will make an order for costs and unless it considers it unjust to do so, must order that:

(1) The claimant be awarded costs up to the date on which the relevant period expired, and
(2) The claimant be ordered to pay the defendant's costs for the period from the date of expiry of the relevant period to the date of acceptance.

Where the claimant's Part 36 offer is accepted late by the defendant, if the parties cannot reach an agreement on the payment of coats, then the court will usually order that the defendant pay the claimant's costs of the proceedings up to the date when the offer was accepted.

Where a claimant accepts the defendant's offer late, the court will require the claimant to pay the defendant's costs on a standard basis from the date when the relevant period expired up to the date of late acceptance. This is a form of punishment or 'costs penalty' imposed on the claimant for accepting the offer late.

If the claimant's behaviour in accepting the defendant's offer late was considered to be unreasonable, then the court may order the claimant to pay the defendant's costs incurred between the expiry of the relevant period and acceptance on an indemnity basis. Failure on the part of the claimant to adequately explain the reason for the late acceptance of the part 36 offer might be considered sufficiently unreasonable conduct.

13.8.1.3 Costs consequences at trial – defendant's offer

If at trial (or perhaps earlier by way of a successful summary judgment application) the claimant obtains a judgment that is more advantageous than the defendant's Part 36 offer, it will be considered justifiable that the claimant did not accept the offer. In those circumstances, the defendant will be required to pay the amount of the judgment and will also be ordered to pay the claimant's costs on a standard basis (see earlier). Interest is also payable on those costs from the date of the judgment.

If the claimant fails to obtain a judgment that is more advantageous than the defendant's Part 36 offer, the court will consider making what is known as a 'split costs' order under r 36.17(3). This is in effect punishment for the claimant having failed to secure a better outcome at trial than the earlier Part 36 offer made by the defendant. An illustration of the possible costs consequences of a claimant failing to beat the defendant's Part 36 offer in tabular format is provided in the case of *Bray v Squeers* in Chapter 5.

13.8.1.4 Split costs order explained

Under r 36.17(3) the court must, unless it considers it unjust to do so, order that the defendant is entitled to the following;

(a) Costs (including any recoverable pre-action costs) from the date on which the relevant period expired (usually 21 days), and
(b) Interest on those costs.

The defendant pays the claimant's costs incurred up to the expiry of the relevant period (usually 21 days after the offer was made) together with interest. The claimant will usually be ordered to pay the defendant's costs from the expiry of the relevant period until judgment on a standard basis. In addition, the claimant will be required to pay interest on those costs.

13.8.1.5 Costs consequences at trial – claimant's offer

If at trial (or perhaps earlier by way of a successful summary judgment application) the claimant does not beat the Part 36 offer he/she proposed, there is no specific penalty.

If the claimant obtains a judgment against the defendant that is at least as advantageous to the claimant as the proposals contained in his/her Part 36 offer, then the court must order that the claimant, unless it considers it unjust to do so, is entitled to the following;

(a) Interest on the whole or part of any sum of money (excluding interest) awarded, at a rate not exceeding 10 per cent above the base rate for some or all of the period starting with the date on which the relevant period expired
(b) Costs (including any recoverable pre-action costs) on the indemnity basis from the date on which the relevant period expired
(c) Interest on those costs at a rate not exceeding 10 per cent above the base rate, and
(d) An additional amount, which shall not exceed £75,000, calculated by applying the prescribed percentage set out in Table 13.1 to an amount which is:
    (i) The sum awarded to the claimant by the court, or
    (ii) Where there is no monetary award, the sum awarded to the claimant by the court in respect of costs.

Table 13.1 Additional amount awarded to the claimant if the claimant beats the defendant's Part 36 offer

Amount awarded by the court	Prescribed percentage
Up to £500,000	10% of the amount awarded
Above £500,000	10% of the first £500,000 and (subject to the limit of £75,000) 5% of any amount above that figure

13.8.1.6 Costs consequences if the claimant loses at trial

If say at trial the claimant loses, in other words, he/she does not establish liability (in a personal injury claim for example) and is not awarded a sum of money after the defendant has made a Part 36 offer, the normal court order as to costs would be for the claimant (as the loser) to pay the defendant's costs from the date when those costs were first incurred by the defendant to judgment. Interest would normally be payable on those costs only from the date of judgment. However, in such circumstances, the provisions of r 36 17(3) would arguably apply, in other words, the claimant could be required to pay interest on the defendant's costs from the expiry of the relevant period of acceptance of that offer. See Chapter 5 for a workable illustration of the situation where the claimant is awarded less at trial than the part 36 offer made by the defendant.

Also mentioned in Chapter 5 was the fact that the Part 36 mechanism is often used as a tactical step, particularly by the defendant who in a personal injury claim, for example, considers themselves to be at risk of liability. By making a Part 36 offer as part of negotiations towards the settlement of the claim, the defendant can apply pressure on the claimant to accept the offer due to the costs consequences that apply. Tactically, the offer should be carefully pitched, and care has to be taken as to the amount of the offer and also the timing of it; the earlier the Part 36 offer is made, the greater the costs consequences will be if the case proceeds to trial many months down the line.

13.9 Security for costs

Because the costs associated with litigation can be considerable and there is a chance that the defendant will defeat the claimant's claim, the defendant can ask the court to provide security for its costs. Rule 25.12 provides that a defendant to any claim may apply for security for his costs of the proceedings. The defendant court can ask the court to exercise its discretion to require the claimant to provide security for the costs that the defendant is likely to be awarded if he/she defeats the claim.

An application for security for costs can be made by the defendant under r 25.12(1) and must be supported by written evidence. When the court makes an order for security for costs, it will determine the amount of security and direct the manner in which, and the time within which, the security must be given.

13.9.1 Conditions to be satisfied

The court may make an order for security for costs under r 25.12 if the following conditions are satisfied:

(a) having regard to all the circumstances of the case, that it is just to make such an order; and,
(b) the claimant is either resident out of the jurisdiction; but not resident in a State bound by the 2005 Hague Convention, or an enactment permits the court to require security for costs;

(c) the claimant is a company or other body (whether incorporated inside or outside Great Britain) and there is reason to believe that it will be unable to pay the defendant's costs if ordered to do so;
(d) the claimant has changed his/her address since the claim was commenced with a view to evading the consequences of the litigation;
(e) the claimant failed to give his address in the claim form, or gave an incorrect address in that form;
(f) the claimant is acting as a nominal claimant, other than as a representative claimant under Part 19, and there is reason to believe that he will be unable to pay the defendant's costs if ordered to do so;
(g) the claimant has taken steps in relation to his assets that would make it difficult to enforce an order for costs against him/her.

13.9.2 The court's discretion factors

The court takes the following into account when considering an application for security of costs from a defendant.

13.9.2.1 The strength of the defence

The court will consider the claimant's likely prospects of success at trial. If the court considers on the basis of information available that the defendant has less than a reasonable chance of successfully defeating the claim, then it is likely that no order for security will be made. For instance, a Part 36 offer to settle the claim made by the defendant may undermine its application for security for costs.

13.9.2.2 The claimant's ability to provide security

The balance has to be struck between the claimant's right to pursue its claim and the unfairness of the defendant in enabling the claimant to do so without requiring the claimant to provide security for its costs. In this case, the European Conventions article 6(1) right of a fair trial may be breached if making an order will mean that the claimant cannot meet its obligations under the terms of the court order.

13.9.3 Procedure

Delay in applying for an order for security for costs may prejudice the defendant's application; it is therefore important that such an application be made as soon as practicable. Otherwise, an application can be made at any time during the lifetime of a case, and it would be wise for the defendant to indicate to the court that it intends to make such an interim application on the directions questionnaire (see Chapter 6). As indicated earlier, the application should be supported by a witness statement which should have three objectives:

(a) Establish that a condition exists
(b) Persuade the court that it should use its discretion to make an order in favour of the defendant, and
(c) Justify the amount of the security sought.

The application will often include the amount already incurred in costs and an estimate of future costs to a certain date provided in a costs budget (see Chapter 6).

If the court grants the application, it will specify in the order the following matters:

(a) The amount of the security
(b) The date by which the claimant must provide it, and
(c) The form it is to take.

The court will usually require the claimant to make a payment into court to the value of the security ordered.

13.10 Fixed and assessed costs

13.10.1 Fixed costs

In certain circumstances, the court may award fixed costs rather than making one of the orders set out in the table displayed in Chapter 7. Part 45 CPR provides guidance on the circumstances and situations where fixed costs can be awarded, and the amount allowed for the receiving party.

13.10.2 Summary assessment

In Chapter 7 we considered the situation where the court makes an order in favour of one of the parties, whereupon the court will make a summary assessment at that stage of the proceedings of the costs of the party in whose favour the costs have been awarded.

Chapter 13 revision points

Costs

- Costs – are fees, charges, disbursements, expenses, and remuneration
- The general rule – the unsuccessful party will be ordered to pay the costs of the successful party
- The indemnity principle – the unsuccessful party will pay the successful party's cost of the proceedings, but only an amount in costs that the successful party is liable to pay to his or her legal representatives
- Basis of assessment:
  - Standard basis – costs allowed which are proportionate to the matters in issue
  - Indemnity basis – costs allowed as a mark court's disapproval of a party's behaviour in relation to its involvement in litigation
- Inter-partes costs orders:
  - Interim – orders which the court will commonly make in proceedings before trial

    - Final – the trial judge orders one party to pay the other party's costs (usually the winner will be awarded costs at trial)
- Qualified one-way costs shifting:
    - Claims involving those for damages arising from personal injury or death
    - Where a claimant has been successful overall, but the defendant is entitled to recover some of its costs due to an interim costs order
- Part 36 and other offers and costs consequences:
    - Acceptance within the relevant period
    - Late acceptance
    - Costs consequences at trial of defendant's offer
    - Split costs orders
    - Costs consequences at trial of claimant's offer
    - Costs consequences if the claimant loses at trial
- Security for costs:
    - Conditions – the seven conditions required for the court to be satisfied
    - Court's discretion factors – strength of the defence and claimant's ability to provide security
    - Procedure – prompt application required

Multiple-choice questions for Part 7

1. There are particular rules and principles that apply to the payment and recovery of costs upon conclusion of litigation.

*Which one of the following **best** explains the indemnity principle?*

A. The unsuccessful party will never be required to pay the successful party's cost of the proceedings, but only those of his or her legal representatives.
B. The unsuccessful party will always be required to pay the successful party's costs of the proceedings, regardless of whether they were incurred unreasonably by his or her legal representatives.
C. The unsuccessful party will pay the successful party's cost of the proceedings, but only an amount in costs that the successful party is liable to pay to his or her legal representatives.
D. The unsuccessful party will be required to pay only those costs that the successful party can show are reasonable compared to the value of the claim.
E. The unsuccessful party of limited means can claim relief from paying all costs incurred unreasonably by the successful party.

2. In a high-value commercial dispute, where the defendant lost at trial after failing to accept the proposed claimant's invitation to engage in either negotiation or mediation during the pre-action protocol period or afterwards, the judge will be able to make an order for costs on an indemnity basis.

*Which one of the following **best** explains the circumstances in which the court will consider making an order for costs on an indemnity basis?*

A. Where a party has acted unreasonably during the course of litigation, but not during the pre-action protocol procedure, the court can mark its disapproval of that party's behaviour by making a costs order on an indemnity basis, and in doing so, those costs will be greater than that usually awarded.
B. It is always possible for the successful party at trial to ask the court to make an indemnity order for costs regardless of the unsuccessful party's conduct prior to or during the course of litigation.
C. Where at trial the unsuccessful party has failed to accept the invitation of the successful party to negotiate or refer the case to mediation, the court will never consider a request by the winning party to claim costs on an indemnity basis.
D. If a party has acted unreasonably by failing to settle the case early and later loses at trial, the court can express its displeasure by imposing an indemnity costs order on the losing party.
E. Where a party has acted unreasonably during the course of litigation the court can mark its disapproval of that party's behaviour by making a costs order on an indemnity basis, and in doing so, those costs will be greater than that usually awarded.

14 Answers to multiple-choice questions

14.1 Chapter overview

This chapter presents the answers to the multiple-choice questions at the end of each part of the book.

14.2 Part 1: Different options for dispute resolution

14.2.1 Question 1

The correct answer is B. As the matter relates to a civil dispute between the solicitor's client and a third party, the solicitor has an obligation under paragraph 2.02(1)(b) of the Solicitors Regulation Authority's (SRA) Code of Conduct to consider the options available to his client; he should discuss whether mediation or some other alternative dispute resolution (ADR) procedure may be more appropriate than litigation, arbitration, or other formal processes.

A is not correct as the N1 claim form, whilst the correct form to be used to commence proceedings for a remedy arising out of a civil wrong, should only be issued and served after a letter of claim has been written and potentially after any applicable pre-action protocol period has elapsed.

C is not correct. This would be the wrong advice because even if the solicitor had suggested ADR, there would be no reason to wait for the building work to start before applying for an injunction to prevent the neighbour from building the structure.

D is not correct. The issue raised by the solicitor's client concerns a civil wrong, the cause of action being founded in tort. As such this is a civil dispute and as it is unlikely that any criminal offence has been committed by the client's neighbour, the police will not wish to become involved.

E is not correct. Whilst the matter is urgent, the solicitor should only recommend this course of action after explaining to his client that there are other alternative dispute resolution options available other than litigation and the threat of court proceedings should only be made as a last resort. Blindly advising a client to ignore ADR and

DOI: 10.4324/9781003218500-21

threaten court proceedings not only goes against a solicitor's code of conduct, but also goes against the spirit of the 'overriding objective'.

14.3 Part 2: Pre-action considerations and steps

14.3.1 Question 1

The correct answer is C. The claimant must serve the claim form, with the particulars of the claim and supporting evidence within four months of the issue of the claim form. The problem is that the claimant's medical appointment is more than four months after the date when proceedings must be served. It is, however, possible to extend the time to serve the particulars of the claim with supportive medical evidence (once that medical report is available), under CPR Rule 7.6(1). The claimant may apply for an order extending the period for compliance with Rule 7.5 which sets out the rules concerning methods of service.

A is not correct. CPR Part 8 procedure is the wrong procedure to use here. Part 7 applies. In any event CPR Rule 8.6. deals with rules of general evidence.

B is not correct. Whilst the court has the power to dispense with service of the claim form under CPR Part 6.16, it may only do so in exceptional circumstances and these circumstances would not comply; this is hence not the correct way to proceed. The defendant will still need to receive the claim form and accompanying evidence in order to file and serve a defence.

D is not correct. Simply writing to the court is insufficient. A formal ex-parte application will have to be made.

E is not correct. There is nothing in the provisions of the Administration of Justice Act 1920 which enables the claimant to do this.

14.3.2 Question 2

The correct answer is B. The Hague Convention on Choice of Court Agreements provides a voluntary worldwide framework of rules on jurisdiction and the recognition and enforcement of judgments in civil and commercial matters. The provisions are incorporated into domestic law under the Private International Law (Implementation of Agreements) Act 2020. Under the Hague Convention, B can insist that the case be dealt with in the USA and if he makes an application to that effect will probably succeed in insisting that the claimant commence proceedings in the US courts.

A is not correct as A's claim is against an individual (B) and not B's company. It is therefore irrelevant that B has business interest in the UK and a registered office of a company he may be a director of there.

C is not correct. It does not matter that the parties do not have a governing law agreement and in any event such causes are more commonly found in trade agreements. As this is a claim founded in tort the parties will not have such an agreement.

D is not correct. Place of service does not decide jurisdiction. The reason provided in the answer to B above should be considered here.

E is not correct. This provision applies where at least one party is from an EU member state and concerns a cause of action arising in tort. The provision provides that the state where the tort was committed or where the harm/damage caused by the tortious action occurred, will be the best forum for the case to be heard. This would be relevant if at least one party were from an EU country, but as neither is, the provision is not the correct one for B to use for insisting that the case be dealt with in the USA.

14.4 Part 3: Commencing, responding to, or progressing a claim

14.4.1 Question 1

The correct answer is D. If A's claim exceeds £100,000, then it can be issued in the High Court, although it does not have to be. PD 7A, para 2.2, however, provides that claims for damages for personal injuries *can* be started in the High Court if the value of the claim is *£50,000* or more. As A's claim has been valued at a figure far in excess of £100,000, and therefore the value of the claim is £50,000 or more, this is the best reason for justifying commencing court proceedings in the High Court.

A does not provide the best reason for justifying choosing the High Court as the venue for issuing proceedings. Simply because the monetary value of A's claim is at least £100,000 does not mean that the claim cannot be issued in the County Court. Claims valued in excess of £100,000 do not have to be issued in the High Court but such claims can be if the claimant wishes.

B is not correct. Although it is often very difficult to place a monetary value on claims for personal injury without expert medical and other evidence to prove financial losses (special damages), a value must be placed on the claim and a figure included in the claim form so that venue can be justified.

C is not correct. A claim exceeding (or is likely to exceed) £25,000, is not a reason for issuing proceedings in the High Court. Indicating on the claim form that a claim is valued at £25,000 will likely mean that the case will be allocated to the multi-track.

E is not correct. Only claims for damages and loss arising from personal injury of a value of £50,000 or more can be issued in the High Court.

14.4.2 Question 2

The correct answer is E. The claim form can be issued even if the defendant's address is not known. The claimant will be required to make an application to the court under CPR Part 6 and the associated Practice Directions to dispense with the service of the claim form.

A is not correct because the claim form can still be issued by the court despite a valid address being included in the claim form.

B is not correct. Whilst CPR Part 6 can be used to request that the court allow you to dispense with service of the claim form, this cannot be done by then posting a notice of issue of proceedings against the defendant in the *Law Society Gazette*.

C is not correct. Whilst you can ask the court to return the claim to to you as the legal representative for service, unless you know the address of the defendant where service can take place, this would be pointless.

D is not correct. You cannot nominate a firm of solicitors to accept service of proceedings regardless of whether you may know the defendant's address.

14.4.3 Question 3

The correct answer is B. It is possible to apply to the court under CPR 19.1 to add or substitute a defendant to the proceedings and under r 19.1, any number of defendants may be joined as parties to the claim.

A is not correct because the claim form can still be issued by the court despite a valid address being included in the claim form.

C is not correct. It is not too late to include another party.

D is not correct. Whilst an order from the court will be required to add a party, the claimant should make the application, not the defendant.

E is not correct. The existing defendant does not have to agree to another party being added as a defendant.

14.4.4 Question 4

The correct answer is C. Leaving the claim form at the defendant's solicitor's office would not constitute a valid method of service.

A is not correct as personal service of the claim form constitutes a valid method of service.

B is not correct as sending the claim form first class post, by document exchange or other service which provides for delivery on the next business day is a valid method of service and constitutes a valid method of service.

D is not correct as sending the claim form via fax or other means of electronic communication is a valid method of service and constitutes a valid method of service.

E is not correct as it is possible to effect valid service of the claim form by using any method authorised by the court. and this constitutes a valid method of service.

14.4.5 Question 5

The correct answer is C. If the claim form was served by first-class post, the second day after it was posted, is considered to be the day of service, i.e., 6 February. The defendant will then have 14 days to acknowledge service indicating an intention to defend, i.e., 20 February. The defence must then be served no later than 14 days thereafter, i.e., by 6 March.

A is not correct. The acknowledgement of service must be served no later than 14 days after the claim form. And if an intention to defend is indicated, then the defence must be served no later than 28 days after deemed service.

B is not correct. Deemed service will not be determined by the fact that the defendant is a limited company (the defendant's entity is irrelevant). Service by first-class post on a limited company at its registered office will be the second day after it was posted; depending on when that is, the defendant will have 28 days in which to file and serve a defence if the claim is to be defended.

D is not correct. Deemed service is not considered to be the day of posting. If the claim form was served by first-class post, the second day after it was posted is considered to be the day of service.

E is not correct. Service of the claim form will be deemed to have taken place on 6 February (not 5 February), i.e., the second day after it was posted.

14.5 Part 4: Case management and any interim applications relevant to a claim

14.5.1 Question 1

The correct answer is E. The court can now serve a notice of proposed allocation requiring on the defendant B to file its directions questionnaire by a specified date, B's failure to do so will mean that the court can then serve a notice on B requiring compliance within seven days. If B then fails to comply with the notice served then its defence will be automatically struck out by the court. It is therefore a two-stage procedure before the draconian step of striking out can take place.

A is not correct. Whilst the court will take the initiative, this is not the correct procedural step as the court will first serve a notice of proposed allocation requiring the defendant B to file its directions questionnaire by a specified date.

B is not correct. The court cannot automatically strike out the defence at this stage as it will need to serve a notice of proposed allocation first. The defence will only be struck out if there is further non-compliance by the defendant.

C is not correct. The value of the claim is irrelevant; the court will consider a party's conduct before considering what procedural step to take.

D is not correct. Whilst A can make an interim application to the court, it will not be granted in his favour at this stage as the court will take the initiative using its general case management powers.

14.5.2 Question 2

The correct answer is B. The claimant can make an application for summary judgment under CPR Part 24 immediately, and on the grounds that the defendant does not have a valid defence; a 'bare denial' of liability is insufficient.

A is not correct. The court cannot automatically strike out the defendant's defence. An application for summary judgment must be made by the claimant.

C is not correct. The claimant does not need to wait for the case to be listed for a case management conference before making an application for summary judgment.

D is not correct. An application for default judgment is the wrong application to make.

E is not correct. The claimant can make an application for summary judgment immediately and does not have to wait until allocation questionnaires have been filed with the court.

14.6 Part 5: The evidence needed and disclosure steps required in commencing, responding to, progressing, or defending a claim

14.6.1 Question 1

The correct answer is D. The witness's statement whilst hearsay evidence (defined by s 1(2) of the Civil Evidence Act 1995 as being 'a statement made, otherwise than by a person while giving oral evidence in proceedings, which is tendered as evidence of the matters stated') is still admissible evidence and relevant to the issues involved in the case. As such the claimant must prepare a notice of proposal to adduce hearsay evidence (a Civil Evidence Act Notice) and arrange for it to be served on the defendant (its legal representatives).

A is not correct. Whilst the witness will be out of the country on the day of the trial, she will not be compelled to attend court to give oral evidence.

B is not correct. The claimant must prepare a notice of proposal to adduce hearsay evidence, not the court.

C is not correct. Whilst the evidence of this witness is hearsay, it is still admissible. As long as the hearsay statement is admissible and relevant the court will allow it to be adduced in evidence.

E is not correct. Whilst the claimant will need to prepare a Civil Evidence Act Notice which must be sent to the court, the claimant does not have to ask the court's permission to adduce this evidence.

14.6.2 Question 2

The correct answer is A. Any genuine efforts through negotiation which take place between the parties, or their respective legal representatives, are considered to be 'without prejudice' or private for the purposes of the disclosure process. The letter does not have to be disclosed as it shows a genuine effort by A to try to settle the dispute and will therefore be considered to be written 'without prejudice'.

B is not correct. Legal professional privilege will not attach to this letter as it was not a communication passing between a party and his/her legal advisers or between a party's legal advisers. This will not be a reason for claiming that the document should not be disclosed.

C is not correct. It does not matter that the letter was written by your client and not by you; it will still be treated as being 'without prejudice' and must be disclosed.

D is not correct. This is not a letter that is likely to incriminate and therefore this is the wrong reason for claiming that the letter need not be disclosed.

E is not correct. Despite the fact that the letter was written prior to the commencement of court proceedings, it will still be considered as being 'without prejudice' and need not be disclosed; it shows a genuine effort by the parties to negotiate.

14.7 Part 6: Preparation of a case for a trial, the trial, and any post-trial steps

14.7.1 Question 1

The correct answer is C. The case summary should not include details of costs. This will be provided in a separate document and produced at the end of the trial.

All the other answers include matters that should be included in the case summary when appearing the case for trial.

14.7.2 Question 2

The correct answer is B. There are grounds for appeal. The grounds for appeal would be that the decision of the judge in ruling out the defendant's evidence was unjust because of a serious procedural irregularity. The correct court to lodge the appeal would be the Court of Appeal.

A is not correct. There are grounds for appeal, but to the Court of Appeal, not the King's Bench Divisional Court

C is not correct. There are grounds. The grounds for appeal would be that the decision of the judge in ruling out the defendant's evidence was unjust because of a serious procedural irregularity.

D is not correct. There are no grounds for a leapfrog appeal to the Supreme Court as the grounds for appeal do not show a point of law of general public importance concerning either the construction of a statutory instrument or a matter already fully considered by the Court of Appeal or the Supreme Court. All parties would also need to consent to the leapfrog and the Supreme Court would need to grant leave.

E is not correct. There are grounds. The grounds for appeal would be that the decision of the judge in ruling out the defendant's evidence was unjust because there was because of a serious procedural irregularity and not an error in law.

14.7.3 Question 3

The correct answer is E. As B is awaiting a payment of about £12,500 from C, a regular customer, A should consider making an application for an order requiring C (the party owing money to the judgment debtor B) to be ordered to pay the judgment creditor A, the amount of the judgment debt and costs direct.

A is not correct. Unless A can identify goods owned by A to the value of the judgment debt, using a warrant of execution to seize goods would probably not be the best method of enforcement.

B is not correct. An attachment of earnings order would not be an appropriate method of enforcement as B is a sole trader and therefore not employed.

C is not correct. It is uncertain that B owns property and an application for a charging order would not be the best method of enforcement in the circumstances.

D is not correct. As the judgment debt is greater than £5,000, applying for B to be made bankrupt might be an option, but it is not the best option and strictly speaking, bankruptcy proceedings are not a method of enforcement.

14.8 Part 7: Procedures and processes relevant to costs involved in dispute resolution

14.8.1 Question 1

The correct answer is C. The indemnity principle is reflected by Rule 44.3(2)(a) CPR 1998, which provides that as a general rule, the unsuccessful party will pay the successful party's cost of the proceedings, but only an amount in costs that the successful party is liable to pay to his or her legal representatives.

A is not correct. The indemnity principle does not mean that the unsuccessful party will never be required to pay the successful party's cost of the proceedings.

B is not correct. The indemnity principle does not mean that the unsuccessful party will always be required to pay the successful party's cost of the proceedings.

D is not correct. Although whilst it is correct that an unsuccessful party will be required to pay only those costs that the successful party can show are reasonable, those costs are not compared to the value of the claim, and this does not reflect the indemnity principle.

E is not correct. Impecuniosity is not a reason for an unsuccessful party to claim relief from paying all costs incurred unreasonably by the successful party. In any event, this is not the indemnity principle.

14.8.2 Question 2

The correct answer is E. Where a party has acted unreasonably during the course of litigation, the court can mark its disapproval of that party's behaviour by making a costs order on an indemnity basis, and in doing so, the costs awarded will be greater than that usually awarded. This will in effect be imposing a penalty on the paying party for failing to negotiate or mediate which may have saved the litigation costs incurred.

A is not correct. Where a party has acted unreasonably during either the course of litigation or during the pre-action protocol procedure, the court can mark its disapproval of that party's behaviour by making a costs order on an indemnity basis.

B is not correct. It is not always possible for the successful party at trial to ask the court to make an indemnity order for costs regardless of the unsuccessful party's conduct prior to or during the course of litigation. The unsuccessful party's conduct must be viewed as having been unreasonable.

C is not correct. The court will consider a request by the winning party to claim costs on an indemnity basis if the unsuccessful party has failed to accept the invitation of the successful party to negotiate or refer the case to mediation

D is not correct. The merits of the claim will be important; simply failing to settle the case early (regardless of the merits) is not good grounds for the court to express its displeasure by imposing an indemnity costs order on the losing party.

Index

Page numbers in **bold** reference tables. Page numbers in *italics* reference figures.

For Product Safety Concerns and Information please contact our EU representative GPSR@taylorandfrancis.com Taylor & Francis Verlag GmbH, Kaufingerstraße 24, 80331 München, Germany